OXFORD WORLD'S CLASSICS

THE OXFORD SHAKESPEARE

General Editor · Stanley Wells

The Oxford Shakespeare offers new and authoritative editions of Shakespeare's plays in which the early printings have been scrupulously re-examined and interpreted. An introductory essay provides all relevant background information together with an appraisal of critical views and of the play's effects in performance. The detailed commentaries pay particular attention to language and staging. Reprints of sources, music for songs, genealogical tables, maps, etc. are included where necessary; many of the volumes are illustrated, and all contain an index.

CHARLES WHITWORTH, the editor of *The Comedy of Errors* in the Oxford Shakespeare, is Professor of English Literature and Director of the Centre for English Renaissance Studies, Université Paul Valéry.

D1026144

THE OXFORD SHAKESPEARE

Currently available in paperback

The rest of the plays are forthcoming

OXFORD WORLD'S CLASSICS

WILLIAM SHAKESPEARE

The Comedy of Errors

Edited by
CHARLES WHITWORTH

OXFORD
UNIVERSITY PRESS

OXFORD
UNIVERSITY PRESS

Great Clarendon Street, Oxford OX2 6DP

Oxford University Press is a department of the University of Oxford.
It furthers the University's objective of excellence in research, scholarship,
and education by publishing worldwide in

Oxford New York

Auckland Bangkok Buenos Aires Cape Town Chennai
Dar es Salaam Delhi Hong Kong Istanbul Karachi Kolkata
Kuala Lumpur Madrid Melbourne Mexico City Mumbai Nairobi
São Paulo Shanghai Singapore Taipei Tokyo Toronto

Oxford is a registered trade mark of Oxford University Press
in the UK and in certain other countries

Published in the United States
by Oxford University Press Inc., New York

First published 2002
First published as an Oxford World's Classics paperback 2003
Reissued 2008

British Library Cataloguing in Publication Data

Data available

Library of Congress Cataloging in Publication Data

Data available

ISBN 978-0-19-953614-6

2

Typeset in Photina MT
by SNP Best-set Typesetter Ltd., Hong Kong
Printed in Great Britain by
Clays Ltd, St Ives plc

PREFACE

THAT this new edition of Shakespeare's shortest play sees the light of day at last is a matter of great relief to its editor. My first debt is to the Oxford Shakespeare general editor, Stanley Wells, whose patience and exemplary editorship have been put to severe test. My scholarly debts to him are manifold and of long standing. Frances Whistler of OUP too has been lenient beyond measure. Christine Buckley's trenchant observations and helpful suggestions are the marks of a copy-editor *sans pareil*, and are gratefully acknowledged.

Among countless friends, colleagues and well-wishers who should be thanked here in their turn, for critical insights or theatrical revelations, for leads, references, material help, and above all for timely encouragement, early and late (with apologies for any unwitting omissions), are Jean-Marie Maguin, Park Honan, Robert Smallwood, Russell Jackson, Susan Brock, Bob Wilcher, Ian Small, Tom Matheson, Alan Brissenden, Gary Taylor, R. A. Foakes, Brian Gibbons, George Walton Williams, David Bevington, Don Beecher, Robert Miola, Laurie Maguire, Jay Halio, Tom Berger, Tom Clayton, Yves Peyré, Luc Borot, Phyllida Lloyd, Owen Teale, Caroline Loncq, Zoë Wanamaker, Niamh Cusack, and the late Jean Fuzier and Philip Brockbank. Colleagues at the Shakespeare Institute, in the English Department of the University of Birmingham (including its successive heads James T. Boulton and Kelsey Thornton), and the Centre for English Renaissance Studies and Research in Montpellier (*UMR 5065 du CNRS*) have been noble in their support. Librarians at the Shakespeare Institute, the University of Birmingham, the Bodleian Library, the Shakespeare Birthplace Trust, and the Folger Shakespeare Library have rendered incalculable help. So many students too, at Birmingham, Stratford, Montpellier, and the Bread Loaf School of English at Lincoln College, Oxford, have contributed perceptions and intuitions, while lecture audiences at various times and places have been more gracious than I had any right to expect. Former editors, still living, of *The Comedy of Errors* will, I trust, find due acknowledgement of their work in this edition; may future ones avoid its shortcomings and profit from any felicities.

Families also contribute in infinite, often indirect ways to the realization of scholarly endeavours. This one is no exception. I owe to Elisabeth, my wife, the decision to continue and complete this work rather than abandoning it as repeated delays and frustrations led me to the brink of doing more than once. That my mother, who first read Shakespeare to me, taught generations of pupils to marvel at his riches, and gave loving encouragement to this project, did not live to see its publication is a cause of deep sorrow. This edition is dedicated to her memory—Margaret Upshaw Whitworth (1913–2000)—and to my father, my sisters (and the memory of another, lost), their sons and daughters, my brother, his children (including twins), my wife, daughter, and two sons— 'such felicity'.

CHARLES WHITWORTH
Montpellier, January 2002

CONTENTS

LIST OF ILLUSTRATIONS

INTRODUCTION

1594/1604—a play for Christmas?

LATE in the evening on 28 December 1594, Innocents' Day, in the hall of Gray's Inn in Holborn, London, a company of players performed a 'Comedy of Errors (like to Plautus his *Menaechmus*)', after a particularly riotous several hours of banqueting and merrymaking presided over by the Prince of Purpoole, as the Inn's Christmas Lord of Misrule was called. The account of the 1594 Christmas revels in *Gesta Grayorum*, published by William Canning nearly a century later in 1688, is not always clear in its details. It seems, however, that some of the entertainments planned that evening for the members of the Inn and their special guests, an 'Ambassador' and his retinue from the Inner Temple, another of the Inns of Court, with a particularly close and 'ancient amity' with Gray's Inn, could not take place due to the great 'pressure of lords, ladies and worshipful personages that did expect some notable performance at that time'; 'there arose such a disordered tumult and crowd upon the stage' that had been set up for the occasion 'that thereby there was no convenient room for those that were actors'. Such was the disruption that 'there was no opportunity to effect that which was intended' and the guests from the Inner Temple left disappointed.[1] The account of the memorable evening concludes, after the mention of the play: 'So that the night was begun, and continued to the end in nothing but confusion and errors, whereupon it was ever afterwards called "The Night of Errors"'. The next night, a mock trial was held in which inquiry was made into the disturbances of the evening of the 28th, and a 'sorcerer or conjurer that was supposed to be the cause of that confused

---

[1] The two Inns frequently shared festive occasions or pooled their resources for special events, as in their production of *The Masque of the Inner Temple and Gray's Inn*, written by Francis Beaumont, for a royal wedding in 1613. On that occasion too there were complications and delays, and performance of the masque, on which considerable effort and expense had been lavished, was postponed for four days (Philip Edwards, ed., *The Masque of the Inner Temple and Gray's Inn*, in *A Book of Masques in Honour of Allardyce Nicoll*, ed. T. J. B. Spencer and S. W. Wells (Cambridge, 1967; repr. 1980), pp. 127–48).

inconvenience' was arraigned. Among other outrages, he was charged with 'foist[ing] a company of base and common fellows to make up our disorders with a play of errors and confusions'. After many pleas and counterpleas he was acquitted, 'and this was the end of our law-sports, concerning the Night of Errors'. Amends were made to the disgruntled guests from the Inner Temple and the 'ancient amity' restored a few days later on 3 January, when a lavish musical show on the theme of Amity, full of classical and allegorical personages, was given in their honour, with more distinguished guests present, including Shakespeare's patron the Earl of Southampton, the Earl of Essex, and Lord Howard of Effingham, the Lord Admiral and patron of the Admiral's Men, principal rivals to his father-in-law's company, the Lord Chamberlain's Men.[1]

There seems no good reason to doubt that the play performed on 28 December 1594 at Gray's Inn was Shakespeare's *Comedy of Errors* and that the company that gave it was the Lord Chamberlain's Men, in existence only since the previous spring. This Christmas season of 1594 was the first in which it and its rival the Admiral's Men, formed at the same time by agreement between Hunsdon and Howard, could perform the function which was their—official—*raison d'être*, namely, presenting plays for the entertainment of the Queen and her court, especially during the prolonged Christmas and New Year season. The two patrons, Hunsdon and Howard, were careful to share the honours equally between their newly formed companies: the Admiral's Men played three times at Court, on 28 December and 1 and 6 January, for which they received £30, while the Chamberlain's played twice at Court (and were paid £20) and once at Gray's Inn, which must have seemed to them almost as prestigious as a Court appearance, in view of the number of high-ranking dignitaries and noblemen in attendance. The two companies continued to share the Court performance monopoly uninterruptedly until 1600.

A number of factors, not all of which are hard facts, converge to suggest further that the play, unique in the Shakespeare canon in several important respects, was composed expressly for that

---

[1] The full text of the *Gesta Grayorum* is reprinted by the Malone Society (1914). Extracts relating to the performance of *The Comedy of Errors* are printed as Appendix B to this edition.

occasion, or at least for that Christmas season: it could possibly have been one of the 'two several comedies or interludes' played at Court by the Chamberlain's Men on the two days preceding their appearance at the Inn, that is 26 and 27 December.[1] The Queen usually returned to Westminster from her country progresses in mid-November, signalling the opening of the Court season. The Master of the Revels, Edmund Tilney (a Howard kinsman), began selecting plays and performers for the Christmas season's Court entertainment in the autumn. The Court dates were presumably fixed well in advance, so it may be fortuitous that the Chamberlain's and not the Admiral's Men (whose patron, Lord Howard, was a member of Gray's Inn) was the company enlisted to play an afterpiece late in the evening of 28 December at the Inn. On the other hand, Shakespeare's young patron, Henry Wriothesley, Earl of Southampton, was also a member of the Inn. The dramatist had recently dedicated two splendid narrative poems, *Venus and Adonis* (1593) and *The Rape of Lucrece* (1594), to Southampton, and the Earl may have had a say in the invitation from the Inn to the company in which his protégé was a shareholder and the new resident playwright.[2] The entry of *Lucrece* in the Stationers' Register in May 1594 coincides to the very month with the creation of the two new playing companies, following the long period of disruption in theatrical activity during the plague years of 1592–4. There is considerable uncertainty about Shakespeare's theatrical career prior to 1594. He may have been a member of the Queen's Men before they broke up in 1592 and he and other players transferred hastily to other companies. But it seems probable that he was picked up by

[1] E. K. Chambers, *The Elizabethan Stage*, 4 vols. (Oxford, 1923), iv. 109, 164 (hereafter *ES*). The Chamber Accounts (dated 15 March) give Holy Innocents' Day, 28 December, as one of the two dates of Court performance. However, the Admiral's Men, Howard's company, performed at Court on that date, when the Chamberlain's Men were at Gray's Inn, so the correct second date for their Court appearance must be 27th (*ES*, iv. 56). The Chamberlain's payees named in the Account are William Kemp, William Shakespeare and Richard Burbage.

[2] Southampton turned twenty-one in October 1594, whereupon he was obliged to pay a huge fine (said to be £5,000) to his guardian, Lord Burghley, for refusing to marry the latter's granddaughter Elizabeth de Vere. The elegant, gregarious, independent-minded young earl was highly visible in and around the Court at this time, and he could well have influenced Hunsdon or Howard or fellow members of the Inn, if any influence were needed, in the choice of entertainers for the Christmas Revels. On Southampton's reputation, see Park Honan, *Shakespeare: A Life* (Oxford, 1998), pp. 172–7.

Hunsdon, along with Burbage and others, from the remains of one of the dissolved companies, perhaps the Earl of Pembroke's (which itself had broken up in 1593), perhaps the Earl of Derby's (Lord Strange's) or the Earl of Sussex's, and that he may have brought with him some plays that he had written or rewritten previously.[1] Certainly Sussex's Men played *Titus Andronicus* three times in late January and early February 1594 at Henslowe's Rose during a brief midwinter remission of the plague.[2] But *The Comedy of Errors* looks like a new composition, purpose-written for the Christmas season, 1594.

It is very unlikely that an outside professional company could have been summoned at the last minute to replace another, aborted performance in the evening's programme, as the *Gesta Grayorum* account may lead us to imagine. The 'trial' of the 'sorcerer or conjuror', who was presumably the member of the Inn responsible for organizing the evening's entertainment (some think it may have been Francis Bacon; he was later a prime mover in the 1613 production by the combined Inns for Princess Elizabeth's wedding) was only a game and it was only pretended that he had 'foisted' a company of professional players upon the assembly without their prior knowledge or approval.[3] The very brevity of *The Comedy of Errors*, one of its many distinguishing features, made it ideal as an afterpiece, a short, boisterous comedy with a joyously festive ending, to cap an evening of carnivalesque gaiety during the Twelve Days of Christmas: nativity and festivity, as well as 'errors and confusions' are prominent motifs in the play. So it was doubtless programmed from the start. It was rather the masque or 'show' in which members and guests were supposed to take part which had to be abandoned due to the great press of people and the gen-

---

[1] Andrew Gurr gathers all the available evidence in his *The Shakespearian Playing Companies* (Oxford, 1996); see esp. Chapter 4, 'Lording it over the players' (pp. 55–77). The Earl of Derby (Lord Strange) died early in 1594, a few months after Sussex. Their deaths left voids in the elite club of aristocratic patrons of theatrical companies, just before the plague began to abate, thus allowing the resumption of playing in the capital from April or May. Hunsdon and Howard seized the opportunity thus fortuitously provided.

[2] *Henslowe's Diary*, ed. R. A. Foakes and R. T. Rickert (Cambridge, 1961), p. 21.

[3] Another possibility might be the conjurer Dr Pinch from *The Comedy of Errors* itself, but it seems more likely that a member of the Inn rather than one of the professional members of the Chamberlain's Men would be the one to take part in such a mock-trial.

eral chaos in the hall. They and not the Chamberlain's Men were 'those that were to be actors', and for whom room could not be cleared on the stage at the appropriate time. The allusion to 'the stage' in *Gesta Grayorum* seems to imply that it was already there in place before the aborted entertainments of the Innsmen gave way to the performance of *Errors* by the professional players. It is unlikely therefore that a formal classical-style set would have been built expressly for the play. The latter calls for at least two houses (*domus* in classical parlance)—the Phoenix, the Abbey—as well as exits to the bay and the town; the Centaur and the Porcupine need not be represented on stage. 'The mart' may simply have been the undefined space of the stage, in front of the screen at the lower end of the hall. Such all-purpose sets were well within the capacities of the great halls of schools, colleges and Inns of Court, and had for decades been frequently erected in such venues.[1]

Assigning the composition as well as an attested performance of *The Comedy of Errors* to the latter part of the year 1594 runs counter to received opinion as to its place in the Shakespeare canon. It was for a long time taken for granted that it was Shakespeare's first comedy, if not his first play. This arbitrary assumption, and the view that the play's brevity, its apparent triviality, the prominence of farce, the absence of 'poetical' passages or memorable characters, and its mechanical plot betrayed it as apprentice work, were mutually confirming: this must be Shakespeare's earliest play because it is short, scholarly, superficial, unpoetical; because it is his earliest play, it is of course immature, lightweight, undemanding, mere entertainment, scarcely serious *drama*. The fact that the earliest reference to it is as part of a frivolous, riotous evening's entertainment for a bunch of law students did not enhance its reputation. Many standard modern works of criticism on Shakespearian comedy begin with *The Comedy of Errors*, implying if not explicitly stating their authors' conviction that it was the first, preceding *The Two Gentlemen of Verona*, *The Taming of the Shrew*, *Love's Labour's Lost* and the rest.

---

[1] For suggestions as to the great-hall staging of another sixteenth-century comedy in which two houses and at least one other exit are called for, see the present editor's introduction to *Gammer Gurton's Needle*, New Mermaids (1997), pp. xxii–xxv. More general discussions are those by Richard Southern, *The Staging of Plays before Shakespeare* (1973), and Alan H. Nelson, *Early Cambridge Theatres: College, University and Town Stages, 1464–1720* (Cambridge, 1994).

But there are internal factors as well as the external ones just summarized which point to a somewhat later rather than a very early date for the play, that is around 1594 and probably towards the end of that year, rather than 1592 or earlier as would have to be the case if it were among Shakespeare's very first dramatic compositions. First, it is extraordinarily well-plotted, even rigorously so, a model of classical-style, five-act structure. There is none of the unevenness or uncertainty that we notice in *The Two Gentlemen of Verona* and *The Taming of the Shrew*, in the handling of their multiple plots and frames, or in the earliest English history plays, *The First Part of the Contention* (*2 Henry VI*), *The True Tragedy of Richard Duke of York* (*3 Henry VI*) and *Henry VI*, Part One, with their plethora of characters and locations and often stilted, declamatory rhetoric. It is often remarked that in only two plays did Shakespeare observe the so-called 'classical unities' of time, place and action; *The Comedy of Errors* is one, *The Tempest*, the last play he wrote apart from a few collaborations with John Fletcher in 1613, is the other. Yet that very fact has been taken as evidence for the alleged immaturity and school-exercise-like quality of the earlier play: Shakespeare, the argument runs, fell back on his knowledge from grammar school of classical comedy, its plots and structures, in this his first solo dramatic composition (i.e. he did not know any better). Later he freed himself from such constraints and hence wrote better and longer plays (including of course *The Tempest*, where the 'unities' have rarely been seen as dimming the brilliance of a virtuoso piece). But for a learned, extremely well-read audience like the gentlemen of the Inns of Court, such a structure in a play whose plot was, furthermore, based closely on two plays by the Roman dramatist Plautus, would scarcely have seemed a weakness. On the contrary, if Shakespeare was composing with such an audience particularly in mind, or indeed the similarly sophisticated one at Court, headed by a queen who prided herself on her scholarship, the tight, classical structure as well as the Plautine plot material must have virtually suggested themselves. The brilliant plot of *The Comedy of Errors* is simply not the work of a novice.

If he chose not to write 'poetically', that is, in a lyric vein, it was because his material or the occasion or both did not warrant it. He does, in fact, employ a variety of verse forms, metres, and moods (including the lyrical, in the one wooing scene, 3.2), as well as prose, in the play's short scope. In that respect, it is a kind of writer's showcase in the dramatic mode; a newly established play-wright showing off somewhat in this, perhaps the first piece to be commissioned from him and his new colleagues, for a special occasion. The rising poet, like the new company of players, was on show. Non-dramatic writers, including Shakespeare himself, and compilers of poetical miscellanies were busily doing the same kind of thing at the time. Collections such as *Breton's Bower of Delights*, *The Arbour of Amorous Devices*, and *The Phoenix' Nest* were published between 1591 and 1594. The years 1592 to 1595 also saw the explosion of the sonnet collection, often containing poems of various lengths in a dazzling variety of forms, besides the standard quatorzain sonnet. In those years, Samuel Daniel, Thomas Lodge, Barnabe Barnes, Giles Fletcher, Thomas Watson, Henry Constable, Michael Drayton, William Percy, Edmund Spenser and others published verse collections; Shakespeare almost certainly wrote many of his own sonnets in this period also. Often a longer, narrative poem was appended to the sonnet sequence: Daniel's *Complaint of Rosamund*, Lodge's *Complaint of Elstred*, Fletcher's *Rising to the Crown of Richard III*, Richard Barnfield's *Legend of Cassandra*, etc. The erotic epyllion, often on an Ovidian subject, of which *Venus and Adonis* is the most famous example, and other similar verse narrative genres were also at the height of their popularity. Besides Shakespeare, many others, including Lodge, Drayton, Daniel, Barnfield, George Chapman, Thomas Heywood, Henry Willoby, and Thomas Edwards, published such works around that time, and Christopher Marlowe had written his brilliant *Hero and Leander* by May 1593, when he was killed in a tavern brawl, aged twenty-nine. Many were dedicated to courtiers and other fashionable young gentlemen about town. The first work in the new mode, Lodge's *Scilla's Metamorphosis* of 1589, bears a dedication to 'the Gentlemen of the Inns of Court and Chancery'. In other words, there is nothing intrinsically improbable in the suggestion that Shakespeare could have written *The Comedy of Errors* especially for the entertainment of the likes of the Earl of Southampton, his friends, fellow Innsmen and/or fellow-courtiers late in 1594, having in the preceding year or so written the modish *Venus and Adonis* and *The Rape of Lucrece* for the delectation of precisely the same discriminating set.

It may nevertheless still be surprising to find *The Comedy of Errors*, known for farce and craziness and virtually nothing in the way of lyricism, pathos or romantic intrigue, placed in such proximity to Shakespeare's so-called 'lyrical' period, that of the sonnets and major narrative poems, and plays such as *Love's Labour's Lost*, *A Midsummer Night's Dream*, *Romeo and Juliet*, *Richard II*, usually ascribed to the years 1594 and 1595, rather than among the works that date from the plague years if not earlier still—*The Two Gentlemen of Verona*, *The Taming of the Shrew*, *Titus Andronicus* and the first historical trilogy (the *Henry VI* group). But recent stylistic and linguistic analyses, notably those carried out by the authors of *William Shakespeare: A Textual Companion*, strengthen such a case in striking ways. For example, in its proportion of prose to verse (12 per cent), *Errors* is closer to *Romeo and Juliet* (13 per cent) than to any other play in the canon—and it has considerably less prose than any of the other first twelve comedies (up to and including *All's Well that Ends Well*).[1] Indeed in this respect, it is closer to the later romances *Pericles* and *Cymbeline* than to any comedies written within ten years of it. In its proportion of rhymed lines in the verse portion, *Errors* with 25 per cent is closest to *Richard II* and *Romeo*, and, interestingly, to three later comedies, *As You Like It*, *Twelfth Night* and *All's Well*; all five of those plays have 18 to 19 per cent of their verse rhymed. Again *Errors* stands out among the first twelve comedies in having more rhyme than all the others, except for the two nearly contemporary, 'romantic' comedies of the 'lyrical' group, *Love's Labour's Lost* and *A Midsummer Night's Dream*. Thus a 'rhyme-group' of works consisting of the two last-named comedies, with *Errors*, *Richard II* and *Romeo*, and of course the two long narrative poems which are entirely in rhyme, and an unknown number of sonnets presumably composed during those years, stand out from the few plays written before them (and thus probably before, or possibly during, the closure of the theatres on account of the plague from mid-1592 to mid-1594), and the next group of plays from *King John* (?1595/6) to *Julius Caesar* in 1599. Indeed, they stand out in this respect also from all other plays, except the three middle comedies mentioned above, before *Timon of*

---

[1] These and the following statistics are gathered from Stanley Wells, Gary Taylor and others, *William Shakespeare: A Textual Companion* (Oxford, 1987), pp. 96–108, 116–17, 266–9 (hereafter *TC*). While a few lines in *Errors* are open to debate as to their status as verse or prose, and modern editions vary in their treatment of them, the totals will not vary enough either way to modify significantly the 12 per cent figure.

Athens (?1605) (*TC*, 96). Chronologically, this 'rhyme-group' belongs to the period from late 1592 to 1595. Statistically, *The Comedy of Errors* stands squarely in that group.

Another linguistic test, that of colloquialism in verse, places *Errors* again among the same group, nearest *Richard II* and *Romeo* among pre-1596 works, with the Sonnets and *Dream* next nearest. In yet another, that of rare vocabulary, *Errors* stands closest to *The Taming of the Shrew*, and to *Richard III* and *Romeo* again. The anomalous closeness to *Shrew*, doubtless an earlier play, which has farcical elements in common with *Errors*, may be due to the former having been among the last plays Shakespeare worked on before the closure of the theatres in 1592, or during the intermittent resumptions of activity in the winters of 1592–3 and 1593–4; that is, it may precede the latter play very nearly in the sequence of *dramatic* composition, though separated from it in time by several months or as much as two years, and by a number of non-dramatic works written in the interim (*TC*, pp. 99, 101–5; 100, 117).

Thus considerable internal as well as external evidence points to the latter half of the year 1594 as the time of composition of *The Comedy of Errors*. We can no longer dismiss it as apprentice work, written by a novice dramatist who had only his recollection of Latin texts studied in school a dozen or more years before to draw upon. In other words, *Errors* and those other plays with which it shares such stylistic, linguistic and poetic features as those outlined above, represent the energetic resumption of regular professional play writing by Shakespeare after the forced interruption of mid-1592 to mid-1594, and it was no doubt among the first in a steady stream of new plays written for his colleagues in the Chamberlain's (later the King's) Men, that did not abate for nearly twenty years.[1]

---

[1] For the suggestion that *Love's Labour's Lost* may allude to the 1594 Gray's Inn Christmas revels in its masque of Muscovites and blackamoors, and in Biron's lines 'Here was a consent, | Knowing aforehand of our merriment, | To dash it like a Christmas comedy' (5.2.460–2), and may thus be close in time of composition to *Errors*, see G. R. Hibbard's introduction to his Oxford Shakespeare edition (Oxford, 1990), pp. 45–7. In any case, *Love's Labour's* contains two of only three occurrences in Shakespeare's works of the word 'Christmas'; see Charles Whitworth, '*Love's Labour's Lost*: Aborted Plays Within, Unconsummated Play Without', in *The Show Within: Dramatic and Other Insets, English Renaissance Drama (1550–1642)*, ed. François Laroque, *Collection Astraea* 4, 2 vols. (Montpellier, 1992), i. 109–25 (p. 119). Another possibility is that *Love's Labour's* was one of the two comedies performed by the Chamberlain's Men at Court at Christmas, 1594, *Errors* being the other, both of them written specially for the season by Shakespeare. The 'Christmas comedy' allusion in the former play would then be self-referring.

The legend of that 'night of errors' at Gray's Inn in 1594 survived and grew in the intervening years, and with it the memory of the play that concluded it. In February 1602, at another Inn, the Middle Temple, a law student, John Manningham, saw another play by Shakespeare, performed in all probability by the Chamberlain's Men. As he recorded in his diary: 'At our feast we had a play called *Twelfth Night, or What You Will,* much like *The Comedy of Errors* or *Menaechmi* in Plautus'.[1] In a unique tenth anniversary revival, 'The Plaie of Errors' by 'Shaxberd' was performed at Court by His Majesty's players—on Innocents' Day, 28 December 1604 (*ES*, iv. 171). No doubt the new king, a lover of plays, demanded that his company's chief dramatist's early Christmas comedy of errors be played for him also. The next year, 1605, Sir Francis Bacon of Gray's Inn, King's Counsel Extraordinary, published his *Advancement of Learning,* in which he likened the surprising subordination of virtue to pleasure in some ancient philosophical systems to 'some comedies of errors, wherein the mistress and the maid change habits'; the generic title of Shakespeare's entertainment (if not its principal plot device, in Bacon's simile) may have continued to echo in the minds of those who saw it.[2]

1623: the text

Although comparatively visible in the annals of performance, with those references in *Gesta Grayorum* and in the Court Calendar for 1594 and 1604, as well as Manningham's quotation of its title in 1602, *The Comedy of Errors* seems not to have been published before it was included among thirty-six plays by Shakespeare in the First Folio in 1623, seven years after the dramatist's death. This is not particularly surprising: if the play was not performed in the public theatres, outdoor or indoor—Theatre, Curtain, Globe, Blackfriars, or another—and thus had no public exposure and consequent notoriety, it would probably not be considered by its owners, the Chamberlain's, later King's Men, or by its author who may have

---

[1] Quoted in full in *Twelfth Night,* ed. Roger Warren and Stanley Wells, The Oxford Shakespeare (Oxford, 1994), p. 1. A facsimile of the passage is printed in S. Schoenbaum, *William Shakespeare: A Documentary Life* (Oxford, 1975), p. 156.

[2] *'The Advancement of Learning' and 'New Atlantis',* ed. Arthur Johnston (Oxford, 1974), p. 150.

had a say in such decisions, as worth offering for sale to a stationer, even at times when forced inactivity due to plague or financial straits for other causes prompted them to sell play manuscripts for publication. It seems unlikely that *Errors* would ever have figured in the commercial repertoire of Shakespeare's company, in view of its marked brevity: at 1,920 lines (of print, not just of dialogue) it is nearly twenty per cent shorter than the next shortest play in the Folio, *The Two Gentlemen of Verona* (2,300 lines).[1] *Errors* was just not substantial enough to provide a full afternoon's entertainment for paying customers at the Theatre, the Shoreditch home of the Chamberlain's Men in the first few years of their existence (1594–7), or at the Curtain, or later at the Globe. Furthermore, its peculiar staging requirements may not have suited it well to the stages of the amphitheatres. By 1608 when the King's Men finally got to use the Second Blackfriars, built by James Burbage more than ten years earlier, and whose facilities might have lent themselves somewhat more readily to the play, a short, fourteen-year-old made-for-the-occasion Christmas comedy would scarcely have been thought viable fare for the private theatre audience used to the diet of sensational tragedies and saucy comedies that comprised the bulk of the repertoires of the boys' companies that had played there for the previous eight or nine years. A special revival at Court of a ten-year-old play, at the express wish of the king, the Company's new patron, was one thing; the exigencies of commercial competition with several other professional companies and theatres, men's and boys', were another. But of course the carefully kept script was included by Shakespeare's colleagues Heminges and Condell when they prepared the contents of the memorial volume published in 1623.

Errors stands fifth in the Folio, in the first section of fourteen plays, the 'Comedies'. It is the only play in the section to bear the label 'comedy' in its title, whereas nearly all of those in the third section, 'Tragedies', including *Cymbeline*, carry titles of the type: 'The Tragedy of —'. The first section includes *The Tempest* and *The Winter's Tale*, now usually grouped with *Cymbeline, Pericles*, and sometimes *The Two Noble Kinsmen*, as 'romances' or 'last plays'. *Errors* follows *The Tempest, Two Gentlemen, The Merry Wives of*

---

[1] Statistics are taken from Charlton Hinman's Norton facsimile of the First Folio (New York, 1968).

Windsor, and *Measure for Measure*. None of these except *Merry Wives*—in a 'bad' quarto of 1602, reprinted in 1619—had been published prior to their inclusion in the Folio. The Folio texts of those four plays seem to have been set from transcripts professionally prepared by Ralph Crane, and their clean state, conducive to relatively trouble-free typesetting, must have prompted Heminges and Condell to place them first in the volume, to make a good early impression upon readers. *The Comedy of Errors* precedes another series of four plays, all deriving, in part at least, from earlier quartos, sometimes annotated from prompt books (*TC*, 145–6; 266); they in turn are followed by five more, none of them previously published. Copy for the play is generally agreed to have been an authorial manuscript, or holograph (foul papers). *Errors* is thus alone among the first nine plays in the Folio in having been set from an authorial manuscript. While it has been argued (by Werstine) that this does not necessarily preclude its having been used as a prompt book, the authors of the *Textual Companion* (266) find little convincing evidence for that hypothesis, and confirm the orthodox opinion of Chambers, McKerrow and Greg. If, as is suggested above, the play was not performed in the public theatre, but only on a few special occasions, the authorial manuscript could have served as prompt book on those rare occasions, and remained otherwise safe and clean in the company's keeping until it was brought out for printing in the Folio, nearly thirty years after its composition. The particularly carefully placed and spaced act divisions in the Folio text may well reflect preparation for performance at Court and similar venues, where pauses would have been taken for refreshment; university plays like *Gammer Gurton's Needle* from Christ's College, Cambridge (*c.*1550–60) share that feature with the Folio *Comedy of Errors*. The printed text of the play is mostly free of the corruptions and confusions that might result from difficult copy, which suggests that the manuscript from which the compositors in Isaac Jaggard's printing shop worked was relatively unproblematic, even if it was still only in the draft state. Thus it was judged suitable to follow the four freshly transcribed texts in the sequence at the beginning of the Folio.

Examples of the kinds of evidence usually cited as revealing unrevised authorial foul papers are to be found in a number of places in the Folio text of *Errors*: inconsistency in speech prefixes and in the names of characters generally, unclear distinctions between characters, imprecise and narrative or descriptive stage directions, references in directions to off-stage locations, super-fluous to staging requirements, and missing entrances or exits. Illustrative examples include the occurrence of '*Iuliana*' and '*Iulia*' for Luciana in 3.2; such identifying phrases in stage directions as '*Adriana, wife to Antipholus Sereptus*' (2.1) and '*a schoolmaster called Pinch*' (4.4); the designation '*Merchant*' (or abbreviations) for three different characters, including Egeon, and '*Angelo*' and '*Goldsmith*' for the same character, at the end of 3.2 and the beginning of 4.1 respectively; such directions as '*All gather to see them*' (5.1), '*Enter Dromio of Syracuse, from the bay*' (4.1), '*Enter three or four, and offer to bind him*' (4.4), and '*Exit one to the priory*' (5.1). (These and other such instances are noted in the commentary to the text in the appropriate places in the present edition.) There seems on the whole to be no contradiction in the hypothesis that Shakespeare's draft manuscript may have served him and his colleagues as their 'book' for the few special performances of the play, and otherwise remained, unrevised, untranscribed and unmarked-up, in the company's possession until Heminges and Condell got it out and handed it over to Jaggard.

The Folio text of *Errors* shows other kinds of mistakes and con-fusions than those attributable to the kind of copy that lay behind it. They were introduced rather during the process of transposition from script to print. Extensive research in the field of composi-torial analysis has taught us much about the working habits of Elizabethan and Jacobean printers and typesetters. The Shakespeare First Folio has inevitably been the principal proving ground and Shakespeare editors and other textual scholars the main beneficiaries of that research. While the introduction to a modern-spelling edition of the play may not be the best place to discuss such technical matters in detail, a brief summary would seem a logical part of the description of that play's first printing, upon which all subsequent printings and editions for nearly four centuries have been directly or indirectly based: the present one is based directly on that 1623 Folio text, as is that in the Oxford *Complete Works*. Beginning with Charlton Hinman's painstaking detec-tive work in his magisterial *Printing and Proof-Reading of the First Folio of Shakespeare*, scholars have determined that three different compositors, designated B, C and D, set the text of the shortest play in the book, each researcher in turn revising and refining the attributions of pages and columns made by his predecessors.[1] *The Comedy of Errors* occupies pages 85 to 100 of the 'Comedies' section, that is, all of quire (gathering) H (twelve printed pages) and the first two leaves (four pages of print) of quire I. Quires F, G and H pose particularly tricky problems and have drawn the attention of textual analysts, due in large part to the complicated pattern of sharing of the work among those three compositors, in addition to the difficulties posed by the practice of setting by formes, involving fine calculations of space available versus copy to be set, or 'casting off'.[2] Some pages and even some columns were set by more than one compositor. A table of the generally agreed attributions of the pages containing the text of *Errors* follows:

Page	Column	Compositor
H1	a + b	C
H1ᵛ	a	C
	b	D
H2	a	D
	b	C
H2ᵛ	a + b	C
H3	a	C
	b	D
H3ᵛ	a + b	D
H4	a	C
	b	D
H4ᵛ	a + b	B

[1] Charlton Hinman, *The Printing and Proof-Reading of the First Folio of Shakespeare*, 2 vols. (Oxford, 1963). Among other important contributions are T. H. Howard-Hill, 'The Compositors of Shakespeare's Folio Comedies', *SB* 26 (1973), 61–106; John O'Connor, 'Compositors D and F of the Shakespeare First Folio', *SB* 28 (1975), 81–117; O'Connor, 'A Qualitative Analysis of Compositors C and D in the Shakespeare First Folio', *SB* 30 (1977), 57–74; Paul Werstine, 'Cases and Compositors in the Shakespeare First Folio Comedies', *SB* 35 (1982), 206–34; and *TC*, pp. 148–50.

[2] Briefly, setting by formes means that (usually) two compositors start setting type from the middle of a gathering, each working outwards; for example, in a folio in sixes like the Shakespeare Folio (three large sheets of paper, each folded once, one inside the other to make six leaves and twelve pages of print) from H3ᵛ and H4 (the sixth and seventh pages), respectively, backward and forward to H1 and H6ᵛ, the first and twelfth pages of the gathering. This entails dividing the copy up, and calculating how much copy will fit into the space available to each compositor (casting off).

H5	a + b	B
H5^v	a	D
	b	D + C
H6	a + b	B
H6^v	a + b	B
I1	a + b	B
I1^v	a + b	B
I2	a + b	B
I2^v	a + b	B

The sharing of a page between two compositors, one of them setting one column and the other the other, is a very rare occurrence in the 'Histories' and 'Tragedies' sections of the Folio, and in the 'Comedies' section is concentrated in quires F, G and H (*Measure for Measure* takes up the two quires F and G), though a few isolated examples are to be found in quires I, K, O and P. It is notable in the above table that Compositor B, a more experienced typesetter than his colleagues C and D, completed the setting of the text of *Errors* from the beginning of quire I, having already set four full pages in H. He shared the remainder of I, again with Compositors C and D.

Those anonymous compositors whom we can distinguish only by letters were the agents who transmitted Shakespeare's text to readers of the Folio, and thence to later printers and editors and readers.[1] At least six, perhaps as many as eight or ten compositors took part in the setting of the Folio. C and D disappeared almost completely after the comedies, and A joined in only at the very end of the section; he and B set most of the histories and B and E most of the tragedies (*TC*, 152–4). Their role was crucial in the production of the Folio and determinant in that of half the plays in the Shakespeare canon, those for which the First Folio provides the sole early text. The parts played by B, C and D in printing the Folio text of *The Comedy of Errors*, and thus in producing the only work we have to call by that title, will be noted and analysed at several significant points in the commentary.

---

[1] D. F. McKenzie's 'A List of Printers' Apprentices, 1605–1640' includes a John Shakespeare, son of a Warwickshire butcher, among William Jaggard's apprentices from 1610 to 1617, when he became a journeyman (*SB* 13 (1960), 109–41). This led Hinman to speculate: 'It is pleasant to wonder if the man who set more than half of the Folio into type (and who also took many liberties with its text) . . . Compositor B was by any chance this same John Shakespeare' (*Printing and Proof-Reading*, ii. 513).

A modern editor of *Errors* has only the First Folio text to turn to for an authoritative basis for his edition. Subsequent Folios, in 1632, 1663 and 1685, were reprinted from their immediate predecessors and thus have no independent authority. In-house editors of those Folios may have corrected some misprints in their copy, but they also introduced errors. Nicholas Rowe, the 'first editor' of Shakespeare, based his 1709 edition on the Fourth Folio of 1685; his edition was thus at four removes from the First Folio. Despite the enormous progress made in the eighteenth century in the study of the Shakespeare text, by brilliant and inspired editors from Pope and Theobald to Johnson, Capell, Steevens and Malone, their texts were usually based on, and departed from, those of their predecessors. Thus their successive editions of *The Comedy of Errors* moved ever further from the earliest surviving text, that of the 1623 Folio, which, while it may have been printed from Shakespeare's own thirty-year-old manuscript, was itself, as we have seen, processed by several anonymous typesetters each of whom brought to his work his own habits and quirks. Our earliest printed text of the play, then, is a collaborative work, just as much as were those performances of it at Gray's Inn in 1594 and at Court in 1604.

Thanks to its inclusion in the First Folio, the legitimate place of *Errors* in the Shakespeare canon has never been seriously challenged. Pope found some passages unworthy of the poet, or rather of his Augustan concept of the poet, and consigned them to smaller print at the bottom of the page. Beginning with Rowe, editors proposed corrections and emendations, many of which have been retained ever since; the collations in the present edition record their readings. Lewis Theobald, in particular, the first 'scholarly' editor of Shakespeare (1733), left his mark on the text not only of *The Comedy of Errors*, but of all the plays, and many of his emendations have become standard, incorporated into editions since his own time. After Theobald, editors found little to dispute or debate in the text of *Errors*, apart from a very few cruxes which have exercised their ingenuity as they have attempted to resolve them and to make sense of nonsense. The most famous of these is the passage at the end of 2.1 in which Adriana, lamenting her husband's supposed desertion, speaks metaphorically of 'the jewel best enamellèd' losing its beauty and of gold being worn by much touching (2.1.109–13). The collations in the present edition for that passage demonstrate the influence of Theobald. Such cruxes as this one have been discussed by scholars and critics other than editors of the play, and their contributions too belong to the history of the text.[1]

Sources and analogues

Plautus, 'Menaechmi'. It has long been agreed that Shakespeare's principal source for *The Comedy of Errors* was the comedy called *Menaechmi* by Plautus, the third-century BC Roman dramatist who, with the second-century playwright Terence, was a mainstay of the Humanist educational curriculum in Renaissance Europe.[2] The earliest mention of Shakespeare's play, by John Manningham in 1602, linked it with Plautus', as we have seen. As Wolfgang Riehle notes, when Thomas Nashe's fictional unfortunate travellers Jack Wilton and the Earl of Surrey, in Nashe's 1594 novel, arrive in Wittenberg and are treated to a magic show by the conjurer Cornelius Agrippa who offers to bring up famous figures from antiquity, the assembled company of learned doctors demand first to see 'pleasant Plautus' (p. 1). His plays were adapted and translated as well as being performed often in the original Latin, in English schools and universities in the sixteenth century. Shakespeare's grammar school education at Stratford would have placed him in early contact with the Roman dramatist.

Plautus' plot of a young man from Syracuse, Menaechmus, who, accompanied by his slave Messenio, travels the world seeking his lost twin and comes at last to Epidamnus where the twin lives, is the basis for Shakespeare's: his Antipholus of Syracuse, accompanied by his slave Dromio, has been seeking his brother for seven years, and arrives in Ephesus where the twin lives. In Act 1, Scene

---

[1] For example, S. A. Tannenbaum, 'Notes on *The Comedy of Errors*', *Shakespeare Jahrbuch*, 68 (1932), 103–24; C. J. Sisson, *New Readings in Shakespeare*, 2 vols. (Cambridge, 1956), i. 88–98; and on the passage in question, Charles D. Stewart, *Some Textual Difficulties in Shakespeare* (New Haven, 1914), pp. 237–40, 241–7, and Gary Taylor, 'Textual and Sexual Criticism: A Crux in *The Comedy of Errors*', *Renaissance Drama*, NS 19 (1988), 195–225.

[2] The major studies of Plautus' influence on Shakespeare are to be found in T. W. Baldwin's *William Shakspere's Small Latine and Lesse Greeke*, 2 vols. (Urbana, Ill., 1944), the same author's *On the Compositional Genetics of 'The Comedy of Errors'* (Urbana, 1965), and more recently, Wolfgang Riehle's *Shakespeare, Plautus and the Humanist Tradition* (Cambridge, 1990), which focuses mainly on *The Comedy of Errors*.

2, Antipholus and Dromio have just arrived in Ephesus and are
being warned of the danger to them, as Syracusans, if they should
be caught and identified, because of the trade war that is going on
between the two city-states. We have learned of the war and its
consequences for Syracusans who find themselves in Ephesus
in the first scene. Plautus began with the local Menaechmus and
a stock character of Roman comedy, the parasite Peniculus, who
is in quest of a free meal (the character is suppressed by
Shakespeare). The travelling twin and his servant appear at the
beginning of Act 2, where they meet the courtesan's cook Cylindrus, who naturally takes Menaechmus for the local twin, the first
of the errors of identity. Plautus carefully accounts in his Prologue
for the twins having the same name, which is of course necessary
for the comedy of errors that ensues.[1] The Syracusan twin had
been called Sosicles, but his grandfather renamed him Menaechmus in memory of his lost brother, stolen from the boy's father by
a childless merchant from Epidamnus (an 'Argument', added to
Plautus' text by a later hand, also mentions the renaming). Shakespeare, in the long opening scene which is his greatly expanded
substitution for the 'Argument' and Plautus' seventy-five-line Prologue, confusingly has Egeon say that his twin infants were so identical that they could only be distinguished by name (1.1.52). It is
worth dwelling for a moment on the Prologue to *Menaechmi*, which
was omitted in William Warner's 1595 translation of the play, and
is rarely mentioned in discussions of Shakespeare's sources.

The Prologue sets the scene, Epidamnus, and specifies that the
father of the twin boys was an old merchant from Syracuse (*Mercator . . . Syracusis senex*). When the boys were seven, the merchant
took one of them with him on a voyage to Tarentum where he had
business, leaving the other at home with his mother. At Tarentum,
during a festival, the boy was stolen by the merchant from
Epidamnus; the father died of grief a few days later. It was when
the news reached their home in Syracuse that the grandfather,
himself called Menaechmus, renamed the remaining twin. The
business of trade and the nautical environment, both prominent in
Shakespeare's opening scene and throughout the play, are clearly
established. Shakespeare changed the setting to Ephesus, but

[1] 'Idem est ambobus nomen geminis fratribus', Prol., 48 (in *Plautus*, trans. Paul
Nixon, Loeb Classical Library, 4 vols. (1916–32); vol. ii (1917), p. 368).

retained Epidamnus, substituting it for Plautus' Tarentum: the city is mentioned several times in his play, and it is there that Egeon's wife is said to have given birth to their twin sons. Plautus' Prologue goes on to inform the audience that the Epidamnian merchant had adopted the twin he had stolen (*geminus surrepticius*), provided him with a wife and made him his heir. The merchant had died when, attempting to ford a rain-swollen river (*fluvium rapidum*) near the city, he was swept away, leaving the boy with his inherited wealth and his wife, living in Epidamnus. In the stage direction at the beginning of Act 2, the Folio text of *Errors* may echo the Latin adjective designating the stolen twin in Plautus' Prologue: Adriana is identified as 'wife to Antipholis Sereptus'. Storms and dangerous bodies of water figure prominently in the dramatic narratives of both Plautus' Prologue and Shakespeare's Egeon.

Shakespeare's major alterations of his principal dramatic source are crucial. The most obvious is his addition of a servant for the Ephesian Antipholus. The servant is also a twin, and also bears the same name—Dromio—as his brother, the servant of the Syracusan Antipholus. The addition multiplies the possibilities of confusion and the number of its victims: in Plautus' play, the local Menaechmus does not have a servant who is a twin, so neither he nor his brother can be mistaken on that score. The slave Messenio can be mistaken as to which Menaechmus is his master, of course, and he is, but not until Act 5, just before the denouement when the twins meet at last. Until that point, it is the citizens of Epidamnus— the wife and the father-in-law of the local Menaechmus, the parasite, the courtesan, her cook and her maid, a doctor—who confuse the twins, and the action of the play is virtually a succession of scenes in which one after another of them makes the obvious mistake. The second servant added by Shakespeare makes the two Antipholus brothers also victims of error; no one is spared. The entire household of the Ephesian Antipholus is deceived by the presence of the Syracusan Dromio. The first error in the play occurs in 1.2 only forty lines into the scene when the local Dromio enters to call his master, as he takes Antipholus of Syracuse to be, home to dinner. The Syracusan Menaechmus in Plautus' play is also puzzled when he is invited by the courtesan to the dinner he supposedly ordered, but the bewilderment of his Shakespearian counterpart is the greater because he thinks that it is *his* Dromio, who had left the scene just twenty lines earlier, who is making this

mad invitation and talking such nonsense about a wife. His confusion and distress, so soon after arriving in what he already knew
was a bizarre and morally decadent city, and has just learned is
also a hostile one, are very important, both for his characterization
and in the rapidly growing feelings of unease, desperation, then
terror, that beset the Syracusan strangers. And the doubling of the
Dromios adds another pair of brothers to be reunited in the play's
family-romance finale. Shakespeare thus reinforced the family
motif central to romance, as he would a few years later reinforce it
in *As You Like It* by making the rightful duke and the usurping duke
brothers and their daughters cousins, whereas his source, Thomas
Lodge's prose romance *Rosalynde*, spoke only of a rightful king
and a usurper, and of the two heroines, their daughters, only
as friends.

The family theme is strengthened also by Shakespeare's handling of the roles of the wife of the local brother and the courtesan.
In Plautus' play, the courtesan, Erotium, not only is named while
the wife remains anonymous, but is much more prominent, receiv-
ing the gifts that the unprincipled Menaechmus of Epidamnus glee-
fully steals from his wife and gives to his mistress. Erotium has
three scenes, one each in Acts 2, 3 and 4, and speaks over seventy
lines; the wife does not appear until Act 4 and has few more lines
than the courtesan. Shakespeare considerably reduces the latter's
role, bringing her on only in 4.3, giving her only thirty lines in all,
and leaving her nameless. Adriana, on the other hand, first
appears in 2.1, in a long scene with her sister Luciana, another
of Shakespeare's additions, replacing Plautus' Senex, the wife's
father. Adriana is in five big scenes, speaks 260 lines, and has
several long speeches, including ones of thirty-seven (2.2) and
twenty-five lines (5.1). The stock jealous wife of Roman comedy
becomes in *The Comedy of Errors* a real woman, jealous certainly,
but also agonized at the thought of her husband's forsaking her,
pleading with him (as she believes; it is the wrong Antipholus, of
course), confiding her anguish in her sister, eager to recover and to
care for her supposedly mad husband in the last act. Shakespeare's
deliberate shift of emphasis from the mistress to the wife and his
addition of yet another pair of siblings, the sisters Adriana and
Luciana, further highlights the family motif, while it also provides
a legitimate love interest for Antipholus of Syracuse. Although
little is made of the blossoming of new love in the romance finale

when all the existing family relationships are so joyously renewed, it replaces the avowedly illicit and vengeful liaison between Menaechmus of Epidamnus and Erotium in Plautus' play. The relationship between Antipholus of Ephesus and the Courtesan is barely sketched by Shakespeare, and enjoyment of anything more than her pleasant company is explicitly denied by Antipholus (3.1.112–14). His vow to give her the chain he had ordered for his wife is provoked by Adriana's infuriating refusal to open the door of his own house to him and his friends (3.1.115–20); he does not steal from her and give her possessions to the Courtesan in revenge for her alleged shrewishness as does his Plautine counterpart. On the whole, Shakespeare softens the harsher, satirical, domestic comedy aspects of *Menaechmi*: he eliminates stock characters like the parasite and the old father-in-law (Senex), reduces the courtesan's role, makes Adriana much more than a two-dimensional stage shrew (as he had done with another shrew, Katherina, in *The Taming of the Shrew* perhaps just a couple of years earlier), gives her a confidante, a sister, and replaces the husband's cynical betrayal of his wife with the wife's desperate fear that she has lost her beauty and hence her husband, with whom she claims to be as one (2.2.113–49).

William Warner.   The summary account of intertextual relations between Plautus' *Menaechmi* and Shakespeare's *Comedy of Errors* does not stop there. On 10 June 1594, a translation of the Plautine comedy was entered in the Stationers' Register, and the work duly appeared bearing the date 1595 on the title-page:

MENÆCMI. A pleasant and fine Conceited Comædie, taken out of the most excellent wittie Poet Plautus. Chosen purposely from out of the rest, as least harmfull, and yet most delightfull. Written in English, by W.W. London. Printed by Tho. Creede, and are to be sold by William Barley at his shop in Gratious streete. 1595.[1]

This is the first known English translation of the play. While it is true that only people with a good school education would have been capable of reading Plautus' play in Latin, merely making it available to a wider non-Latin reading public was not Warner's

---

[1] From the edition of Warner's *Menaechmi* in Geoffrey Bullough, ed., *Narrative and Dramatic Sources of Shakespeare*, 8 vols. (1957–75), i. 12.

primary aim. As the title-page makes clear, this is a faithful adaptation, 'taken out' of Plautus, and 'written' by W.W. True, the
epistle of 'the Printer to the Reader' states that the 'writer' had
'Englished' several of Plautus' comedies 'for the use and delight of
his private friends, who in Plautus' own words are not able to
understand them'. But the printer goes on to explain that the
author's intention was neither to produce a mere translation, nor
to 'notoriously vary from the Poet's own order'. His purpose was
rather that of the Humanist educators who had throughout the
century adapted Roman comedy for the intellectual recreation of
their pupils. As it is expressed in the Prologue to Nicholas Udall's
mid-century school comedy *Roister Doister* (*c.*1552), an adaptation
of Plautus' *Miles Gloriosus*:

> What creature is in health, either young or old,
> But some mirth with modesty will be glad to use,
> As we in this interlude shall now unfold? . . .
> Knowing nothing more commendable for a man's recreation
> Than mirth which is used in an honest fashion.
>
> For mirth prolongeth life and causeth health . . .[1]

The printer offers the book to the reader as 'a public recreation
and delight', and begs his indulgence for the 'little alteration' of
the original because 'as it is only a matter of merriment', it 'can
breed no detriment of importance'. The title-page has already
announced that this play has been selected as being 'least harmful
and yet most delightful'. Others would follow if the readers greeted
this 'little labour' with 'courteous acceptance'. Whether they did
or not we do not know, but no further Plautus translations were
immediately forthcoming.

There is virtually unanimous agreement that 'W.W.' was
William Warner (1558–1609), a minor late Elizabethan man of letters and a lawyer by profession.[2] As an author, Warner is known
principally for his elaborately structured prose romance *Pan his*

---

[1] From *Three Sixteenth-Century Comedies*, ed. Charles Whitworth, New Mermaids
(1984), p. 93.

[2] Warner's latest biographer dissents. Ursula F. Appelt finds the styles of
Warner's acknowledged works and the *Menaechmi* translation too different to war-
rant the attribution of common authorship ('William Warner', in *Dictionary of
Literary Biography*, vol. 172: *Sixteenth-Century British Nondramatic Writers*,
Fourth Series, ed. David A. Richardson (Detroit, 1996), 244–8 (p. 245)).

Syrinx (1584) and for his massive part-historical, part-literary compilation in verse, *Albion's England*, first published in four books in 1586, and swelling to sixteen in the posthumous edition of 1612. There has, however, been considerable disagreement as to the degree to which, or whether at all, Shakepeare knew and drew from Warner's *Menaechmi* for his *Comedy of Errors*.[1] The coincidence of dates as well as their common source makes it difficult to maintain the assumption that neither author knew a thing about the other's work: Warner's translation was entered for publication the month after the Lord Chamberlain's company was formed, and several months at most before Shakespeare presumably began writing his comedy for the Christmas season's entertainments at Court and/or Gray's Inn. The work is said to have circulated, with others, in manuscript among Warner's acquaintances. The *Gesta Grayorum* account of the 'Night of Errors' likens the play performed that evening to 'Plautus his *Menaechmus*'. Warner was a lawyer of the common pleas, and doubtless had connections with members of one or more of the Inns of Court, if he himself was not an Innsman. Finally, his publications of 1584 and 1586, *Syrinx* and *Albion's England*, were both dedicated to Henry Carey, Lord Hunsdon, the Lord Chamberlain; later editions were dedicated to Hunsdon's son and successor as Chamberlain, George Carey. Warner lived in Hertfordshire, near the Hunsdon estates.

The delay of half a year or more between the book's entry in the Register and its publication in 1595 may appear puzzling, but is not unusual in the annals of Elizabethan printing. Perhaps even it was the notoriety of the Gray's Inn 'Night of Errors' that prompted Thomas Creede to get Warner's version of 'Plautus his *Menaechmus*' quickly into print, or Warner himself to deliver a long-promised manuscript to the publisher Barley. Creede already had at least indirect connections with Shakespeare in 1594: he printed that year *The First Part of the Contention betwixt the two Famous Houses of York and Lancaster* (later published in the First Folio as *Henry VI*, Part Two); though unauthorized and probably a memorial reconstruction, the text was entered in the Stationers'

---

[1] For example, Baldwin insisted that Shakespeare did not use Warner at all, but worked solely from the Latin (*Compositional Genetics*, pp. 47–8 and *passim*), Bullough thinks that he 'may possibly' have read Warner, though echoes are few (i. 3–4), and Riehle is 'convinced that Shakespeare did indeed use Warner' (280).

Register in March 1594. Creede also printed for Barley in the same year *The True Tragedy of Richard III* (entered June 1594), an anonymous work which if nothing else is more or less contemporary with Shakespeare's own *Richard III*, and he attributed his 1595 quarto (entered July 1594) of *The Lamentable Tragedy of Locrine* to 'W.S.'. Creede went on to print several other plays, including the first quarto of *Henry V* and Qq2–5 of *Richard III*, as well as becoming a thorn in the side of the dramatist, printing further unauthorized copies and attributing others' works to Shakespeare on several occasions.[1] It is conceivable that Shakespeare could have seen the manuscript of Warner's *Menaechmi* in Creede's shop, though his direct, personal connections, if any, with the printer at this time or any other are very uncertain. In any case, from this Hunsdon–Warner–Creede nexus, a manuscript copy of the Plautus translation could have found its way into Shakespeare's hands sometime between the spring and winter of 1594.

Internal evidence is not conclusive, however. While a few phrases and expressions in *Errors* find parallels in Warner's *Menaechmi*, it is clear that Shakespeare was not depending in any slavish or systematic way upon Warner's text. Riehle points out some evidence of possible borrowing (279–83); for example, that the Folio's odd form 'Epidamium' for Epidamnus may be a corruption, due perhaps to compositors' misreading of Shakespeare's handwriting, or to the latter's carelessness, of Warner's form of the name, 'Epidamnum', which he uses throughout. Like Shakespeare, Warner calls the courtesan a 'gentlewoman', a deliberate 'upgrading' of Plautus' *meretrix*. Riehle further notes that both Warner and Shakespeare change the bracelet that Menaechmus of Epidamnus gives to Erotium, to a gold chain, one of the more prominent stage properties in *The Comedy of Errors*. Robert S. Miola, however, finds this unconvincing as evidence: both readers and adapters of Plautus might have come up with the same word for the Latin *spinter*. He concludes that 'there is simply no proof that Shakespeare used Warner for this play'.[2] Neither, however, is

---

[1] Jean-Marie and Angela Maguin have a very useful brief section in their recent biography, on Shakespeare's printers and his possible access through them to many of the books he so obviously knew and used in the composition of his works (*William Shakespeare* (Paris, 1996), pp. 388–95). On Creede, see pp. 393–4.

[2] Robert S. Miola, 'The Play and the Critics', in *'The Comedy of Errors': Critical Essays*, ed. Miola (New York and London, 1997), pp. 3–51; p. 5.

there is any necessary contradiction in Riehle's conclusion that 'Shakespeare not only used the original *Menaechmi* but also worked with Warner's English version when he wrote his *Errors*' (283). In view of the July 1594 Stationers' Register entry, it is less likely that Warner heard about or even attended the 'Night of Errors' at Gray's Inn before making his adaptation of Plautus, than that Shakespeare saw in manuscript and echoed in his title a phrase in the last line of Warner's version of Plautus' 'Argument': 'Much pleasant error'. The reader of the latter in the present edition may compare the two contemporary Elizabethan texts for himself (Appendix C).

Plautus, 'Amphitruo'. Shakespeare's debt to Plautus did not stop with his use of the twins plot from *Menaechmi*. He must have had at hand a collected edition of Plautus in Latin, for he also drew upon another play by the Roman dramatist, the mythological farce *Amphitruo*. No English translation of that play was available. It has been, however, one of the most popular and durable of Plautus' plays, spawning dozens of adaptations and imitations as well as translations into modern languages. The title of Jean Giraudoux's 1929 French version, *Amphitryon 38*, wittily acknowledges the numerous previous renditions. In the seventeenth century, Dryden in England and Jean de Rotrou and Molière in France, among others, wrote adaptations. An English translation by Lawrence Echard finally appeared a century after Shakespeare's play, in 1694. The brilliant farcical centrepiece of *The Comedy of Errors*, Act 3, Scene 1 (124 lines), in which Antipholus of Ephesus, with servant and dinner guests, is locked out of his own house by his wife who believes he is inside dining with her, and those within and those without engage in a violent slanging match, is constructed largely from two scenes of *Amphitruo*, the very long Act 1, Scene 1, and the long Act 2, totalling some 770 lines in all, or two-thirds of the entire play (there is however a gap in the manuscript). Here too there are two pairs of identical twins, but they are the result of supernatural skulduggery, not natural childbirth, and here too, a master, servants and a wife are deceived. Amphitryon, a victorious Theban general, returns home from war and sends his slave Sosia ahead of him to announce their arrival to his wife Alcmena. Sosia finds his double guarding the house, issuing insults and threatening serious bodily harm if he attempts to force an entry. The double is Mercury who, in Sosia's likeness, is guarding the door while his master Jupiter, in Amphitryon's likeness, is inside making love to the unsuspecting Alcmena, who is delighted to have her husband safely back at home, especially as she is pregnant: actually she is expecting twins, one of whom, Hercules, is the son of Jupiter, while the other is Amphitryon's son; the off-stage birth of the two boys is related by a nurse. Jupiter has made the night stand still. When Amphitryon arrives (Act 2), he becomes furious with his slave who insists insanely that he, Sosia himself, is already inside the house. In both scenes, the themes of madness and loss of one's identity are explicit, as is knockabout farce, particularly in 1.1 where Mercury/Sosia repeatedly beats the real Sosia for continuing to insist that he is who he is and that he lives in the house being guarded by his pugnacious double. Sosia's bewildered insistence that his name *is* Sosia and that he *is* Amphitryon's slave and that this *is* his house clearly lies close behind Dromio of Ephesus' similar protestations in Act 3, Scene 1 of Shakespeare's comedy. The words *os* (face) and *nomen* (name) fly about in the scene in Plautus' play as they do in Shakespeare's. Both Dromios and Antipholus of Syracuse at different times echo Sosia's desperate doubts as to his own identity: 'Ubi ego perii? Ubi immutatus sum? Ubi ego formam perdidi?' ('Where did I lose myself? Where was I transformed? Where did I drop my shape?') (l. 456).[1] Amphitryon too claims to be bewitched and not to know who he is any more (l. 844).

Shakespeare makes one brief but vital scene from Plautus' two, an excellent example of the dramatist's compression of source material that was too copious for his needs. He was to do it repeatedly in later plays, especially when adapting romance narrative material. The imposture by the two mischievous gods and their occupation of Amphitryon's house account for the whole plot of Plautus' play, while in Shakespeare's, the scene is just an episode in the play of errors. Here he crafts his one central farcical scene from the two episodes in which the slave Sosia, first alone then in the company of his master, attempts to gain entry to their house. But this second Plautine comedy left its mark in other ways on Shakespeare's play, and is a more important source than it has usually been reckoned to be. It seems likely that the Sosia–Mercury pair may have first given Shakespeare the idea of doubling the ser-

---

[1] In *Plautus*, trans. Nixon, vol. i (1916), p. 48. Bullough prints extracts from *Amphitruo* (i. 40–9).

vants in his play, making two pairs of twins with the same names, with the resulting increase in confusion that has already been mentioned. He must have been reading the two works by Plautus at virtually the same time in a collected edition, and moving from one to the other was a natural process. Furthermore, the motif of loss of identity and the fear of madness in oneself and the suspicion of it in others, a central element in Shakespeare's play, is present throughout *Amphitruo* as it is not in *Menaechmi*. Shakespeare's other sources, romance narrative and biblical accounts, contributed to the theme certainly, but it is clearly there also in the second play by Plautus. The one Roman play is urban domestic comedy, the other is farce (though that is a modern critical term and not a classical one),[1] the only extant burlesque of a mythological subject in Roman drama (Plautus called *Amphitruo* a *tragicomoedia*). The farce of *The Comedy of Errors*, so prominent that the play has commonly been defined as being only that, comes mainly from *Amphitruo*, but the two Plautine genres are fused in Shakespeare's play, giving it a unique quality that is irreducible to one or the other type. But even they and Warner's adaptation of *Menaechmi* are not sufficient to account fully for its other major dimension, namely romance, particularly in the Egeon plot that frames and ultimately subsumes the Roman comedy, the ambiance of strangeness and unease in the city of Ephesus, and the related theme of metamorphosis.

'Apollonius of Tyre': Gower or Twine? The ancient story of Apollonius of Tyre, possibly originating in a Hellenistic Greek romance in about the third century, enjoyed continuous popularity throughout Europe from late antiquity until the Renaissance. A sixth-century bishop of Poitiers, Venantius Fortunatus, alluded to Apollonius as the type of the exile, so the story must have been well known by that time.[2] The earliest surviving version is in Latin prose: no fewer than 114 manuscripts of the *Historia*

---

[1] *OED*'s earliest citation of the term as designating generally a dramatic mode (rather than a specific genre, that of late medieval French *farce*, virtually unknown in England apart from one or two examples by John Heywood from the 1530s) is from Dryden's epilogue to Etherege's *Man of Mode* (1676).

[2] *Patrologia Latina*, lxxxviii. 227. Cited in Michael Swanton, ed., *Anglo-Saxon Prose* (1975), p. 158; this volume contains a modern prose translation of the Old English version of *Apollonius* (158–73).

Apollonii are extant, dating from the ninth century to the seven-teenth.[1] Later versions abound, in Latin and in the vernaculars; it is alluded to in the *Carmina Burana*, in a Provençal romance, in the poetry of Chaucer, Robert Henryson, Chrétien de Troyes, and Hans Sachs, the German *Meistersinger*. It came down to the Renaissance in England by two parallel routes: the *Gesta Romanorum*, a large, extremely popular fourteenth-century compilation of exemplary legends and stories, and John Gower's *Confessio Amantis*, the major work in English by the late fourteenth-century poet and friend of Chaucer. But there had been Old English and Middle English ver-sions much earlier; only fragments of those remain. Gower devotes most of Book 8 of the *Confessio* to the Apollonius story. His own source for the legend was not the *Gesta*, but a twelfth-century ver-sion in Godfrey of Viterbo's *Pantheon*. Chaucer too knew the story, and referred to it in the Introduction to his *Man of Law's Tale*, but did not leave a version of it. Gower's work was printed by William Caxton in 1483, then twice in the sixteenth century by Berthelette, in 1532 and 1554, and not again until the nineteenth century. It has traditionally been assumed that Shakespeare got his frame story of Egeon and his narrative of his shipwreck and loss of his wife and one of his sons, and of his ultimate reunion with his wife and both his sons in Ephesus, directly from Gower. While it is pos-sible that Shakespeare had access forty years later to a copy of the 1554 edition of *Confessio Amantis*, or indeed that he saw it in manu-script, it would be a departure from his normal practice of using very recently published works, fiction and nonfiction, as sources.[2] Also, Shakespeare had the habit of moving in his reading from one section or episode in a source collection to others in the same vol-ume, returning to them later for other works: he did so when he read Plutarch and the English chronicles, the tragedies of Seneca, Ovid's *Metamorphoses* and the short story collections of Painter and Cinthio, for example. Allusions to and borrowings from Chaucer's works occur throughout Shakespeare's œuvre, from *The*

---

[1] Elizabeth Archibald's *Apollonius of Tyre: Medieval and Renaissance Themes and Variations* (Cambridge, 1991) includes a text and translation of the *Historia Apollonii* and appendices listing later versions and allusions.

[2] John H. Fisher lists forty-nine extant manuscripts of the three versions of *Con-fessio Amantis* in his standard study, *John Gower, Moral Philosopher and Friend of Chaucer* (1964), pp. 304–5. Presumably even more were extant in the sixteenth century.

Rape of Lucrece in 1594 to *The Two Noble Kinsmen* in 1613; and then, there were no fewer than ten editions of Chaucer between 1532 and 1594, the year *Lucrece* was published.[1] Certainly Shakespeare and/or his collaborator (probably George Wilkins) had seen a copy of Gower's work by the time they wrote *Pericles* in 1607 or 1608: Gower is the Chorus in the play; much is made of his great age and the antique fame of his book, and his octosyllabic couplet is imitated in most of the Chorus's speeches. But no other tale or excerpt from *Confessio Amantis* figures among Shakespeare's known sources, or even probable or possible sources, as collected by Geoffrey Bullough in his *Narrative and Dramatic Sources of Shakespeare*, or as surveyed by Kenneth Muir.[2] It would have been atypical at least if Shakespeare, had he known the 1554 edition of Gower's *Confessio Amantis* as early as 1594, had not returned to it at all between then and the time of his collaboration on *Pericles* some thirteen or fourteen years later. Furthermore there is really very little of the Apollonius legend in *The Comedy of Errors*.

I think it just as likely that Shakespeare found the Apollonius narrative and took the little he needed for his considerably abbreviated and altered sketch of it in *The Comedy of Errors* in a popular work much nearer to hand than *Confessio Amantis*: a recent prose version, Lawrence Twine's *Pattern of Painful Adventures*, entered in the Stationers' Register in 1576, but probably not published until 1594, when it was apparently issued twice; there was another reprint in 1607. The two dates are particularly timely where the composition of Shakespeare's two Apollonian plays, *Errors* and *Pericles*, is concerned. The *Pattern* is a main source, with Gower, for *Pericles*, and for Wilkins's prose narrative based partly on the play, *The Painful Adventures of Pericles, Prince of Tyre*, published in 1608, the year before the quarto of the play. The printer of Twine's novel, Valentine Simmes, had just set up shop in 1594. Twine's book was among the very first he printed. Though the first issue bears no date, it does bear Simmes's name, and it must not therefore date from 1576 or any other year before 1594; the second issue does bear the date '1594'. He must have acquired the manuscript among the stock he bought from the original licensee, William Howe, and

---

[1] Ann Thompson, *Shakespeare's Chaucer: A Study in Literary Origins* (Liverpool, 1978), pp. 220–1.

[2] Kenneth Muir, *The Sources of Shakespeare's Plays* (1977; New Haven, 1978).

brought it out quickly to get his name on a title-page and before the reading public.[1] Simmes was to become, like Creede, at least indirectly associated with Shakespeare through the printing of several of his plays, beginning with quartos of *Richard II* and *Richard III* in 1597.

Twine's source was not Gower, but the *Gesta Romanorum* in one of its many Latin editions; an English translation by Richard Robinson (1577) omitted the Apollonius story. Certain details are unique to the *Gesta* and Twine (Archibald, 191). In outline, the plot has Apollonius (Apollinus in Gower), King of Tyre, sail to Antioch to woo the daughter of Antiochus. He must answer a riddle first (many hopeful suitors have failed and have paid with their heads), and discovers the horrible truth that Antiochus is married to his own daughter in an incestuous union. Apollonius flees, returns home, then, when Antiochus despatches assassins to kill him, flees again, to Tarsus where he saves the city from famine. He sails again, is shipwrecked in Cyrene, is helped by fishermen and goes to the court at Pentapolis where he so impresses King Altistrates that he wins the hand of the princess Lucina. They marry, she becomes pregnant, they leave to return to Tyre. Another shipwreck occurs. Lucina is thought to be dead and is thrown overboard in a rich casket. Apollonius is left with his infant daughter, born on board ship. He returns to Tarsus with the infant whom he names Tharsia and entrusts her to his friends Stranguilio and his wife Dionisiades, leaving her nurse Ligozides to care for her. On her deathbed the nurse tells Tharsia whose daughter she really is. Dionisiades becomes jealous of Tharsia's beauty which eclipses that of her own daughter and plots to have her killed. As the hired murderer Theophilus is about to stab Tharsia near the tomb of her dead nurse, pirates arrive and 'rescue' her. They take her to Machilenta (Mytilene in Gower and *Pericles*) and sell her to a bawd who takes her away to the brothel. The governor of the city,

---

[1] Simmes in fact printed Twine's *Pattern* for 'widow Newman'. The only other publication recorded for her is Richard Barnfield's *Affectionate Shepherd*, also in 1594, printed by John Danter for her and 'J. G[ubbin]'. Simmes printed a book of psalms and prayers in association with Howe in 1594 before, apparently, taking over his shop, or at least his presses. Perhaps the Widow Newman acquired the shop and stock herself, and hired Simmes to print *Pattern*, which was among the unprinted manuscripts that had been in Howe's possession at the time he sold his business. Simmes also printed the 1607 edition.

Athanagoras, coming to the brothel to deflower the new recruit, takes pity and relents upon hearing her story, and becomes her protector. Apollonius, wandering the seas in a catatonic state of despair and near-madness, arrives at Machilenta. Athanagoras sends the young maiden Tharsia to sing to him, hoping that her wondrous gifts may be able to rouse him from his stupor. She succeeds and as she tells her story, Apollonius comes to realize that she is his own daughter. Athanagoras shares their joy, and is married to Tharsia with her father's blessing. They all set sail for Tarsus to exact revenge upon the wicked Stranguilio and Dionisiades, but an angel appears to Apollonius in his sleep and commands him to go to Ephesus, to the temple of Diana, and there recount all his adventures 'with a loud voice'.[1] He does so (Twine duly has him summarize, in inset narrative, the entire story thus far; p. 472), and there the priestess, who is none other than Lucina, not dead at sea, but miraculously revived by a learned doctor and his pupil in Ephesus where her casket had washed ashore, recognizes him. The family is whole again, with the next generation assured in the marriage of Athanagoras and Tharsia. In the four remaining chapters, they all sail, first to Antioch where, the wicked king having died, the people had elected Apollonius as their king *in absentia*, then to Tyre, then to Tarsus, finally to Pentapolis to see Lucina's old father. Apollonius and Lucina have a son, and when at last they die in very old age, their son and daughter and her husband inherit their lands and wealth.

The above summary contains the main plot elements common to nearly all branches of the legend. Many details have been omitted from this outline of the story, as Twine retold it. It is sufficient I think to show just what, if anything, Shakespeare may have borrowed from it for *The Comedy of Errors*. The parts of Shakespeare's play that resemble, however distantly, the Apollonius story are Egeon's long narrative in the first scene (beginning at line 36) when he is under arrest in Ephesus and the Duke demands to know what brought him, a Syracusan, to a hostile city, and the final scene (5.1.130–end) when Egeon, being led to execution, is reunited with his long-lost wife Emilia and the two of them with their children. That plot is suspended while the Plautine comedy of errors unfolds with the arrival of the Syracusan

---

[1] The text of Twine's novel is reprinted in Bullough, vi. 423–82 (p. 471).

Antipholus and Dromio in Ephesus in the second scene. We may notice first of all that Shakespeare's names come neither from Gower nor from Twine—Apollonius/Apollinus becomes Egeon, Lucina (Twine; unnamed in Gower) his wife, Emilia (though 'Lucina' may be echoed in 'Luciana', the name of Adriana's sister, a character invented by Shakespeare). They are the parents of twin sons named Antipholus, not a daughter called Thaise (Gower) or Tharsia (Twine). Egeon and Emilia are reunited in Ephesus— Shakespeare's alteration of Plautus' settings, Epidamnus and Thebes, becomes crucial—but the rest of their Mediterranean map bears little resemblance to that of Apollonius: instead of Tyre, Antioch, Pentapolis, Tarsus, and Mytilene, Egeon names Syracuse, Epidamnus, Corinth, and Epidaurus in his narrative. Shakespeare had no use for the initial episodes in the Apollonius saga, the voyage to Antioch and the encounter with the incestuous king and his daughter (though as the play begins, Egeon *is* under sentence of death, as were those suitors for the hand of Antiochus' daughter who failed to solve the riddle, and as was Apollonius himself after he had fled from Antioch), nor for the Tarsus episodes, nor for the account of Apollonius' shipwreck at Pentapolis where he met his wife, nor of course for the brothel episode since his plot has the twin sons from Plautus and not the daughter of the *Historia Apollonii*.

It is apparent also that in planning his comedy, Shakespeare first went to *Menaechmi*, then to *Amphitruo* for Act 3, Scene 1, and only subsequently grafted the frame plot from the Apollonius legend on to the rest, deftly integrating them at the end: Egeon's twin sons replaced Apollonius' daughter in the opening narrative, as they were already in the mix, so to speak. Shakespeare adapted and dovetailed some elements of the Apollonius story to fit the story he had already adapted from Plautus; indeed, as we have seen, the Prologue and the Argument to *Menaechmi* contain something like parts of the narratives of Egeon and Apollonius, notably the quintessential romance device of the broken family. It would seem to have been necessary only for Shakespeare to recall the general pattern of the Apollonius narrative, substituting details from the Plautine plots he had already adopted and adapted. Egeon's nearer literary ancestry, rather than Apollonius of Tyre, is perhaps a composite, the father of the Menaechmus twins, who dies of grief at Tarentum when one of them is kidnapped, and the Epidamnian merchant who steals then adopts his son; perhaps also, since Antipholus and Dromio of Syracuse have grown up living with Egeon, the grandfather who in Plautus changes the remaining twin's name. Like his Plautine counterparts, Egeon is a merchant, not a king, and like one of them, he is from Syracuse, not Tyre. He had business interests in Epidamnus; the kidnapper and adoptive father of one Menaechmus is from Epidamnus, where Plautus set his play. Other fragments of romance in the background of *The Comedy of Errors* Shakespeare probably made up himself, or recalled from yet other works he had read. For example, Antipholus of Ephesus announces that he had been brought from Corinth to Ephesus by Duke Menaphon, uncle of the present duke Solinus (5.1.366–9); he was not stolen from his father as Menaechmus of Epidamnus had been. Maybe Shakespeare retained only the name from Robert Greene's pastoral romance, *Menaphon*, published in 1589, in which there is a shipwreck from which a lady and her infant son are saved by shepherds, and are later reunited with both her father the king and her banished husband, the boy's father. On the other hand, it was Corinthian fishermen, according to Emilia, who had taken the infants Antipholus and Dromio from her all those years ago after a ship from Epidamnus had rescued them from the sea (ll. 356–60; she does not say how she came to Ephesus). These elements may derive from the Apollonius story, with alteration: there is shipwreck in the Apollonius legend but not in Plautus, pirates take Tharsia from the hands not of her rescuers but of her would-be assassin, and they take her to Machilenta (Mytilene) and not Corinth, etc. But of course, very importantly, Shakespeare retained from his reading of the Apollonius narrative in whatever form the account of the separation of husband and wife at sea and their ultimate reunion—at Ephesus. Thus the romance dimension of Shakespeare's play derives from multiple sources, including the so-called Plautine farce, and permeates the text, both in numerous details and in general ambiance. More will be said about this in the following section of the Introduction.

There is no detail of Egeon's narrative in 1.1 or in the family reunion scene in 5.1 which must have come from Gower and could not have come from Twine. In fact, nothing in the opening account of Egeon's mishaps (1.1.36–93, 99–119, 123–35) really need be traced specifically to the Apollonius story in whatever version. As we have seen, the places he mentions do not figure in the famous legend, and the salient details, set out as a list here, hardly correspond to Apollonius' career:

(*a*) Egeon's birth and marriage in Syracuse, his business trip to Epidamnus, his wife's following him a few months later, the birth there of their twin sons and of the twin slaves at the same time in the same place, bought by Egeon to attend on his sons;

(*b*) The return voyage to Syracuse, the storm and desertion of the ship by the crew, their expedient in tying themselves, each with one of each pair of twins, to a mast which then split upon a rock, with the mother and her charges being rescued by a ship from Epidamnus—says Emilia (5.1.356–7); 'by fishermen of Corinth, as we thought', says Egeon (1.1.110)—but it was Emilia's two infant charges who were subsequently taken by force from the Epidamnians by 'rude fishermen of Corinth' (5.1.358–9), which accounts for the mother's ignorance of her son's presence in Ephesus (he had been brought there from Corinth by Duke Menaphon), and the father and his two infants by 'another ship' (1.1.111) which, unable to overtake the other, bent its course 'homeward' (l. 116), wherever that was (Epidaurus, Corinth, Epidamnus, Syracuse . . .) (Fig. 1);

(*c*) His remaining son's and servant's desire to seek their brothers, their departure from Syracuse seven years before, Egeon's own departure to search for them five years ago, his arrival now in Ephesus, unaware of the state of war between the city and his own Syracuse, and the dire fate that awaits him at the end of this very day.

What the two narratives have in common are: (1) a shipwreck somewhere in the Mediterranean; (2) the separation of husband and wife, with a child remaining with the father; (3) the subsequent safe arrival of the wife at Ephesus (Emilia fills in this part, which Egeon could not know, but she gives no details), and much later, the reunion of the couple there.

Nor in the other part of the romance frame of the play is there much left of the Apollonius story. Egeon is reunited with his two sons ashore in Ephesus as he is being led to execution, not on board ship at Machilenta where Apollonius' daughter comes to sing to him in his catatonic state. Music is not involved: *Errors* is unique among Shakespeare's comedies in not having songs or other music indicated anywhere. Egeon is reunited first with one son and

1. Francis Wheatley's painting *The Rescue of Aemilia and the Infants Antipholus and Dromio of Ephesus from Shipwreck* (1794) is testimony to the power of story-telling in dramatic works: the scene depicted is not shown in Shakespeare's play. It is related in Egeon's narrative in 1.1 in which he describes the rescue of Emilia and the two babies with her by 'fishermen of Corinth, as we thought' (l. 110).

servant, the Ephesian ones who do not know him, then almost immediately with the other pair and with his wife who has sheltered the Syracusans in her abbey. Here is the play's one outstanding similarity to the Apollonius narrative: Egeon finds his wife Emilia, whom he had lost at sea, as abbess of a Christian convent in Ephesus, where Apollonius had found his wife Lucina, as priestess in the temple of Diana, years after he had buried her at sea, as he thought. There has been in Emilia's case no rescue from a casket and revival from the dead by Cerimon and his pupil Machaon, or adoption by the doctor and entry into the temple of Diana where Lucina vows to live in chastity and piety in memory of her husband and child. Emilia merely relates very succinctly her rescue from the sea by a ship from Epidamnus and the kidnapping of the two babies by fishermen of Corinth, and nothing about how she came to 'this fortune that you see me in' (5.1.362), that is, being an abbess in Ephesus. Lucina, in Twine's version, 'discoursed unto her lord and husband Apollonius, of all the strange accidents that happened unto her after his casting her forth into the sea . . . how she was . . . for preservation of her honesty, placed among the nuns in the Temple of Diana, where he there found her' (Bullough, vi. 474; spelling modernized).

It is true that Gower once refers to Apollonius' wife as an 'abbess', while 'abbess' and 'abbey' both occur a number of times in Shakespeare's play, but Twine mentions 'nuns' several times. Twine has Apollonius relate his adventures at the temple as the angel had commanded him (p. 472). His narrative is the prelude to the joyful reunion of husband and wife, mother and child. Egeon's comparable narrative in Act 1, Scene 1 of the play is also the prelude to the multiple reunions and general joy at the end of the play's day. It is a résumé of the years-long saga of perils and misadventures that have preceded this, the final chapter of the romance: the remainder of *The Comedy of Errors* is that final chapter of the romance, in the dramatic rather than the narrative mode. Not only does Twine, like Shakespeare but unlike Gower, have his romance hero recount his own story just before its denouement takes place, he also explicitly Christianizes the pagan tale, by having the characters repeatedly give thanks to God and bless his name on virtually every page, despite the temple of Diana (which he calls a 'church' several times), evoking in the last sentence of the tale 'the everlasting kingdom that never shall have end' to which Lucina follows her husband, 'which so far exceedeth the kingdom, which forthwith she left unto her young son Altistrates to inherit, as heavenly joys surmount the earthly, and the bright sun surpasseth the smallest star' (p. 482; spelling modernized). This not only recalls and nearly echoes the images of rebirth and joy and thanksgiving at the end of *Errors*, appropriate to the Christmas season for which it may have been written and first performed, it also helps to account for the shift of scene by Shakespeare from Epidamnus to Ephesus.[1]

Acts and Ephesians.   While it may have been Twine's (or possibly Gower's) rendition of the Apollonius story with its denouement in Ephesus that first suggested to Shakespeare the substitution of that famous city of antiquity for Plautus' Epidamnus, a convergence of other sources must have reinforced the choice.[2] In the first place, the name 'Epidamnus' would not have been particularly well known to Elizabethans, beyond those familar with Plautus and perhaps some other classical texts where it may have occurred. The Romans had renamed the city, on the Adriatic coast of what is now Albania, 'Dyrrachium' (it is called 'Durrës' today). Shakespeare seems to have been uncertain of the correct form of the Latinized Greek name, probably spelling it 'Epidamium', since two different compositors of the Folio text, B and C, spell it that way in its seven occurrences. But the place had a dubious reputation, at least according to Plautus' Messenio, who near the beginning of Act 2 of *Menaechmi*, urges his master, in view of the thin state of his purse, to leave quickly and return home. As Warner renders it:

This town Epidamnum is a place of outrageous expenses, exceeding in all riot and lasciviousness and, I hear, as full of ribalds, parasites, drunkards, catchpoles, coneycatchers, and sycophants as it can hold. Then for courtesans, why here's the currentest stamp of them in the world. . . . The very name shows the nature: no man comes hither *sine damno*.

Warner does not translate the Latin *sine damno*, which means 'without injury, harm or loss', thus retaining the Latin pun on the

---

[1] It would doubtless be frivolous to imagine that Twine's very name caught Shakespeare's eye, its likeness to 'twin' making a near-echo to the central devices of the *Menaechmi* and *Amphitruo* plots. Shakespeare's twins Judith and Hamnet were nine years old in 1594.

[2] While most of Plautus' plays are set in Athens, there are three notable exceptions (besides *Amphitruo*): *Menaechmi* (Epidamnus), *Curculio* (Epidaurus), *Miles Gloriosus* (Ephesus). All three place-names occur in *The Comedy of Errors*. Ephesus figures too in several of the Hellenistic romances, besides *Apollonius*: it is the setting for the climactic action in Achilles Tatius' *Clitophon and Leucippe* (translated into English by William Burton in 1597). In another ancient romance, Xenophon of Ephesus' *Ephesian Tale* (?second century AD), unknown to the Elizabethans, the story begins and ends in Ephesus. And 'The Widow of Ephesus' is one of the most famous short stories in Petronius' *Satyricon*.

form *Epidamno* in the previous line, a pun repeated by Menaechmus in the following line: 'Ne mihi damnum in Epidamno duis' ('[For fear] of your doing me some damage in Epidamnus'). This reputation for wildness and immorality is applied explicitly to Ephesus by the newly arrived Antipholus of Syracuse in the parallel scene in *Errors*, 1.2:

> They say this town is full of cozenage,
> As nimble jugglers that deceive the eye,
> Dark-working sorcerers that change the mind,
> Soul-killing witches that deform the body,
> Disguisèd cheaters, prating mountebanks,
> And many suchlike libertines of sin.
> If it prove so, I will be gone the sooner.
> I'll to the Centaur to go seek this slave.
> I greatly fear my money is not safe.
>
> (1.2.97–105)

Antipholus' fear for the safety of his money is shared by his counterpart Menaechmus, who demands his purse from Messenio, lest the latter be tempted to spend it on courtesans.

Shakespeare could find warrant for transferring the description from Epidamnus to Ephesus in New Testament accounts of the difficulties Saint Paul faced when he attempted to preach the Christian gospel there. In Acts 19, Luke speaks of 'exorcists'— the marginal gloss in the Geneva Bible adds 'or conjurers'—who undertake to cure men possessed of evil spirits (verse 13), those who practise 'curious arts' (19), and of the whole city being 'full of confusion' (29). Verse 32 could well stand as a summary of the last two scenes of the play: 'Some therefore cried one thing, and some another, for the assembly was out of order, and the more part knew not wherefore they were come together'.[1] Artisans and craftsmen are prominent in Luke's Ephesus: perhaps Demetrius the silversmith, who made miniature replica temples or statues for the devotees of Diana and who aroused the townspeople against Paul and his followers (24–9), gave Shakespeare the hint for Angelo the goldsmith who makes trinkets for the servants of Venus and pays

---

[1] Quotations are from the Geneva Bible (1560; first printed in England in 1575), in the facsimile edition published by the University of Wisconsin Press (Madison, 1969). Spelling is modernized.

an officer to arrest Antipholus of Ephesus (4.1.76). In a lengthy speech, the 'town clerk' (Acts 19: 35–41) speaks of accusations and sedition, and invokes Ephesian law as does Duke Solinus in the play's opening scene. Before going to Ephesus, Paul had been at Corinth (Acts 18).

In the book of Acts, Luke relates Paul's various missionary journeys to churches throughout Asia and the Mediterranean. Luke's narrative often resembles Egeon's: he lists countries and towns on the itinerary, and incidents on the voyages, including storms and shipwreck. In the 1560 Geneva Bible, a full-page map of the Mediterranean is printed on an interleaf at the end of Acts, on the verso of a page listing all the countries, islands and towns included on the map (reproduced as Fig. 2). There one finds Ephesus, of course, and also Syracuse, Corinthus and Grecia. Epidamnus (Dyrrachium) and Epidaurus are not mentioned. The first town in the alphabetical list is Amphipolis, which bears a tantalizing resemblance to 'Antipholus', Shakespeare's name for Plautus' Menaechmus twins. The point is not to suggest that Shakespeare looked at the map in the Geneva Bible before writing Egeon's account of his travels in search of his son, or indeed any of the rest of the play. It is rather that recollections or rereadings of Acts may have reinforced and sharpened his recent experience of reading Plautus and Twine's *Pattern of Painful Adventures*, and confirmed Ephesus as his choice for the setting of his comedy of confusion.

In his letter to the Ephesians, Paul admonishes them to respect and honour each other in Christian love.[1] Chapter 4 concludes with the plea: 'Let all bitterness, and anger, and wrath, crying, and evil speaking be put away from you, with all maliciousness. Be ye courteous one to another, and tender-hearted, forgiving one another . . .' (31–2). Much of Chapters 5 and 6 is devoted to precepts on domestic relations: 'Wives, submit yourselves unto your husbands . . .' (5: 22); 'For the husband is the wife's head . . .' (5:

---

[1] If Paul was the author of the epistle. Biblical scholars still debate the question; a doubt was first voiced by Erasmus in the sixteenth century. One argument against Paul's authorship is the large number of words found in Ephesians but not in any of his other known letters. One of those words is *diabolos* (devil), which Paul never uses, preferring the name 'Satan'. For modern scholarly discussions of the issue, see the Introduction to Ephesians by Francis W. Beare in *The Interpreter's Bible*, 12 vols. (New York, 1951–7), vol. x: *Corinthians, Galatians, Ephesians* (1953), 597–601; and C. Leslie Mitton, *Ephesians*, The New Century Bible Commentary (1973; 1981), pp. 2–11.

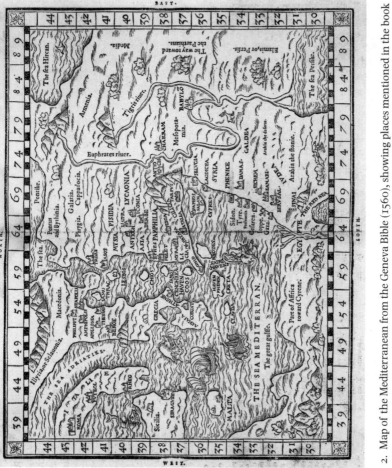

2. Map of the Mediterranean from the Geneva Bible (1560), showing places mentioned in the book of the Acts of the Apostles. The map is on the verso of an interleaf inserted between the end of Acts and the beginning of Romans (leaves 69–70).

23), 'Husbands, love your wives . . .' (5: 25); 'So ought men to love their own wives, as their own bodies; he that loveth his wife, loveth himself. For no man ever yet hated his own flesh, but nourisheth and cherisheth it' (5: 28–9); 'For this cause shall a man leave father and mother, and shall cleave to his wife, and they twain shall be one flesh' (5: 31). These fundamental principles resonate through the dialogues between Adriana and Luciana which open and close Act 2, Scene 1, and Adriana's lengthy monologue at 2.2.115–49, while verses 28–9 may lie somewhere behind the notoriously corrupt and much-emended passage at 2.1.110–14 of Shakespeare's play. In Chapter 6, children are enjoined to honour and obey their parents, and servants to obey their masters with good will, while fathers and masters, for their part, ought not to provoke or threaten their children and servants.

The apostle warns the Ephesians specifically against the devil and the 'unfruitful works of darkness' at 4: 17 and 5: 11 respectively. In Chapter 6 there are further warnings against the forces of evil—the 'principalities', 'powers', 'princes of the darkness of this world' and 'spiritual wickednesses' (6: 12)—that are the enemies of the 'blessèd power' invoked by Shakespeare's beleaguered Antipholus of Syracuse at 4.3.44. Dromio of Syracuse's fearful report of the 'drudge' or 'diviner' who tried to seduce him contains an echo of Paul's famous admonition to 'Put on the whole armour of God' (Ephesians 6: 11), and in particular 'the breastplate of righteousness' (14) and 'the shield of faith' (16): 'And I think if my breast had not been made of faith, and my heart of steel . . .' (3.2.150). Had Shakespeare been thumbing through the Geneva Bible just before he wrote *The Comedy of Errors*, his eye might have been caught by a passage in the epistle to the Galatians, on the page just overleaf from the beginning of Ephesians, where Paul is enumerating the 'works of the flesh', among which are 'idolatry, witchcraft, hatred, debate, emulations, wrath, contentions, seditions, heresies, envy, murders, drunkenness, gluttony, and such like' (5: 19–21). And on the facing page, in a large boldface running title, he would have seen the words 'Free & bond', which could well stand as an epigraph for a main theme of his play.

The lexical field adumbrated in Antipholus' speech quoted above—sorcery, witchcraft, conjuration, enchantment, deceit—is a substantial element in the play's texture: the words *conjure* and *conjurer* together occur six times in *Errors*, more than in any other play in the canon (including all cognate forms of the words); *witch* and *witches* together occur six times in the play, *sorcerer(s)/sorceress* three times (more than in any other play except *The Tempest*), *mountebank(s)* twice (in a total of five occurrences in the entire canon). *Devil/devil's* occurs seven times, and *Satan* three, more than in any other work; that name appears only eight times in Shakespeare. The concentration of words relating to magic, the weird, and the supernatural, diabolical as well as divine, not only reflects Shakespeare's familiarity with New Testament writing concerning Ephesus and its reputation in biblical times, it also contributes crucially to the ambiance of wonder, confusion, and fear that permeates the play. This 'romance' atmosphere will be examined in more detail in the following section.

From two Roman comedies by Plautus, a contemporary English translation of one of them (possibly), an ancient legend in a modern retelling (probably), and a vivid recollection of New Testament accounts of Ephesus (as well perhaps as some literary ones), Shakespeare put together one of his most tightly constructed plays. Far from the mere slavish imitation of Plautus dredged up from schooldays that it was long dismissed as being, *The Comedy of Errors* is an exceptionally skilful composition, wrought from a variety of dramatic and nondramatic sources, judiciously selected and blended, the work of a *playwright*, a maker of plays. The radical mix of romance, farce and domestic comedy into such a coherent whole is unique not only among Shakespeare's works, but in the dramatic literature of his age.[1]

Farce, City Comedy and Romance

E. M. W. Tillyard, in his generally sympathetic if not unequivocally enthusiastic discussion of *Errors*, followed the well-established tradition, in both criticism and stage production, of assuming its 'core' or essence to be farce and its comedy as being that exaggerated kind peculiar to farce. The critical tradition dates from

[1] E. M. W. Tillyard was among the first critics to appreciate the skill and sophistication with which Shakespeare grafted 'romantic framework' on to 'farcical core', and accorded a lengthy chapter to the play, even though he thought, like most earlier critics, that *Errors* was probably Shakespeare's first comedy if not his first play (*Shakespeare's Early Comedies* (1965; repr. 1983), pp. 46–72).

the time of Coleridge at least. He insisted on the uniqueness of
the play in the Shakespeare canon, defining it as 'a legitimate
farce', distinct 'from comedy and from other entertainments' by
'the licence . . . required . . . to produce strange and laughable
situations': 'A comedy would scarcely allow even the two
Antipholuses . . . but farce dares add the two Dromios'.[1] While on
the page, farce may be conveyed by vigorous dialogue and in stage
directions and a sympathetic reader may react to it, only on the
stage does it come into its own, there for all to see. From the low
comedy that crept into the Restoration theatre and was decried by
Dryden and other guardians of dramatic decorum (see p. 27 n. 1
above), to vaudeville and the popular French farces of the late nineteenth century by masters like Labiche, Feydeau and Courteline, to
the slapstick of early American cinema, farce has always had to be
seen to be (dis)believed. It relies on visual gags, facial expressions,
large gestures, exaggeration, repetition, grotesque business such
as pratfalls, ear-wringing and nose-pulling. That generations of literary critics, many of whom rarely or never went to the theatre,
could have affirmed so emphatically that *The Comedy of Errors* is a
farce is just one of the misfortunes of its critical and theatrical
history.

What critics usually have in mind when they label the play as
farce is the increasingly hectic and crazy action in the middle acts
generated by the presence in Ephesus of two sets of identical twins,
and in particular the physical violence of which the two servant
Dromios are the main victims. Their increasingly irritated and
uncomprehending masters, the Antipholus brothers, resort to
beating and threats of such punishment on several occasions—
there are specific directions in the Folio only at 2.2.23 and 4.4.45—
and there is much talk of beating, especially by the Dromios. *Beat,
beaten* and *beating*, always in the primary sense of physical blows
(as opposed to the beating of the heart, for example, or of the sea
upon the rocks), occur a total of fourteen times in *Errors*, more
than in any other play in the canon. There is further vigorous
action in 3.1 when Antipholus and Dromio of Ephesus and their
dinner guests try to enter their own house, where their Syracusan
twins are already ensconced, and in 4.4 when the exorcist Pinch

---

[1] From *Samuel Taylor Coleridge: Shakespeare Criticism*, ed. Thomas Middleton
Raysor, 2 vols. (1960), i. 213; quoted by Miola, p. 18.

and his assistants catch and bind the supposedly possessed Ephesian master and servant. But to categorize the *whole* play as 'farce', even 'the only specimen of poetical farce in our language, that is intentionally such', as Coleridge did, solely because there are twins and people mistake them or because masters sometimes beat servants, would seem to be wilfully to ignore its other facets. Perhaps critics' uneasiness about its authenticity, dating from Pope, could be resolved by isolating it in a separate genre from all of Shakespeare's other plays. After all, there are apparently identical twins, of opposite sexes, in *Twelfth Night*, one of whom is married to a woman who thinks she has married the other, who is in fact a girl—yet few critics have called that wonderful comedy a farce. Beatings are administered and characters are otherwise physically assaulted in a comical context in many other plays: *The Taming of the Shrew*, *The Two Gentlemen of Verona*, *Love's Labour's Lost*, even *The Tempest*, but those plays have not generally been relegated to the literary outer darkness connoted by the term 'farce'. As for improbable or 'unbelievable' endings, if that is what some may have in mind as justifying the label, one need look no further than some of Shakespeare's other comedies—*Twelfth Night*, *As You Like It*, *Much Ado About Nothing*, *Measure for Measure*—or any of the late plays, with their multiple, complex, truly incredible revelations and resolutions—*The Winter's Tale*, *Pericles*, and above all, *Cymbeline*.

Farce is essentially a dramatic genre, viewerly, spectator-friendly; romance is essentially literary, readerly, a narrative genre, making large demands upon the imagination whereas farce leaves little or nothing to it. In performance, drama occurs in the present, is immediate, visual as well as aural, shows as much as or more than it tells. Narrative is usually in the past tense, most often in the third person, and the narrator must supply descriptions of places, actions, persons and their states of mind; such work is done by actors, directors, designers, composers and set-builders in the theatre. Romance in particular relies on the scene-setting, mood-making, spell-binding voice of the narrator. 'Once upon a time, long ago' is the romance narrator's typical opening gambit, but not the dramatist's, whose action begins in the present, *in medias res*. Even if a narrator does not start his story at the beginning, as many authors of prose romance have done, from the Greeks Chariton and Xenophon of Ephesus to the Elizabethans Sidney, in his original *Arcadia,* and Lodge, in his *Rosalynde,* but rather at a decisive moment in the plot, as both Heliodorus in his *Ethiopian Story* and Sidney in his partially-revised *Arcadia* did, he must eventually go back and fill in, in his own voice or in that of one or more characters, the prior history necessary to the hearer's or reader's understanding of all that will occur. And of course he is free to move from one place and one character or group of characters to another and back again—the *entrelacement* of French medieval romance—confident that the hearer/reader will follow. Both the time-scale and the geographical space of romance can be vast.

But the task is much more difficult for the dramatic author who, as Shakespeare so persisted in doing, attempts to put romance matter on the stage. There is not time for all that scene-setting, back-tracking, gap-filling, digressing and explaining, and there is normally, in the dramatic mode, no narrator on hand to do it. Consider some of Shakespeare's ploys to resolve the problem of the intractability of romance story: he uses prologues, epilogues, choruses, frames, or simply great lumps of narrative within the play. The forward action stops, and someone tells the story or the necessary part of it that is supposed to have taken place previously and/or elsewhere, up to the present moment, when the present-tense of drama resumes: Orlando at the beginning of *As You Like It* and Oliver in Act 4, Scene 3 of the same play, Othello with his striking story about story-telling in Act 1, Scene 3, Prospero in the second scene of *The Tempest,* the succession of Gentlemen in Act 5, Scene 2 of *The Winter's Tale.* Samuel Johnson complained that in his narrative passages Shakespeare

affects ... a wearisome train of circumlocution, and tells the incident imperfectly in many words, which might have been more plainly delivered in few. Narration in dramatic poetry is naturally tedious, as it is unanimated and inactive, and obstructs the progress of the action; it should therefore always be rapid and enlivened by frequent interruption. Shakespeare found it an encumbrance ...[1]

If that is so, Shakespeare repeatedly brought it upon himself by choosing to dramatize romance material. Only once did he (and his collaborator) simply put a narrator on stage and leave him there

[1] Preface to Johnson's edition of Shakespeare (1765); reprinted in Brian Vickers, ed., *Shakespeare: The Critical Heritage,* 5: *1765–1774* (1979), 67.

throughout, to sort out for the spectator/auditor the tangled threads of the too-complicated plot, that of the Apollonius of Tyre story: Gower in *Pericles*. It is a striking recognition of the peculiar nature of the material that in the most quintessential romance in his entire dramatic canon, Shakespeare and his colleague in effect handed the famous story back to a story-teller, and a real, historical one besides. Gower refers repeatedly to his tale or story, calling it a play only in the very last line: 'Here our play has ending'. (Then George Wilkins, who was probably Shakespeare's collaborator, wrote his prose version, 'being the true history of the play of *Pericles*, as it was lately presented by the worthy and ancient poet, John Gower', thrusting the romance firmly back into its more natural, narrative mode.[1]) The Apollonius story was simply too much to handle in conventional theatrical terms. As we have already seen, just that story, or one very like it, is told by Egeon in the first scene of *The Comedy of Errors*. Furthermore, the denouement of that story, its concluding chapter as it were, constitutes the final three hundred lines or so of the play.[2]

The farcical action is framed, overarched and subsumed by the romance plot, as the latter absorbs the characters from the former: in the family romance finale, both sets of twins as well as a husband and wife are reunited, two sons are restored to their parents, the misunderstandings between another husband and wife are resolved, as is a potential rivalry between sisters, a new pair of lovers is formed, legitimately now (and Dromio of Syracuse gratefully escapes a snare set for him by a man-hungry kitchen wench). Egeon himself, the narrator of his and his family's tragic mishaps in the first scene, becomes a character in the dramatic

---

[1] Shakespeare's exploitation of the differences and tensions between the telling/hearing function peculiar to narrative, and the showing/seeing one peculiar to drama, particularly in the late romances but with reference also to *The Comedy of Errors* among other plays, is the subject of a published lecture by the present editor, *Seeing and Believing in Shakespeare* (Rome, Ga., 1993). Stanley Wells's 'Shakespeare and Romance' (in *Later Shakespeare*, ed. John Russell Brown and Bernard Harris, Stratford-upon-Avon Studies, 8 (1966), 49–79) contains a suggestive reading of *The Tempest* as romance, with Prospero as a romance narrator (pp. 70–8).

[2] The similarities and differences in Shakespeare's handling of very similar if not identical romance narrative material in *Errors* and *Pericles*, and the narrators' respective roles in the two plays, are discussed in some detail in Charles Whitworth, '"Standing i' th' gaps": Telling and Showing from Egeon to Gower', in *Narrative and Drama*, vol. 2 of *Collection Theta: Tudor Theatre*, ed. André Lascombes (Bern, New York and Paris, 1995), pp. 125–41.

conclusion to his own story, absorbed in the stories told by others, suffering errors and confusion and anguish as they have done, then being saved from death, then rejoicing with them in the rescues and reunions. The language of the final scene both recalls Egeon's account of the twins' birth in his opening narrative, and anticipates that of the finales of other, later family romances: both Pericles and Cymbeline, for example, like the Abbess in *The Comedy of Errors*, use images of rebirth when they are reunited with children whom they had believed dead.[1] And the last *coup de théâtre* of all looks forward to the 'resurrection' of Hermione in the final scene of *The Winter's Tale*: the revelation of Emilia as Egeon's wife. We had known that both sets of twins were in Ephesus since the first of the 'errors' in Act 1, Scene 2. Their eventual reunion was just a matter of time. But Shakespeare keeps from us the fact that the Abbess, who does not appear until the final scene anyway, is Emilia, Egeon's wife, mother of the Antipholus twins, alive and safe; the last we heard of her was in Egeon's tragic tale of their separation at sea years before. Even in *Pericles*, we witness the rescue of Thaisa from the sea well before the end when she is reunited with her husband. But the romance ethos and atmosphere seep into the rest of the play too, infusing even the 'farcical core' and the city comedy with mystery, weirdness and awe. Indeed, this early comedy is much more nearly kin to the true romances and the romance-based comedies of Shakespeare's later career than has usually been acknowledged.

Egeon's seemingly interminable narrative, 'the wearisome train of circumlocution', ends, and he is led away to await his fate: the past has caught up with him. The dramatic present of theatre succeeds the narrative past of romance, and the second scene opens in the midst of a conversation, in mid-sentence in fact ('Therefore . . .'), begun before the three characters, Antipholus and Dromio of Syracuse and the First Merchant, burst upon the scene and into the story. 'Once upon a time' gives way to *in medias res*. The very verbs and temporal indicators change, from the past, mostly distant, of Egeon's story, to the immediate present,

---

[1] 'Thou that begett'st him that did thee beget, | Thou that wast born at sea, buried at Tarsus, | And found at sea again!' (*Pericles*, 21.183–5); 'O, what am I? | A mother to the birth of three? Ne'er mother | Rejoiced deliverance more' (*Cymbeline* 5.6.369–71).

indicative and imperative: 'Therefore give out' (1.2.1), 'This very day' (3), 'Is apprehended' (4), 'not being able' (5), 'Dies' (7), 'There is' (8). The shift is radical—plot, mode, time-scale, everything. Nevertheless, we soon begin to understand that the two apparently unrelated plots *are* related, and also that the threat of death to the weary old man with which the first scene ended will not be carried out, as the elements necessary to forestall it and bring about the happy denouement begin immediately to assemble: tragicomedy (or romance), not tragedy, will be the genre. The very subject of the conversation into which we intrude in the second scene is what we have just witnessed in the first, the dire sentence pronounced against Egeon. The frequent reminders of the time of day—in eight of the play's eleven scenes—keep Egeon and his impending doom on the edge of the spectator's consciousness while he is absent from the stage, from the end of 1.1 to well into Act 5, just under a third of the way through the final scene. Shakespeare's pointed observation of the unity of time—all of the action occurs between late morning and late afternoon of the same day—signals the end of the romance, its final chapter.

In the only other Shakespeare play whose time-scale is explicitly limited to one day, *The Tempest,* Prospero interrupts in the second scene the dramatic action begun by the storm in the first to tell Miranda the story of their lives and misadventures up to that moment. His narrative serves exactly the same purpose as Egeon's in the first scene of *Errors.* It is very nearly the same length (about 150 lines; *Tempest* 1.2.37–187) as Egeon's 'sad stories of [his] own mishaps', and like his, it is punctuated by questions and remarks from his auditor. In the later play too, the action that unfolds constitutes the final chapter of the story related by the father to his daughter, and that action begins with the arrival on the scene of the first of the other characters from the story who must together act out its conclusion. A similar strategy is evident in the early comedy. This is just one of the ways in which the Egeon romance plot 'overarches' the inner plot drawn from Plautus. Coincidences and links begin at once to appear: Antipholus and Dromio are from Syracuse, which provides the opportunity for the Merchant to tell them about their fellow countryman who has just been condemned to death (and to suggest that they 'give out' they are from somewhere else). Within a few minutes, the amount of money returned to Antipholus by the Merchant in the opening lines—

'There is your money that I had to keep' (1.2.8)—and entrusted by the master to his servant, is mentioned: a thousand marks (1.2.81). That sum, we just heard, is exactly what is needed by Egeon to pay his ransom (1.1.21).

Money and trade will be prominent motifs throughout the play: Ephesus, for all its reputation as a strange and dangerous place, is also a working commercial centre, where the making of profit and the doing of deals is everyday and everybody's business. The enmity between Ephesus and Syracuse has arisen from a trade war: merchants are in the thick of it. The Duke defends the business interests of his subjects with terrible rigour. No sooner does the old merchant Egeon leave the stage to seek the pecuniary means to save his life than another merchant ostentatiously hands over just that sum to Egeon's son. The First Merchant excuses himself from accompanying Antipholus on a visit of the town because he has an appointment with 'certain merchants' of whom he hopes 'to make much benefit' (1.2.24–5). Antipholus himself proposes to 'Peruse the traders' (13) while on his sightseeing tour, presumably because they are one of the things the city is famous for. Several merchants, a goldsmith and a businesswoman (the Courtesan) figure among the dramatis personae. Buying and selling seem to be going on all the time. Creditors repeatedly demand payment of bills, people get arrested in the street for debt, send for money to pay fines, pay officers to arrest others. Money, purses and articles of barter (a chain, a ring) are prominent properties in any production of the play. Dromio of Syracuse's first exit is on an errand to put his master's money away safely at their inn; his absence is the occasion of the first 'error' when his twin comes to call his supposed master home to dinner. The word *money* occurs twenty-six times in Shakespeare's shortest play, more than in any other work in the canon. *Marks* (the amount of money) and *mart* also occur more times than in any other play. *Gold* and *golden* are found more often only in *Timon of Athens*, *ducats* and *merchant(s)* more times only in *The Merchant of Venice*. The rare *guilders* occurs only in *Errors*, where it appears twice. This extraordinary density of vocabulary relating to financial and commercial affairs, with the busy to-and-fro of the marketplace, makes *The Comedy of Errors* a true city comedy. The city itself, Ephesus, has a personality, is not just a setting, but a presence in the play's world, like Venice in *The Merchant of Venice*, Vienna in *Measure for Measure*, or Rome in *Julius*

Caesar.[1] But the comparison should be made also with such romance never-never lands as the wood outside Athens, the Forest of Arden, Illyria, or Prospero's island. Whatever moved Shakespeare to replace Plautus' Epidamnus with the Ephesus of romance and the New Testament, it gave him two cities in one, a twin: the bustling, mundane metropolis of urban comedy, and the weird and wonderful setting of romance.

The imagery of romance also carries over from the first scene to the second and thence to the rest of the play, binding the separate plots and the broken family together. Egeon's tale is of the sea and shipwreck, of a family torn apart, carried away from one another, helpless before the stupendous powers of nature. The motif, expressed in imagery of the sea and the loss of oneself in that vast element, is the theme of Antipholus' first soliloquy:

> I to the world am like a drop of water
> That in the ocean seeks another drop,
> Who, failing there to find his fellow forth,
> Unseen, inquisitive, confounds himself.
> So I, to find a mother and a brother,
> In quest of them unhappy, lose myself.
>
> (1.2.35-40)

The objects of his hopeless search and subjects of his despairing meditation, his mother and his brother, are those very ones who were lost to Egeon and his remaining son, this same Antipholus. In fact, Egeon in his long tale in the first scene, and Antipholus in his short reflection in the second, speak of the same lost members of their family, and both speak the language of the sea, the former referring literally, in his factual narrative, to a particular large body of water, the latter, in his dramatic soliloquy, likening himself, in simile, to a single drop in an even vaster gulf, the ocean. *Errors* has more occurrences of the word *sea(s)*—plus one compound, *seafaring* (also *ocean* and *gulf* once each)—than any of the comedies and romances except the obvious sea-story ones, *The Tempest*, *The Winter's Tale*, *Pericles*, and *The Merchant of Venice*, which has the same number; *Errors* has one more than *Twelfth Night*. The *bay* is mentioned three times in dialogue and once in a

---

[1] Gail Kern Paster has a stimulating section on *Errors* as city comedy in her *The Idea of the City in the Age of Shakespeare* (Athens, Ga., 1985), pp. 185–94.

Folio stage direction. Only in *Pericles* in the entire canon do *ship(s)* and its compounds occur more often. *The Comedy of Errors* is not just farce, not just adapted Roman domestic or city comedy, it is also romance, sea-romance, family romance, and not only in the Egeon frame plot.

Adriana, the scolding but devoted wife of Antipholus of Ephesus, echoes the other Antipholus when she addresses him, mistaking him for her wayward husband:

> For know, my love, as easy mayst thou fall
> A drop of water in the breaking gulf,
> And take unmingled thence that drop again
> Without addition or diminishing,
> As take from me thyself, and not me too.
>
> (2.2.128–32)

The conjugal conflict of domestic comedy is expressed by the distressed wife in the same terms as her unknown brother-in-law's anguish in his isolation and despair. Storm, shipwreck and loss at sea, the very stuff of romance, become metaphors for spiritual and emotional incompleteness, hopelessness, self-doubt, loss of one's identity. The sea/water motif swells and surges into all corners of the play, in floods, tears, streams, waves. In an unexpected passage of formal verse in cross-rhymed quatrains and couplets, which set it off from the blank verse and prose on either side of it, Antipholus of Syracuse, infatuated by Adriana's sister Luciana, imagines that she is a mermaid, enticing him to perdition, to lose himself in a watery bed:

> O, train me not, sweet mermaid, with thy note
>   To drown me in thy sister's flood of tears.
> Sing, siren, for thyself, and I will dote.
>   Spread o'er the silver waves thy golden hairs,
> And as a bed I'll take them, and there lie,
>   And in that glorious supposition think
> He gains by death that hath such means to die.
> Let love, being light, be drownèd if she sink.
>
> (3.2.45–52)

Later in the scene, in a grotesque prose counterpart to Antipholus' lyrical wooing, Dromio tells him of his terror at the advances of the immense kitchen wench, the spherical 'Nell'. Her sweat and grime are too much even for Noah's flood to wash away (106–9). In his geographical anatomization of her, the English Channel and its chalky cliffs, armadas of Spanish treasure ships, and such faraway lands across the seas as America and the Indies, are evoked (116–44). The scene ends with Antipholus' resolution to take the first ship available and flee this increasingly disturbing place. Salt water washes over and through the whole fabric of the play.

Sinking and drowning, dissolution, transformation, meta-morphosis, madness—these and related processes and states con-stitute a central motif, running through the play from beginning to end. They occur and recur, weaving a dense web of associations and allusions, criss-crossing and bridging the various plot ele-ments, making one whole. Words such as *changed* and *transformed* echo throughout. The mood is sometimes humorous, sometimes fearful, sometimes anguished. Adriana wonders if age is diminish-ing her beauty, causing her husband to seek his pleasure with other women (2.1.88–102). When old Egeon's son does not know him, he supposes that grief and 'time's extremity' must have changed him beyond recognition (5.1.297–9). Both use the rare word *defeatures*, its only two occurrences in Shakespeare. Dromio of Syracuse is convinced he is an ass in the scene with Antipholus just mentioned (3.2.77), and that the 'drudge', 'diviner', or 'witch' who claims him for her betrothed would, had he not been resolute and fled, have turned him into another kind of beast:

And I think if my breast had not been made of faith, and my heart of steel,
She had transformed me to a curtal dog, and made me turn i'th' wheel.

(150–1)

'I am transformèd, master, am not I?' wails the same bewildered Dromio earlier (2.2.198), convinced he is an ape (201). Luciana tells him that he is merely an ass (202), having already called him 'snail' and 'slug' a few lines before (197), as he muttered nonsense about goblins, elves, sprites, and being pinched black and blue (193–5). He even *feels* like an ass: ''Tis true: she rides me, and I long for grass. | 'Tis so, I am an ass' (203–4). In the very next scene, the other Dromio is told by his master 'I think thou art an ass', and replies in much the same way as his brother: 'Marry, so it doth appear | By the wrongs I suffer and the blows I bear' (3.1.15–16); he confirms his metamorphosis a few scenes later: 'I am an ass indeed. You may prove it by my long ears' (4.4.30–1). The worka-day city of Ephesus itself is curiously animate: its buildings and houses bear the names of exotic fauna—Centaur, Phoenix, Tiger and Porcupine. More than thirty names of animals, real and legendary, generic and specific, occur in the play.

The Duke makes explicit the idea of metamorphosis (and in so doing looses its hold upon fevered imaginations) in the final scene when he exclaims 'I think you all have drunk of Circe's cup' (5.1.270). No one has, of course. But the allusion to the goddess–enchantress of ancient legend recalls her transformation of Odysseus' men into swine in Book 10 of the *Odyssey*, most famous of all classical sea-romances. It also recalls the 'siren' and 'mermaid' of Antipholus' rhapsody in 3.2 when he was under the spell of Luciana's 'enchanting presence and discourse', and his subsequent determination to 'stop [his] ears against the mermaid's song' (169): it was Circe who gave Odysseus advice on how to avoid the deadly Sirens' song by stopping his men's ears with wax so they could not hear it as they sailed past (*Odyssey*, Book 12). Apart from one in Act 5 of the First Part of *Henry VI* (a passage which may not have been written by Shakespeare), this is the only allusion to Circe, by name at any rate, in the canon.

Madness, the fear of it in oneself and the conviction of it in others, is a closely related theme, as are magic and conjuring. Even before anything bizarre or distressing happens to him, Antipholus of Syracuse voices in his first soliloquy his trepidation at finding himself in Ephesus, with its renowned 'libertines of sin', eye-deceiving, body-deforming, mind-changing, soul-killing (1.2.98–102). The lexical group of words formed from and including *mad*—*madness*, *madly*, *madman*, etc.—are more frequent in Shakespeare's shortest play than in any others except his longest, *Hamlet*, and *Twelfth Night*, a play which has more than that and a pair of twins in common with the earlier comedy. The theme was already there, of course, in *Menaechmi*: the local brother's relations and acquaintances think he is mad as he seems not to know any of them, and a doctor is sent for to cure him, the ancestor of Shakespeare's schoolmaster–exorcist Dr Pinch. The treatment prescribed for the supposedly mad Ephesian master and servant is exactly that imposed upon the allegedly mad Malvolio in *Twelfth Night*: 'They must be bound and laid in some dark room' (4.4.95). The furious frustration of Antipholus of Ephesus is exactly that of Malvolio: to those who are convinced that one is mad, nothing one can say—especially 'I am not mad' (4.4.59)—will change their minds. The frantic comic tension that has built up in *The Comedy of Errors* prior to Act 4, Scene 4, creates a quite different atmosphere from that in *Twelfth Night* when Malvolio's tormentors insist that he is mad, but the utter conviction and deadly earnestness of everybody (including, particularly, the grieving wife Adriana) give the underlying theme of supposed madness a potential gravity and disquieting edge missing from the later play. In *Twelfth Night*, Malvolio's alleged madness is a prank, which deteriorates into a cruel joke. He is the unfortunate butt. Everyone knows that Malvolio is not really mad (not in the way the conspirators pretend he is anyway), the threat ends with the joke, though the distasteful impression of mental cruelty may remain, as is seen in much modern criticism and many modern productions, in which Malvolio is made an almost tragic figure. Feste's Sir Topas is a much more sinister exorcist than the pompous mountebank Pinch. Everyone concerned *does* believe that Antipholus and Dromio of Ephesus are mad, no one is pretending or playing a game. Only the denouement resolves that problem and saves the two from further attempts at 'curing' them. Of course, the farcical frenzy has reached such a peak, and Pinch is so inept, that any real threat remains well below the surface in performance. It is there nevertheless, part of the pervasive romance atmosphere.

Still another aspect of the madness theme, different from both the supposed madness of Antipholus and Dromio of Ephesus and the alleged madness of Malvolio, is the fear that one is mad, or going that way, oneself. This is the predicament of the Syracusan pair from early on in the action. It reinforces strongly their isolation in a strange country, particularly that of Antipholus, who is given several soliloquies in which he expresses his fears. Such fears, such isolation, generating self-doubt, failure of the will, the temptation to surrender, and sometimes madness itself, are common to romance heroes from Odysseus of Ithaca to Apollonius of Tyre to Lancelot du Lac to Frodo Baggins of the Shire, struggling on in his lonely mission in the hostile Land of Mordor, and Luke Skywalker facing the evil forces of the Empire. For some of those heroes, as for Antipholus of Syracuse, the absence of family, the uncertainty even that he has a family any more, is a main factor in their despair and sense of isolation. Antipholus is peculiarly vulnerable because he is lonely, and is susceptible to the least suggestion that he may be losing his senses and his self. Ephesus is definitely not the place to be when one is in that frame of mind. Egeon is not the only one who finds danger in that strange, hostile city. For Antipholus too is a romance hero, wandering, searching, isolated, fearful, half-believing already the things he has heard about Ephesus and resolved to be gone as soon as possible, yet held there as if by magnetism. Before the end of Act 2, Scene 2, though he suspects some 'error' that 'drives our eyes and ears amiss' (2.2.187), he is ready, until he knows 'this sure uncertainty', to 'entertain the offered fallacy' (188–9), that is Adriana's insistent invitation to be her husband and come in to dinner, though he may wonder: 'What, was I married to her in my dream?' (185). In just such terms, another twin, Sebastian in *Twelfth Night*, a stranger in Illyria, when enjoined by Olivia to go with her to her house, marvels 'Or I am mad, or else this is a dream', and resolves still to sleep (4.1.60–2). Later, while he hopes that 'this may be some error but no madness' (4.3.10), he is driven to conclude the contrary: 'I am mad, | Or else the lady's mad' (15–16). In any case, 'There's something in't | That is deceivable' (20–1).[1] The close parallels between the predicaments and reactions of Antipholus of Syracuse and Sebastian, even to the very language and images in which they express themselves, illustrate well the kinship between the 'early' and the 'middle' comedy written some seven years later. Surely the twinship of Sebastian and Viola in the later play, whichever source he may have drawn it from and despite the differences in plot (and gender), triggered recollections and produced echoes in Shakespeare's mind of passages composed for the earlier one. We do not hesitate to affix the label 'romance' to *Twelfth Night*. The fear-of-madness motif is common to both plays.

The vulnerability of Antipholus is strikingly emphasized by the scenes in which he is seen in the company and under the spell—as he believes—of a woman. These imagined enchantresses succeed each other in a sequence of neatly distributed scenes, one per act: Adriana in 2.2, Luciana in 3.2 (in which we also hear of Dromio's encounter with the terrible 'Nell', another sorceress), the Courtesan in 4.3, the Abbess (his mother) in 5.1; another element in the play's tight and tidy structure. And as prelude to the

---

[1] Menaechmus Sosicles in Plautus' comedy thinks that Erotium the courtesan is either 'mad or drunk' (*aut insana aut ebria*) when she hails him as her lover (Warner, Act 3).

sequence, there is the soliloquy in 1.2 in which Antipholus voices his fear of sorcerers, witches and the like. His case is similar to that of a hero of Arthurian romance, Perceval, one of the Grail knights. Brought up by his mother in ignorance of chivalry (his father, the famous King Pellinor, had been killed, and the widow tries to protect her sons from a similar fate), his encounters with women—his mother, his saintly sister, the fiend in female guise several times—underline his naïvety and his susceptibility to error. During his Grail quest, he narrowly avoids succumbing to temptation on several occasions when beautiful women, always of course fiends in human form, attempt to seduce him. When Antipholus of Syracuse, convinced that he and Dromio are bewitched, calls for divine aid—'Some blessèd power deliver us from hence' (4.3.44)— the Courtesan appears, not a heavenly rescuer, but the fiend herself. In Adrian Noble's 1983 RSC production, she rose spectacularly from beneath the stage floor, scantily and seductively clad in red, black, and white. The terrified Antipholus recognizes her immediately: 'Satan, avoid! I charge thee, tempt me not!' (48); then, to Dromio, emphatically: 'It is the devil' (50). Epithets such as 'Satan', 'devil', 'fiend', 'sorceress', 'witch', ten or more of them in a thirty-line passage, are hurled at the supposed 'devil's dam' (48–79). In the very next scene, 4.4, Satan is hailed again by the would-be healer Pinch, who exhorts him to leave his abode in the allegedly mad Antipholus of Ephesus. The madness theme is now given expression in satanic terms. One brother sees the devil in the woman standing before him, the other is believed by all who know him to have the devil in him. Divine aid will come, and in female form, bringing safety and relief from the fear of madness, when the Abbess appears and gives her unknown Syracusan son and his servant sanctuary. In contrast to his brother, Antipholus of Ephesus is always seen in the company of men only—his servant (or the other, wrong, one), friends, business associates, creditors, the officer who arrests him—until the conjuring scene (4.4), when at last he *is* surrounded by women—his wife, his sister-in-law, the Courtesan—who insist that he is mad. The same woman, the Abbess, mother to this Antipholus also, will resolve that error too. The two brothers are further distinguished by the fact that the Syracusan has no fewer than six soliloquies and asides, totalling fifty lines, while the Ephesian has none. The one, isolated, fearful, impressionable, is the vulnerable romance protagonist, the other, irascible, defiant, impetuous, the jealous husband of domestic comedy.

A complex of related motifs, made up of opposite or complementary states or processes, underlies and reinforces the more prominent and explicit ones, such as metamorphosis, loss of identity and madness. Losing and finding, closing and opening, binding and freeing, spellbinding and spellbreaking, condemning and pardoning, separating and uniting, beating and embracing, dying and being (re)born, and other such pairs are the play's thematic sinews. And binding all of *them* together, ensuring that the positive, hopeful one of each pair—finding, freeing, pardoning, uniting, embracing—prevails in the end, is Time. 'The triumph of Time', the subtitle of Robert Greene's short romance *Pandosto*, published in 1588 and used by Shakespeare as his main source for *The Winter's Tale*, could well stand as a subtitle for all romances, including *The Comedy of Errors*. Time, of which we are repeatedly made aware as it ticks away, bringing the happy end of the story ever closer, and its nevertheless ineluctable ravages, the work of its 'deformèd hand', are the subject of two comic exchanges, between Antipholus and Dromio of Syracuse (2.2), and between the same Dromio and Adriana at the end of 4.2. Dromio is Time's spokesman, and at the very end of the play, he defers to his brother, his 'elder', in acknowledgement of its inexorable rule over all persons and things, despite such apparent anomalies as twinship. It was noted earlier that the time of day is mentioned frequently, some ten times, in eight of the play's eleven scenes, and that does not include the two comic duologues just referred to and a few other general references to the hour, clocks, sunset, etc. In only two other plays in the canon, *As You Like It* and *Henry IV*, Part One, both considerably longer than *Errors*, does the word *clock* occur more often, and in only a small number of plays, a half-dozen or so, does *hour(s)* occur more often.

As the time of day, five o'clock, set for Egeon's execution, is announced—'By this, I think, the dial point's at five' (5.1.118)– the Duke and the old man return to the stage for the first time since the end of the first scene. The Abbess has just withdrawn into the abbey into which the Syracusan pair had fled (5.1.37). The Ephesian pair had previously been forcibly removed into the Phoenix to be bound and laid in a dark room (4.4.131). Both pairs of twins are hidden away, the farce is suspended, and the main romance plot resumes. A new order intervenes in the person of the Abbess, one of genuine divine authority, not Pinch's sham, and the solemn temporal authority of the Duke reasserts itself after the anarchic disorder of the previous scenes. The farce is suspended, but the comedy continues and bridges the two plots: Adriana throws herself prostrate at the Duke's feet, impeding his progress towards the place of execution, literally halting the tragic progress in its tracks. At this moment the two plots meet and merge, for Adriana pleads with the Duke to intercede on her behalf with the Abbess to get her husband, whom she believes to be in the abbey, restored to her. Just as the First Merchant in 1.2 links the Egeon frame and the inner play by informing the newly arrived Antipholus and Dromio of Syracuse of another Syracusan's fate, so now another member of the city's thriving commercial community (Angelo the goldsmith in the present edition) announces the arrival of the Duke and Egeon at the appointed time, signalling the opening out of the action to embrace both plots. His interlocutor is sure that they are to witness the final act of a tragedy: 'See where they come. We will behold his death' (5.1.128). But this is romance, not tragedy. To be sure, the unravelling will take some three hundred more lines, and there will be further supposes, surprises, reversals and irruptions, even some pathos, as when Egeon pleads with the wrong son and servant, the ones who have never known him (286–330). Again, the parallel with *Twelfth Night* is evident: in the later play, Antonio, under arrest and in mortal danger, pleads desperately with the supposed Sebastian whom he had befriended earlier. But it is the uncomprehending Viola in her disguise as Cesario whom he addresses (*Twelfth Night* 3.4.325–64). The finale of *Errors* is one of Shakespeare's most eventful and complex, a true romance denouement, anticipating those of later plays such as *As You Like It*, *Twelfth Night*, *All's Well that Ends Well*, *Cymbeline* and *The Winter's Tale*.[1] At 430 lines, it is considerably longer than the final scenes of all but three of the other comedies and romances in the canon: *Love's Labour's Lost*, *Measure for Measure* and *Cymbeline*.

Time, which Dromio claimed had gone back an hour (4.2.53),

---

[1] Stanley Wells compares details in 'Reunion Scenes in *The Comedy of Errors* and *Twelfth Night*', *Wiener Beitrage sur Englischen Philologie, 80: A Yearbook of Studies in English Language and Literature 1985/86*, pp. 267–76.

has in fact gone back years, to when the family of Egeon and Emilia was whole, before the tragic events narrated by the husband and father a couple of hours earlier took place, thirty-three or twenty-five years ago, it matters little. The boys, all four of them, were infants then, new-born. It is, fittingly, the Abbess, the holy mother, who gives explicit utterance to the metaphor of nativity, describing this moment as one of rebirth:

> Thirty-three years have I but gone in travail
> Of you, my sons, and till this present hour
> My heavy burden ne'er deliverèd.
> The Duke, my husband, and my children both,
> And you the calendars of their nativity,
> Go to a gossips' feast, and joy with me.
> After so long grief, such felicity!
>
> (5.1.402–8)

The imminent death with which the play began is transfigured into birth; then we met with things dying, now with things new-born. The stern, death-dealing Duke of Act 1, Scene 1, becomes the generous, life-giving magistrate, refusing the ransom offered by Antipholus of Ephesus for his new-found father: 'It shall not need. Thy father hath his life' (392)—so much for Ephesian law which he had been so scrupulous to enforce in the opening scene. Patron already to one Antipholus, the Duke becomes godfather to both at their re-christening. The ever-moving clock in Theodor Komisarjevsky's famous 1938 Stratford-upon-Avon production (see below, pp. 68–9) should have been whirling furiously backward at this point, turning back the years, for in the biggest and best of the comedy's errors, Time has indeed gone back, all the way from death to birth, from the intense dramatic denouement to the expansive romance narrative 'Once upon a time', from the end of the play to the beginning of the story. That, essentially, is what happens in romance.

Four centuries of 'Errors' on the page and on the stage

Nevertheless, the play seems to have been either played as farce, or denatured and transformed into a saccharine love comedy with many cuts and the addition of music, for a very long time. In the early nineteenth century, around the time Coleridge was proclaiming its uniqueness as 'poetical farce', the playwright and show producer Frederick Reynolds mounted a musical extravaganza in London which set the tone of productions for much of the following century and a half. After those early documented performances in 1594 and 1604, the play seems to have had no stage life to speak of until the eighteenth century. No doubt its brevity, perhaps too its low-comic and farcical aspects did not recommend it to later seventeenth-century playgoers, after the Restoration in any case. We have seen that Dryden denounced that kind of theatre. *The Comedy of Errors* was apparently not one of the many Elizabethan plays to be adapted for the Restoration stage. Little is heard of it in the theatre until the mid-eighteenth century, when heavily adapted and 'arranged' versions began appearing on London's stages. A farce, *Every Body Mistaken*, had appeared as early as 1716; it seems to have been loosely based on *Errors*. A two-act comedy, *See if You Like it, or 'Tis All a Mistake*, opened at Drury Lane in 1734, and apparently had a long life both there and at Covent Garden. It competed with at least one other heavily adapted version, which may have been the first of Thomas Hull's several reworkings, from 1762. So, albeit in considerably altered, emended and augmented form, something vaguely reminiscent of Shakespeare's play was around to entertain audiences through most of the eighteenth century.

Some years before Coleridge made his solemn pronouncement upon the genre of *Errors*, W. Woods adapted it for performance at the Theatre Royal, Edinburgh, giving his three-act version the title *The Twins, or Which is Which?*, and defending the liberties taken with the original: 'the characters and incidents in general of this entertaining piece would rank with much more propriety under the title of *Farce*. It would also . . . obtain a great advantage in representation by being shortened'.[1] Despite being by far the shortest play in the canon! Woods (who played Antipholus of Ephesus) went on to opine that 'the similarity of character, and quick succession of mistakes, must render the subject very liable to pall upon an audience during the exhibition of five acts; whereas, by being reduced to three, the judgement will not be so much offended, having less time to reflect on the improbability of the events.' Woods's

---

[1] Quoted in G. C. D. Odell, *Shakespeare from Betterton to Irving*, 2 vols. (New York, 1920; repr. New York, 1966), ii. 48.

text was published in London in 1780. His version temporarily superseded that of Thomas Hull at Covent Garden in August 1790. Hull's may be considered the first major, serious adaptation for the contemporary theatre. His latest version was first presented at Covent Garden in January 1779. Hull, attempting to rescue the play from its perceived hopeless (and incomprehensible) triviality and vulgarity, had sentimentalized it by expanding the wooing scenes, for example in Act 3, Scene 2, where he interpolated some sixty lines before returning to something like Shakespeare's text, which he nevertheless curtailed radically (Odell, ii. 46–7). Much of the text is, in Odell's acerb terms, 'Hull undiluted by a word of Shakespeare' (46). But it did represent an attempt to make something other than a slapstick show of the play, and it seems to have pleased the London theatregoing public, as John Philip Kemble's revival nearly thirty years after its first performances testifies: when Kemble revived *Errors* in 1808, it was Hull's text with a few modifications that he staged.[1]

That year, the dramatist and novelist Elizabeth Inchbald published a twenty-five volume collection called *The British Theatre; or A Collection of Plays, which are acted at the Theatres Royal, Drury Lane, Covent Garden, and Haymarket*. In volume i, she printed Hull's version of *Errors* 'as performed at the Theatre Royal, Covent Garden . . . from the Prompt Book', and refers in her 'Remarks' to his 'judicious alterations and arrangements'. She performed a genuine piece of theatre-historical work, providing complete cast lists for each play in her large collection. We learn, for example, that Charles Kemble, younger brother of John Philip and father of Fanny Kemble, played Antipholus of Ephesus. We discover also that Hull had identified two Merchants; the distinction was apparently not made by editors before Alexander Dyce (1857). Nevertheless, Inchbald enthusiastically joined the ranks of the doubters and detractors:

This play is supposed, by some commentators, to have been among Shakespeare's earliest productions; whilst others will not allow that he

---

[1] Kemble liked to give names to Shakespeare's anonymous minor characters; the Second Merchant in *Errors* is named Chares in his version of Hull (Odell, ii. 56). He made a particular effort to revive the least known of Shakespeare's works; *The Two Gentlemen of Verona* was also staged by him at Covent Garden in the same season, 1808.

had any farther share in the work, than to embellish it with additional words, lines, speeches, or scenes, to gratify its original author, or the manager of the theatre . . . As it is partly decided that the work is not wholly Shakespeare's, full liberty may be taken to find fault with it. Of all improbable stories, this is the most so. The Ghost in 'Hamlet', Witches in 'Macbeth', and Monster in 'The Tempest', seem all like events in the common course of nature, when compared to those which take place in this drama. Its fable verges on impossibility, but the incidents which arise from it could never have occurred.

Meanwhile on the Continent, in Vienna, *The Comedy of Errors* was undergoing a different kind of transformation, to the opera stage, at the hands this time of more than competent adapters, the Anglo-Italian composer Stephen Storace (1762–96) and the great Italian librettist Lorenzo Da Ponte (1749–1838). Storace, a friend and almost certainly a pupil of Mozart's and brother of Nancy Storace (1765–1817), the soprano who created the role of Susanna in *The Marriage of Figaro*, produced his opera on a libretto by Da Ponte, *Gli Equivoci*, based on a French translation of *Errors*, in 1786, the same year as *Figaro*. Da Ponte was librettist for that Mozart opera also, as well as for *Don Giovanni* (1787) and *Così fan tutte* (1790). It is intriguing to speculate that Mozart must have seen and heard Storace's opera based on Shakespeare's least musical comedy, and may well have advised his younger friend on the score. Winton Dean has high praise for Da Ponte's text, though he worked from a French translation of the play: 'by far the most skilful' of late eighteenth-century Shakespearian librettos; he was after all adept at *opera buffa*.[1] Da Ponte cut the Egeon–Emilia intrigue and the Courtesan, and had Euphemio and Dromio of Syracuse shipwrecked on the shore of Ephesus. Nancy Storace was Sofronia (Adriana). Another of Mozart's Vienna circle, the Irish tenor Michael Kelly, who created the operatic role of Euphemio (Antipholus) of Ephesus in *Gli Equivoci* (as well as Basilio in *The Marriage of Figaro* in the same year), wrote in his highly entertaining *Reminiscences* (1826) that 'it became the rage, and well it might, for the music of Storace was beyond description beautiful'.[2] The

---

[1] In Phyllis Hartnoll, ed., *Shakespeare in Music* (1964), p. 100. Further material on the opera is to be found in Roger Fiske, *English Theatre Music in the Eighteenth Century* (Oxford, 1973), pp. 495–6.

[2] Ed. Roger Fiske (Oxford, 1975), p. 120. I am grateful to Stanley Wells for this reference and for additional details on Storace's opera.

composer himself must have thought so too: he borrowed from his own score in at least two later operas in English, *No Song, No Supper* (1790) and *The Pirate* (1792) (*SMC*, 215).[1] By coincidence, in 1786, the same year as Storace's *Gli Equivoci*, the French opera composer André-Ernest-Modeste Grétry (1741–1813) produced *Les Méprises par Ressemblance* at Fontainebleau, with libretto by Joseph Patrat. The text, drawn mainly from *Menaechmi*, seems also to contain borrowings from *The Comedy of Errors* (*SMC*, 217–18).

Making *The Comedy of Errors* palatable to early nineteenth-century audiences—which implies of course that it was felt to be unpalatable as it stood in its original form, as represented in the grand editorial tradition, deriving in a straight line from the folios and those early editions of Rowe, Pope and Theobald—was the concern not only of more or less 'legitimate' theatrical producers like Hull, Woods and Kemble. In 1819, Frederick Reynolds 'laid violent hands', as Odell puts it, upon *Errors*, and turned it into a musical spectacle of vast proportions. Reynolds's advertisement indicates the scope of his intentions:

The admirers of Shakespeare having long regretted, that most of his *Lyrical Compositions*, have never been sung in a Theatre, the Comedy of Errors (one of the shortest and most lively of his Comedies) has been selected as the best vehicle for their introduction,—A few additional scenes and passages were absolutely necessary for this purpose; and however deficient these may be found, it is hoped they will be readily pardoned, as having served to bring on the stage, more of the 'native wood notes wild' of our Immortal Bard! (Odell, ii. 131–2)

Shakespeare's least musical comedy had that deficiency corrected at last, and with a vengeance. The title-page of the 1819 edition specifies the types and sources of the musical embellishments: 'Songs, Duets, Glees, and Choruses, Selected entirely from the Plays, Poems and Sonnets of Shakespeare . . . The Overture and new Music composed, and the Glees arranged, by Mr. Bishop. The Selections from Dr. Arne, Sir J. Stevenson, Stevens, and Mozart' (Odell, ii. 131). A hunting scene is interpolated in Act 3, only to allow the singing of 'When icicles hang by the wall' from *Love's Labour's Lost*. A drinking party in Act 4 at the house of Balthasar

---

[1] On Storace's life and career and that of Nancy, see *The New Grove Dictionary of Music and Musicians*, ed. Stanley Sadie, 20 vols. (1980), xviii. 179–82.

('a character certainly harmless enough as Shakespeare left him', quipped Odell) provides the setting for a rendition of 'Bacchus, monarch of the vine' from *Antony and Cleopatra*. Other songs include: 'It was a lover and his lass', 'Blow, blow, thou winter wind', and 'Under the greenwood tree' (*As You Like It*), 'Sweet rose, fair flower' and 'Beauty is but a vain and doubtful good' (*The Passionate Pilgrim*), 'Willow, willow' (*Othello*), 'Tell me where is fancy bred' (*The Merchant of Venice*), 'Take, O take those lips away' (*Measure for Measure*). Lines from Marlowe's 'Come live with me and be my love' (printed in *The Passionate Pilgrim*) are sung by Adriana, and the show ends in a medley of songs from *A Midsummer Night's Dream* and *The Tempest*. Henry Rowley Bishop, a prolific composer and arranger, is remembered today chiefly for 'Lo, here the gentle lark', for soprano and obbligato flute, which he took from *Venus and Adonis* (l. 853 ff.) and inserted forcibly into Reynolds's extravaganza that passed under the title of *The Comedy of Errors*.[1]

Many found Reynolds's enormities just the thing to save a silly, incredible play. The critic for the *European Magazine* wrote in December 1819:

The revival of a comedy of Shakespeare, with interpolated songs, this evening, was a dramatic epoch, and it seems the favourite expedient of managers, after a run of unpopularity, to recommend them once more to the public good will. If this was the idea in which 'The Comedy of Errors' was revived, its reception has amply justified the hazard. It was attended by the most crowded house since the beginning of the season, and the audience were throughout in a unanimous temper to applaud. We will not repeat the plot, for who does not read Shakespeare? . . . No illusion of the stage can give probability to the perpetual mutations of four persons, paired in such perfect similitude, that the servant mistakes his master, and the master his servant: the wife her husband, and the husband his wife. All this so strongly contradicts common experience, that it repels us even in description; but on the stage, with the necessary dissimilarity of countenance, voice, manner, and movement, that occurs between the actors, however disguised by dress, the improbability becomes almost offensive.[2]

---

[1] On Bishop and his music for Shakespearian spectacles, those of Reynolds in particular, see Hartnoll, ed., *Shakespeare in Music*, esp. pp. 75–6.

[2] Reprinted in Gāmini Salgādo, ed., *Eyewitnesses of Shakespeare: First Hand Accounts of Performances 1590–1890* (Hassocks, 1975), pp. 68–9.

The anonymous reviewer, with all his refined sensibilities, is carried away by his own rhetoric: no husband mistakes his wife, because the wife in question, Adriana, has no twin. Even the farce, let alone what little may have been left of the romance, if anything, failed to work for the dyspeptic critic. But he, and the audience too apparently, put up with the absurdity of the pairs of twins 'for the sake of the music, which was abundant, and in general happily selected', though the selection of songs 'might have been more appropriate to the scene'. He concluded that 'the drama . . . bids fair to attain a higher popularity than it has ever done before, when bereft of its new musical accompaniments' (69).

Thus within a few decades, we find Coleridge defending *Errors* as a unique Shakespearian work, a 'poetical farce'; Woods arguing that the play is indeed a farce, and needs to be shortened so that its absurd plot may be comprehensible and thus acceptable to a modern audience who couldn't put up with a full-length version; Elizabeth Inchbald alternately snorting at the absurdity and sniffing at the distasteful beating of servants ('a custom that is abolished, except in the West Indies'); and Reynolds and Bishop, to the general applause of critic and spectator, inflating the thing and stuffing it with extraneous music of all sorts, covering up the farce and smothering any remaining hint of a coherent narrative line or dramatic suspense beneath 'songs and scenery', of which it was found to be in dire need.

While theatrical producers, even the more serious ones, who deigned to take up the play at all decked it out in a variety of borrowed finery, critics before Coleridge had had little that was good to say about it, being mostly content to note its Plautine provenance. Gerard Langbaine had ventured a little further than that as early as 1691, preferring Shakespeare's to Warner's version: 'This play is founded on *Plautus* his *Maenechmi*, and if it be not a just translation, 'tis at least a paraphrase, and I think far beyond the translation, call'd *Menechmus*, which was printed 40. *Lond.* 1595'.[1] Early eighteenth-century critics—Rowe, Gildon, Dennis—all commented on the Roman derivation of *Errors*, citing this as proof that Shakespeare knew Latin; unlike Langbaine, they apparently took no notice of Warner's version, or considered

---

[1] Gerard Langbaine, *An Account of the English Dramatick Poets, or Some Observations and Remarks* (Oxford, 1691), p. 455.

the possibility that Shakespeare may have known it. Both Rowe and Gildon mention 'the doggerel' of some of the verse of the play.[1] Warburton, in his edition of 1747, placed *Errors* with *The Taming of the Shrew* in 'Class IV' of the comedies, as being 'certainly not of Shakespeare'.[2] Pope, as we have already seen, had relegated some passages, mostly of the despised 'doggerel' in the Dromios' speeches, to the bottom of the page and small print as being probably unauthentic. As far as I can discover, Warburton was the first to deny Shakespeare's authorship of the entire play. From that outer darkness it struggled to return to the fold. Later in the century, Johnson and Farmer, among others, were concerned mostly with the question of whether or not Shakespeare read Plautus in Latin or got his plot from Warner's translation of 'the only play of Plautus which was then in English'. As late as 1817, shortly before Coleridge attempted to salvage it, as farce anyway, Hazlitt, placing *Errors* last in his *Characters of Shakespear's Plays*, began his very brief remarks by saying: 'This comedy is taken very much from the Menaechmi of Plautus, and is not an improvement on it. Shakespear appears to have bestowed no great pains on it, and there are but few passages which bear the decided stamp of his genius'.[3] If the play's theatrical fortunes began to improve by the middle of the nineteenth century, its reputation remained low, as did those of a number of the comedies; the later nineteenth century admired the great tragedies, including the Roman plays, and the actor-managers found roles more suited to their talents and showmanship in them and in some of the history plays than in the comedies, with a very few exceptions, such as Shylock and Benedick. Actresses, on the other hand, found more challenges in the comedies and romances—Kate, Titania, Portia, Beatrice, Rosalind, Viola, Innogen, Hermione, Miranda. But Adriana and Luciana could hardly compete as star vehicles in such company.

Samuel Phelps, manager of Sadler's Wells from 1844 to 1862, restored something like Shakespeare's texts to the London stage, supplanting the often grossly overlaid and mangled versions that

---

[1] *Shakespeare: The Critical Heritage*, ed. Brian Vickers, vol. ii (1974), 194, 197, 218, 225, 240.

[2] *Shakespeare: The Critical Heritage*, ed. Brian Vickers, vol. iii (1975), 226.

[3] William Hazlitt, *Characters of Shakespear's Plays* (1817); Everyman Library (1906), p. 253.

had become traditional. Odell is categorical: 'Phelps gave more of Shakespeare in a play than did any other of the actor-managers for two hundred and fifty years' (ii. 281). Among his many 'firsts' were the first production of *Pericles* (1854) since the Restoration, and the first *Antony and Cleopatra* (1849) for nearly a century. He staged all but a few of Shakespeare's plays, and *Errors* was one that benefited from his exceptionally responsible treatment of the texts. Phelps's 1855 production at the suburban Sadler's Wells was one of his triumphs in a decade that saw his restorations of, among others, *Timon of Athens, Henry V, Pericles, Love's Labour's Lost* and *The Taming of the Shrew*. Phelps must have been an extraordinarily versatile performer as well as a sensitive and intelligent director: besides reviving roles such as Timon, Henry V, Pericles and Antony, he is said to have excelled as Lear, Othello—and Bottom, in his own outstanding 1853 production of *A Midsummer Night's Dream*.[1] His *Errors* may be considered the first serious attempt at rehabilitation of the play on the London professional stage. It was followed in 1864, the tercentenary of Shakespeare's birth, by another textually faithful production at the Princess's Theatre, played without an interval and including all the scenes from the original text. The main attraction was the Irish identical twins, Charles and Henry Webb, as the two Dromios (Odell, ii. 300–1). It was a gimmick, to be sure, and the Webbs got top billing in the publicity, but Shakespeare's text was again staged more or less as it had been written, and as it had probably not been staged in London between its few recorded Elizabethan and Jacobean performances and Phelps's revival in the previous decade.

The Comedy of Errors reached the Shakespeare Memorial Theatre's Stratford stage in 1882. The director, Edward Compton, played Dromio of Ephesus. In a preface to the Memorial Theatre acting edition published at the time, C. E. Flower makes a point about the text of the 'Comedy, or as we should now call it, Farce' being fully restored. So the tradition of *Errors* as farce died hard. On the critical front, little changed. Editions continued to appear at frequent intervals, of course: they included the major Cambridge Shakespeare of Clark, Glover and Wright (1863–6) and its satellite

---

[1] Later, in a 1864 production at Drury Lane of the two parts of *Henry IV*, he played Falstaff in Part One and doubled the King and Justice Shallow in Part Two (Odell, ii. 300).

Globe Shakespeare, used worldwide as a college text for generations, the Arden Shakespeare edition by Henry Cuningham in
1907 and John Dover Wilson's New Shakespeare (Cambridge) in
1922. *Errors* was respectable, merely by virtue of being included
in respectable, new scholarly editions of Shakespeare's works. It
could be read like all the others, though the critics had little to say
about it. It could also be seen now and again at the theatre: there
were revivals at Stratford in 1905, 1914 and 1916, then none until
1938. In those productions, the different actor-directors took different parts: Sir Frank Benson was Antipholus of Syracuse in 1905,
Patrick Kirwan was Dromio of Syracuse in 1914, and Sir Philip Ben
Greet played Dromio of Ephesus in 1916; Greet had taken the same
role in a production that he co-directed at Terry's Theatre, London,
in 1899.

   In 1938 began a series of remarkable, memorable productions
of *Errors* in Stratford. That year, the Russian director Theodor
Komisarjevsky staged the play on a large, stylized but vaguely
Mediterranean set, which he designed—'a romantic huddle of
pink and green and grey and yellow houses' wrote the *Times*
reviewer; 'a scene of dolls' houses in pastel shades . . . a Christmas
pantomime as it might be staged in Moscow' mused Clive McMann
in the *Daily Mail*—with the main buildings named in the text
clearly marked (Fig. 3). W. A. Darlington in the *Daily Telegraph* saw
'an Ephesus outside time and beyond geography'. Timelessness,
zaniness and an atmosphere of comic anarchy pervaded the production, and they became hallmarks of productions both in Stratford and elsewhere in the following half-century. Komisarjevsky
peopled his Ephesus with additional characters: a usurer, an inn-
keeper, a tailor, a fisherman, two sailors, two ladies, four officers,
an attendant for the Duke—and Nell. A prominent feature of the
production, remarked upon by many reviewers, was the clock on a
tower at the centre of the set, referred to previously: from time to
time, it would strike an hour that did not correspond to the position
of the hands, which would then whirl round to catch up. The
director-designer's awareness of the crucial importance of time in
the play is abundantly clear from the prompt books, in which
specific directions concerning the clock are frequent: 'CLOCK 12'
(end of 1.1); 'CLOCK 1. Turn hands of clock quickly to 2' (end of
1.2); 'CLOCK strikes 3' (end of 2.2); 'CLOCK 4' (end of 3.2); 'Clock

3. Komisarjevsky's set for his 1938 Stratford production. Act 5, Scene 1,
the Abbess's first entrance. Komisarjevsky put all the locations named in
the play on stage, creating a packed urban scene: the Centaur is at the
left, with the ladder, then the priory, with the clock, a prominent feature
of the production, the Phoenix in the middle, with an arrow pointing 'To
the bay'. A sign indicates the Tiger (mentioned at 3.1.96); the
'Porpentine' is on the far right.

chimes up to 8' (4.2.53 in the present edition, altered by Komisarjevsky to 'It was *nine* ere I left him, and now the clock strikes
eight'); '4 QUARTERS. CLOCK 9' (end of 4.4); '4 QUARTERS. CLOCK 10'
(5.1.118 in the present edition).[1] His way with troublesome bits
of text was more peremptory: for example, he simply cut the
notorious passage at 2.1.110–14. Like their predecessors more than
a century earlier who had applauded Reynolds's adaptation of a
tiresome play, some reviewers congratulated Komisarjevsky for

---

[1] I am grateful to the custodians of the Royal Shakespeare Theatre archives at the
Shakespeare Centre Library for allowing me to consult the prompt books of Komisarjevsky's and other productions of the play in their keeping.

overcoming the apprentice playwright's shortcomings: 'The producer, happy to find his author at his worst, throws him away and substitutes a dancing and timeless farce. It is mime, music, madness, what you like; the one thing it is determined not to be is Shakespeare's play. On that barren and tedious farce it superimposes the wittiest and gayest extravaganzas' (Lionel Hale, in the *News Chronicle*, 13 April 1938). The *Yorkshire Post* critic commended Komisarjevsky, who 'with some authority, decided that [the play] was rubbish, and to show his contempt, has burlesqued it into a French farce'; the critic was sure that the 'studied affront to Bardolators' would be 'Stratford's biggest box office success to date, wail the purists never so much'. Critical commonplaces die hard. Thus, well into the twentieth century, the play's patent feebleness was felt to justify any liberties in production (if produced it must be), just as it always had. That condescension and that permissiveness continued, with rare exceptions, to characterize critical response and stage revivals.

Other notable productions have marked the second half of the twentieth century, as *The Comedy of Errors* has continued to please audiences, if not always jaundiced reviewers. Clifford Williams staged the play at Stratford in 1962, and his production was still being revived ten years later (Fig. 4). Most critics of course stuck to their preconceptions: 'However can you stage such a conglomeration of improbabilities?' (*Gloucester Echo*, 12 September 1962); 'It is no mistake to see nothing more in *The Comedy of Errors* than an endearing Shakespearian frolic' (*Birmingham Dispatch*). A few reacted more sensitively to Williams's effort: finding it 'less fanciful than the earlier one by Komisarjevsky', the reviewer in *The Tablet* remarked the 'underlying note of seriousness established in the opening scene by a moving performance by Tony Church as Aegeon . . . beautifully spoken and played with touching sadness'. While Edmund Gardner in the *Stratford-upon-Avon Herald* (14 September 1962) still thought the play 'early, flawed, unsubtle stuff', he admitted that 'it still works'. This relatively positive appraisal seems to have been due to both Williams's intelligent reading of the play and the outstanding ensemble playing of the Royal Shakespeare Company: 'a skin-tight, integrated display of ensemble work . . . that kind of acting which mixes physical slickness with complete understanding of comedy's vocal nuances'. It is striking that critics began seeing more in the play when directors

4. Members of the original cast of Clifford Williams's often-revived 1962
RSC production. From lower left clockwise: Ian Richardson (Antipholus
of Ephesus), Ian Hewitson (Dromio of Ephesus), Pauline Letts (Emilia),
Tony Church (Egeon), Barry MacGregor (Dromio of Syracuse), Alec
McCowen (Antipholus of Syracuse). A general resemblance between
actors, identical costumes and hairstyles is more than sufficient to signal
twinship in the theatre.

and actors *showed* that there was more in it than slapstick, or 'a
neat box of tricks for getting laughs' (*Wolverhampton Express and
Star*, 12 September 1962). Harold Hobson in *The Sunday Times* (16
September 1962) praised Alec McCowen, whose 'bewildered impu-
dence and sudden snatches of fear, finds more in Antipholus of
Syracuse than one would have thought possible'. Hobson, in the
same review, also put his finger on a crucial dimension of
Williams's production: 'The wild comedy of irrational recognitions
is given consistency and a curious force by the suggestion that
there is behind it something vaguely disquieting.'

It may be more than mere coincidence that academic critics
too began to treat the play seriously, and to recognize its potential

depths, at around the same time as first Komisarjevsky then Clifford Williams gave it serious, large-scale stagings in their respective Stratford productions of 1938 and 1962. H. B. Charlton accorded a full chapter to *Errors* in his *Shakespearean Comedy* of 1939, and in the same year G. R. Elliot published an influential article on 'Weirdness in *The Comedy of Errors*' that drew attention to that hitherto neglected aspect (*University of Toronto Quarterly*, 9, 95–106). It was in 1938 too that Richard Rodgers's musical comedy *The Boys from Syracuse* was staged, with book by George Abbott (who also directed), lyrics by Lorenz Hart, and choreography by George Balanchine. Though the libretto retained but a couple of lines from Shakespeare's text, that great Broadway success doubtless brought the play indirectly to the attention of many American theatregoers. A film version was released in 1940.

By the early 1960s, further critical studies had ensured the place of *Errors* in the canonical fold, after several centuries of disdain or, at best, patronizing tolerance: among them, T. W. Baldwin's *William Shakspere's Five-Act Structure* (1947); Bertrand Evans's *Shakespeare's Comedies* (1960); Harold F. Brooks's important article, 'Themes and Structure in *The Comedy of Errors*' (in *Early Shakespeare*, Stratford-upon-Avon Studies 3, 1961). At the same time, the second, revised edition of Dover Wilson's New Shakespeare text (1962) and R. A. Foakes's new Arden Shakespeare edition (1962) brought the latest serious scholarship to bear upon the play. In 1965, Baldwin produced the first full-length study of Shakespeare's shortest play: *On the Compositional Genetics of 'The Comedy of Errors'*. From the sixties onward, *Errors* has figured regularly in studies of Shakespearian comedy, though often, as has been remarked, it has been tacitly assumed if not explicitly stated to be the dramatist's first essay in the genre.[1] In the same period, successive editors too, in both separate editions of the play and collected works of Shakespeare, have written critically informed,

---

[1] For example, among many others, in E. M. W. Tillyard's *Shakespeare's Early Comedies* (1965); the Penguin Shakespeare Library anthology of criticism, *Shakespeare's Comedies*, ed. Laurence Lerner (Harmondsworth, 1967); Alexander Leggatt's *Shakespeare's Comedy of Love* (1974); Kenneth Muir's *The Sources of Shakespeare's Plays* (1977); Ruth Nevo's *Comic Transformations in Shakespeare* (1980); and Robert Ornstein's *Shakespeare's Comedies: From Roman Farce to Romantic Mystery* (1986), where the title itself implies that *Errors* was the first (and of least consequence).

insightful introductions and commentaries that accord full recognition to its multiple facets and skilful construction; among them have been such scholars as Paul A. Jorgensen, Stanley Wells, Harry Levin, David Bevington, and Anne Barton in her excellent introductory note to the play in the Riverside Shakespeare. The play's coming of age, so to speak, in the critical arena as in the theatrical one, may perhaps be measured by the nine essays from the 1980s and 1990s selected by Robert Miola for inclusion in his volume of criticism on the play, as opposed to just six from the near century and a half, from 1836 (Coleridge) to 1974 (Leggatt); a compiler's choice, to be sure, but he obviously found much very recent, and comparatively little earlier, criticism of the play worthy of inclusion in the first full-length critical collection devoted solely to the one play. Miola himself and Wolfgang Riehle are among recent critics who have returned to the classical sources of *The Comedy of Errors* and reassessed Shakespeare's debt to them.[1]

The last three decades of the twentieth century have seen a number of significant productions, in Great Britain as elsewhere. In Stratford alone, starting with the Williams production, each decade since the 1960s has been marked by at least one major RSC revival: 1976 (Trevor Nunn), 1983 (Adrian Noble), 1990 (Ian Judge), 1996 (Tim Supple), 2000 (Lynne Parker)—all in the main house, except for the outstanding Supple production of 1996 in The Other Place (Fig. 5).[2] Clearly the intimate space of that venue, and the sensitive direction of Tim Supple, which gave full scope to the actors' art, allowed the shadows and nuances of the play to emerge as they cannot, indeed, must not, in a popular main house spectacular. Like their predecessors Komisarjevsky, Williams, Nunn and Noble in their different ways, Ian Judge in 1990 and

---

[1] Robert S. Miola, *Shakespeare and Classical Comedy: The Influence of Terence and Plautus* (1994); Wolfgang Riehle, *Shakespeare, Plautus and the Humanist Tradition* (1990).

[2] It is not possible in the introduction to an edition to give detailed accounts of all significant productions. Reviews of the first three listed above (including one of Adrian Noble's 1983 production by the present editor) may be found in the volume of criticism on the play edited by Miola. Of the Tim Supple production, which rediscovered the depths of romance anguish without in the least neglecting the high comedy and farce, a perspicacious account by Robert Smallwood is to be found in *Shakespeare in the Theatre: An Anthology of Criticism* (ed. Stanley Wells, 1997). Further reviews of modern productions will be found in such periodicals as *Cahiers Élisabéthains*, *Shakespeare Quarterly* and *Shakespeare Survey*.

5. From Act 4, Scene 4, Tim Supple's Other Place production (1996).
Design by Robert Innes Hopkins. From left, the principals are Sarah C.
Cameron (Adriana), Maeve Larkin (Courtesan), Eric Mallet (Dromio of
Ephesus), Simon Coates (Antipholus of Ephesus).

Lynne Parker in 2000 answered handsomely to the latter requisite.
The former, however, compromised the very structure of the
play by doubling the Antipholus and Dromio twins, necessitating
transparent substitutions at the end, the romance denouement
when the pairs of brothers are reunited, thus cheating the audience of one of the major thrills of recognition toward which the
play builds from the beginning. To double the twins may work in
film: the BBC television version of 1984 did so, with Michael
Kitchen as both Antipholuses and Roger Daltrey as both Dromios.
But that is a different medium, and not the one for which
Shakespeare wrote his plays. On stage, such a choice leaves only
cheating—a double who remains facing upstage, away from the
audience—as the unhappy solution at the crucial moment when
the twins meet for the first time. (A similar problem arises when
Hermione and Perdita are played by the same actress in *The
Winter's Tale*.) Lynne Parker's energetic production, in which different actors played the twins, nudged and winked the audience

through a medley of movie and music hall sketches, gorged with technical tricks, gratuitous turns and gimmicks. Actors often forgot, or were not obliged to remember, what play they were in; often it did not matter, nor did the period: in the accelerated hysteria at the end of Act 4, characters from *Henry IV*, Part 1, which was playing in the adjacent Swan Theatre, joined in the chase (Falstaff, and a bewildered soldier in fifteenth-century armour), an in-joke for patrons who might have seen the other show. Zaniness ruled. The hodge-podge of styles recalled, distantly, the Komisarjevsky classic of sixty years earlier. A businesslike, *tailleur*-suited Luce greeted the audience with an extratextual prologue in verse, warning them of dire consequences should their mobile phones ring during the performance. Angelo became an Eastern rug merchant, present in almost every scene. The Second Merchant was a mad Cossack wielding a huge sabre. Pinch and his associates seemed to belong to some voodoo sect, and wore long beaked masks like those of medieval European plague doctors. The girlish Courtesan of Nina Conti managed to position herself just once over a draught vent downstage which made her full skirt billow, *à la* Marilyn Monroe. As a spectacle, of sorts, it worked. The laughs were frequent, loud and long. Shakespeare's text was not permitted to generate many of them.

Stratford playgoers in 2000 with longish memories of RSC productions may have had a mild *frisson* at seeing Paul Greenwood as the aged Egeon: he had played the younger generation, as Antipholus of Syracuse, in Noble's 1983 version, identified then as the Ephesian Antipholus' twin by his blue face; the Dromios (Richard O'Callaghan and Henry Goodman) had clown faces with red noses. The circus motif was evident too in the suspended cradle which served as a balcony, or merely the interior, of the Phoenix; in 3.1, Antipholus of Ephesus (Peter McEnery) hung from the underside of the cradle while his twin and his wife embraced exaggeratedly above (Fig. 6). (Zoë Wanamaker (Adriana) has spoken of the panic induced by the failure of the cradle to descend at one matinée performance; she and Jane Booker (Luciana) had to improvise movement and business upon entering at stage level in 2.1. Such an accident illustrates both the hazards of high-technology in the theatre, and the continuing necessity for the age-old actor's ability to improvise on the spot.) In the scene, Dromio of Syracuse, stage right, sat behind and held a free-

6. Act 3, Scene 1, Adrian Noble's 1983 RSC production. From left:
Richard O'Callaghan, behind door (Dromio of Syracuse), Peter McEnery,
hanging from cradle (Antipholus of Ephesus), Henry Goodman (Dromio
of Ephesus), Geoffrey Beevers (Balthazar), Timothy Kightley (Angelo).
Above, Paul Greenwood (Antipholus of Syracuse) and Zoë Wanamaker
(Adriana).

standing door, and listened to the fracas 'outside' through the
mail-slot. The slanging/farting match between the Dromios took
place via that aperture. In 3.2, Antipholus of Syracuse hung
upside down from a window to woo Luciana; she was perched on a
ladder, just out of reach. Ladders, lifts, bicycles, special sound
effects from the pit orchestra—there were gimmicks aplenty in this
production too. And music. Trevor Nunn's famous 1976 musical
version had been tremendously successful. With an outstanding
cast—Judi Dench, Francesca Annis, Roger Rees, Mike Gwilym,
Michael Williams, Nikolas Grace, Richard Griffiths, Griffith Jones,
Brian Coburn, among others—and music by Guy Woolfenden, it
became a classic and was later filmed for television. Nunn solved
the Luce–Nell puzzle by having both, the one a lady's maid, the

other a kitchen wench. Both it and the BBC version are available on video. The BBC had already presented an operetta version with music by Julian Slade as early as 1954, in which Joan Plowright had taken the part of Adriana; it was revived at the Arts Theatre, London, in 1956.

The Comedy of Errors has had a life on stages other than those of Stratford and London's West End, of course. In December 1894, William Poel produced an elaborate Elizabethan-style reconstruction in the hall of Gray's Inn where the première had probably taken place 300 years earlier. In 1994, another anniversary performance was given at the Inn, directed by Anthony Besch. This was in fact a reprise of the 1954 musical version seen on BBC television. Composer Julian Slade provided new music for this Gray's Inn revival. In 1970, Frank Dunlop transposed Syracuse and Ephesus into London and Edinburgh at the Young Vic, where automobiles and bicycles circulated on the set. There have been a remarkable number of productions of *Die Komödie der Irrungen* in Germany, where it seems to have remained popular throughout the twentieth century: *A Shakespeare Music Catalogue* alone lists more than forty German stage productions with incidental music between the 1930s and the 1980s (192–211). A notable production at the Bristol Old Vic by Phyllida Lloyd in 1989 had a direct influence on Ian Judge's RSC version a year later. Lloyd did not make the mistake that Judge was to make, that of doubling the two sets of twins, and her rendition, based on a close reading of the text, was full of wonder as well as weirdness. Her Antipholuses, Owen Teale and Brian Hickey, and Dromios, Colin Hurley and Sean Murray, were of course not identical, but identical costumes *implied* twinship, as they always do in the theatre. Anthony Ward's stunning skewed set featured a Magritte-like skyscape and doors at first-floor level which opened into empty space. The door of Adriana's house in 3.1 was free-standing: first one Dromio, the one inside, propped it up, then the other, outside, caught it as the other let it fall. The device, a piece of pure theatricality, borrowed no doubt from Noble's 1983 RSC version, resolved the problem and allowed the audience to see inside and outside simultaneously. The necessary letter-slot was provided, through which insults and farts were exchanged, and through which the enraged Nell (Luce) applied a vacuum cleaner to the outside (her) Dromio's crotch. Even in 1989, critics could still be terribly vague about the play's action, or woefully inattentive to the performance, as if befuddled themselves by its manifold 'errors': the *Financial Times* reviewer (21 February) of the Bristol production names the wrong actor in the part of Angelo, says that Adriana makes her entrance in a swimming pool (it was Luciana), that the Abbess comes out leading the Ephesian Antipholus (it is of course the Syracusan twin, who had taken refuge in the abbey), and that Shakespeare unforgivably marries off the Abbess and Egeus—a double howler: they are already married, have been for many years, and he is called Egeon. Finally, he says, we shall never know which Dromio ends up with Nell (Luce), when it is perfectly clear at the end that the Syracusan resigns her, with relief, to his Ephesian twin.

Caroline Loncq, who played Luciana in both the 1989 Bristol Old Vic and the 1990 RSC productions, reported that her RSC colleagues were struck, when shown photographs of the set of the former, by its similarity to that designed by Mark Thompson for the RSC show. Clearly the first influenced the second. But instead of Phyllida Lloyd's close and careful work on the text—a literary adviser was called upon, members of the cast were shown copies of the Folio text in rehearsal, were encouraged to observe the original, or at any rate, the earliest surviving form of the text which they were learning, and to compare various editions' readings of troublesome passages—the RSC director went for ill-judged doublings, gratuitous tricks and over-the-top gags, a vaudeville potpourri. The Abbess wore an extravagant headgear which made her look like the Flying Nun. Any hint of lyricism or pathos in the text was stamped out or sent up. 'The Travesty of *Errors*' was the jaundiced verdict of some spectators. But once again, the unjaundiced majority loved it. Another ill-advised attempt at doubling the pairs of twins was Kathryn Hunter's version at the new Globe in 1999. Reviewers found it clumsy and distracting.[1]

---

[1] Peter J. Smith: '[the production] remained superficial and smugly pleased with the easy comic solutions it offered . . .; the play was reduced, for the most part, to a comic vehicle for the performances of Vincenzo Nicoli as the Antipholuses and, especially, Marcello Magni as the Dromios . . . [and] to the level of a school-leavers' review' (*Cahiers Élisabéthains*, 56 (Octobre 1999), 105–7). Lois Potter: 'In my experience, doubling the parts of the Antipholus and Dromio twins tends to make the play less funny, displacing attention from the plot to the logistics involved in the doubling itself . . . I felt sorry for the actors playing the doubles' (*Shakespeare Quarterly*, 50 (1999), 515).

It is not possible to go further than the year 2000 in a review of the fortunes and misfortunes of *The Comedy of Errors*. The play is firmly established in the canon and in theatrical repertoires. Doubtless its boisterousness, high jinks and farce will continue to attract directors and audiences. Perhaps some may also continue to find and respond to its subtler aspects, the very real shadows and depths of romance. The stage history of *The Comedy of Errors*, which has been sketched in rudimentary form here, testifies to its peculiar blend of the seemingly incompatible extremes of farce and romance. It was argued earlier in this Introduction that romance is essentially a non-theatrical mode, while farce *is* essentially theatrical. It is scarcely surprising then that producers of the play in the theatre have gone for the farce and have, for the most part, let the romance go. The curious penchant of Shakespeare throughout his career for the unlikely tales of romance as matter for stage plays has been remarked upon. That first audience at Gray's Inn at Christmas 1594 may well have been, given the prevailing atmosphere, more in a mood to applaud the frenzied farce than in one conducive to imaginative and sympathetic response to the distressing predicaments in which Egeon, both Antipholuses, Adriana and, to a lesser degree, some of the other characters find themselves. No director is likely to be foolish enough to try to turn *Errors* into the sombre, laughless 'dark comedy' that *As You Like It* and *Twelfth Night* often masquerade as nowadays in the theatre, even less to make of it topical-political drama like *The Taming of the Shrew* or *The Merchant of Venice*. But the best modern productions, such as those of Williams, Lloyd, and Supple, have shown that the tragicomic element can be respected and rendered movingly, without sending up or grotesque hamming, and without in the least denying or denaturing the farce and the domestic comedy. If directors, designers and actors, as well as readers, critics and playgoers, continue to give the play a fair chance, it will without doubt emerge more clearly as a comedy on a par with, if different from—as each of his works is different from all the others—Shakespeare's best in that kind.

EDITORIAL PROCEDURES

THE second section of the Introduction above sets out in detail the characteristics of the First Folio text of the play. An editor of *The Comedy of Errors* is happily spared the difficulties encountered by editors of works by Shakespeare which survive in multiple early editions, where sometimes several quartos and the Folio texts must be compared, weighed and sifted, and decisions made about the relations between them and the relative authority of each. Such a complicated textual history as faces and may well daunt the editor of *Hamlet, Romeo and Juliet, Richard III* or *Pericles*, for example, is not an obstacle to the editor of *Errors*. As a Folio-only text, such problems as it poses are internal ones, due to the nature of the copy used by the printers, and to what they did with and to that copy in the process of setting it in type. Among the eighteen plays apparently first published in the 1623 Folio, *Errors* is notably less problematic than some, such as *Timon of Athens, 1 Henry VI*, or *The Taming of the Shrew*, but somewhat more so than, say, *As You Like It* or *Twelfth Night*. The probability that Shakespeare's foul papers provided the copy and the participation of three compositors in the setting of the text mean that the editor will have considerable work to do to establish a reliable text. Audacious though it may appear, he will necessarily be rectifying Shakespeare's own errors, or at least compensating for his occasional lapses as they are discernible in the text, and anticipating his thought at times, and at others he will be tidying up, as best he can at such a great distance in time, behind those anonymous, often fallible typesetters. I have given some space in the commentary to discussion of textual matters, more so than has usually been allotted to them in previous editions of the play, in the hope, not of providing a definitive text—such a hope is vain—but of setting out the main problems posed by the text and airing them as thoroughly as possible, in the light of research carried out in the last few decades by textual scholars.

Oxford Shakespeare editorial principles have been observed in this edition; those principles, where modernization of spelling and punctuation are concerned, are set out in Stanley Wells and Gary Taylor, *Modernizing Shakespeare's Spelling, with Three Studies in the*

Text of 'Henry V' (Oxford, 1979), and in the guidelines furnished to editors. In the first phase, a full modernized text was established based directly upon the Folio. Later, though working primarily from the text of the play presented in the Oxford *Complete Works*, ed. Wells and Taylor (1986), I felt free to depart from its readings in a number of instances; where it matters, the reasons for doing so are set out in the notes. Stage directions whose content and/or placement are uncertain, and disputable speech prefixes, are printed in broken brackets ⌈ ⌉. While some directions have been expanded to make the stage action clearer, all Folio directions, which may derive directly from Shakespeare's draft, have been retained. Such obvious indications as *aside* and *to Adriana* (for example), have usually been added silently where they were not present in earlier editions. Although this is not a variorum edition, where long-standard textual readings have been departed from, the departures are recorded in the collations, and if necessary defended in the notes.

Abbreviations and References

All Shakespeare references are to the Oxford Shakespeare *Complete Works*, ed. Stanley Wells and Gary Taylor (1986), unless otherwise indicated. Place of publication is London unless otherwise indicated.

EDITIONS OF SHAKESPEARE

F, F1	*Mr. William Shakespeare's Comedies, Histories, and Tragedies . . .* (1623) (First Folio)
F2	Second Folio (1632)
F3	Third Folio (1663)
F4	Fourth Folio (1685)
Alexander	Peter Alexander, *The Complete Works* (1951)
BBC TV	*The Comedy of Errors*, The BBC TV Shakespeare (1984) (the Alexander text)
Bevington	David Bevington, *The Comedy of Errors*, The Bantam Shakespeare (New York, 1988)
Cambridge	W. G. Clark and W. A. Wright, *The Works*, Cambridge Shakespeare, 9 vols. (Cambridge, 1863; third edition, W. A. Wright, 1891)

Capell	Edward Capell, *Comedies, Histories, and Tragedies*, 10 vols. (1767–8)
Collier	John Payne Collier, *Works*, 8 vols. (1842–4)
Collier 1858	John Payne Collier, *Comedies, Histories, Tragedies, and Poems*, 6 vols. (1858)
Craig	Hardin Craig, *Works* (New York, 1951; 1961; revised edition, D. Bevington, 1973)
Cuningham	Henry Cuningham, *The Comedy of Errors*, Arden Shakespeare (1907)
Delius	Nicolaus Delius, *Works*, 7 vols. (Elberfeld, 1854–60)
Dorsch	T. S. Dorsch, *The Comedy of Errors*, New Cambridge Shakespeare (Cambridge, 1988)
Dyce	Alexander Dyce, *Works*, 6 vols. (1857)
Dyce 1866	Alexander Dyce, *Works*, 9 vols. (1864–7)
Foakes	R. A. Foakes, *The Comedy of Errors*, Arden Shakespeare, new edition (1962)
Hanmer	Thomas Hanmer, *Works*, 6 vols. (Oxford, 1743–4)
Harness	William Harness, *Works*, 8 vols. (1825)
Hudson	Henry N. Hudson, *Works*, 11 vols. (Boston, 1851–6)
Johnson	Samuel Johnson, *Works*, 8 vols. (1765)
Jorgensen	Paul A. Jorgensen, *The Comedy of Errors*, in The Pelican Shakespeare, general editor, Alfred Harbage (New York, 1969)
Keightley	Thomas Keightley, *Works*, 6 vols. (1864)
Kittredge	George Lyman Kittredge, *Works* (Boston, 1936)
Knight	Charles Knight, *Works*, 8 vols. (1838–43); 12 vols. (1842–4)
Levin	Harry Levin, *The Comedy of Errors*, Signet Classic Shakespeare (1965)
Malone	Edmond Malone, *Works*, 10 vols. (1790)
Munro	John Munro, *Works*, London Shakespeare, 6 vols. (1958)
Oxford	*The Complete Works*, Oxford Shakespeare, Stanley Wells and Gary Taylor, general editors (original-spelling edition, Oxford, 1986; modern-spelling edition, Oxford, 1986)
Pope	Alexander Pope, *Works*, 6 vols. (1723–5)
Pope 1728	Alexander Pope, *Works*, 8 vols. (1728)
Rann	Joseph Rann, *Dramatic Works*, 6 vols. (Oxford, 1786–94)

Ritson	Joseph Ritson, *The Plays of William Shakespeare, With Notes. In Eight Volumes.* A projected edition by Ritson; a specimen first page (104 lines) of *Errors* from the projected vol. ii survives. The title-page is dated 1787.
Riverside	*The Riverside Shakespeare*, G. Blakemore Evans, textual editor (Boston, 1974)
Rowe	Nicholas Rowe, *Works*, 6 vols. (1709)
Rowe 1709	Nicholas Rowe, *Works*, 6 vols. (second edition, 1709)
Rowe 1714	Nicholas Rowe, *Works*, 8 vols. (third edition, 1714)
Singer	S. W. Singer, *Dramatic Works*, 10 vols. (1826; 1856)
Sisson	Charles J. Sisson, *Works* (1954)
Staunton	Howard Staunton, *Works*, 3 vols. (1858–60)
Steevens	George Steevens (with Samuel Johnson), *Works*, 10 vols. (1773)
Steevens 1778	George Steevens (with Samuel Johnson), *Works*, 10 vols. (1778)
Tetzeli	Kurt Tetzeli von Rosador, *The Comedy of Errors/Die Komödie der Irrungen* (Bern and Munich, 1982)
Theobald	Lewis Theobald, *Works*, 7 vols. (1733)
Warburton	William Warburton, *Works*, 8 vols. (1747)
Wells	Stanley Wells, *The Comedy of Errors*, New Penguin Shakespeare (Harmondsworth, 1972)
White	Richard Grant White, *Works*, 12 vols. (Boston, 1857–66)
Wilson	John Dover Wilson, *The Comedy of Errors*, The New Shakespeare (Cambridge, 1922)
Wilson 1962	John Dover Wilson, *The Comedy of Errors*, The New Shakespeare, second edition (Cambridge, 1962)

OTHER ABBREVIATIONS

Abbott	E. A. Abbott, *A Shakespearian Grammar*, third edition (1876)
Bullough	Geoffrey Bullough, ed., *Narrative and Dramatic Sources of Shakespeare*, 8 vols. (1957–75)
Cercignani	Fausto Cercignani, *Shakespeare's Works and Elizabethan Pronunciation* (Oxford, 1981)
Clayton	Thomas Clayton, 'The Text, Imagery, and Sense of the Abbess's Final Speech in *The Comedy of Errors*', *Anglia*, 91 (1973), 479–84

Dent	R. W. Dent, *Shakespeare's Proverbial Language: An Index* (1981)
Eagleson–Onions	C. T. Onions, *A Shakespeare Glossary*, enlarged and revised throughout by Robert D. Eagleson (Oxford, 1986)
ES	E. K. Chambers, *The Elizabethan Stage*, 4 vols. (Oxford, 1923)
McKerrow	R. B. McKerrow, *Prolegomena for the Oxford Shakespeare: A Study in Editorial Method* (Oxford, 1939)
Miola	Robert S. Miola, 'The Play and the Critics', in *'The Comedy of Errors': Critical Essays*, ed. Miola (New York and London, 1997), pp. 3–51
N & Q	*Notes and Queries*
New Readings	C. J. Sisson, *New Readings in Shakespeare*, 2 vols. (Cambridge, 1956)
O'Connor	John O'Connor, 'A Qualitative Analysis of Compositors C and D in the Shakespeare First Folio', *SB* 30 (1977), 57–74
ODEP	*The Oxford Dictionary of English Proverbs*, compiled by William George Smith, third edition, ed. F. P. Wilson (1970)
OED	*Oxford English Dictionary* (Compact Edition, 1971; repr. 1976)
SB	*Studies in Bibliography*
SMC	Bryan N. S. Gooch and David Thatcher, eds., *A Shakespeare Music Catalogue*, 5 vols. (Oxford, 1991); i. 192–218 (for *The Comedy of Errors*)
TC	Stanley Wells and Gary Taylor, with John Jowett and William Montgomery, *William Shakespeare: A Textual Companion* (Oxford, 1987)
Tannenbaum	Samuel A. Tannenbaum, 'Notes on *The Comedy of Errors*', *Shakespeare Jahrbuch*, 68 (1932), 103–24
Tilley	Morris Palmer Tilley, *Dictionary of the Proverbs in England in the Sixteenth and Seventeenth Centuries* (Ann Arbor, 1950)
Walker	W. S. Walker, *A Critical Examination of the Text of Shakespeare*, 3 vols. (1860)
Werstine	Paul Werstine, '"Foul Papers" and "Prompt Books": Printer's Copy for Shakespeare's *Comedy of Errors*', *SB* 41 (1988), 232–46

Whitworth	Charles Whitworth, 'Rectifying Shakespeare's *Errors*: Romance and Farce in Bardeditry', in Ian Small and Marcus Walsh, eds., *The Theory and Practice of Text-Editing: Essays in Honour of James T. Boulton* (Cambridge, 1991), pp. 107–41. Reprinted in Miola, *'The Comedy of Errors': Critical Essays* (1997), pp. 227–60. References are to the prior publication.
Fr.	French
L.	Latin

The Comedy of Errors

THE PERSONS OF THE PLAY

Solinus, DUKE of Ephesus

EGEON, a merchant of Syracuse, father of the Antipholus twins

ANTIPHOLUS OF EPHESUS ⎫
ANTIPHOLUS OF SYRACUSE ⎭ twin brothers, sons of Egeon

DROMIO OF EPHESUS ⎫ twin brothers, and bondmen of the
DROMIO OF SYRACUSE ⎭ Antipholus twins

ADRIANA, wife of Antipholus of Ephesus

LUCIANA, her sister

LUCE, Adriana's kitchen-maid

ANGELO, a goldsmith

BALTHASAR, a merchant

A COURTESAN

Doctor PINCH, a schoolmaster and exorcist

FIRST MERCHANT, who befriends Antipholus of Syracuse

SECOND MERCHANT, Angelo's creditor

Emilia, an ABBESS at Ephesus

Jailer, messenger, headsman, officers, and other attendants

The Comedy of Errors

I.I *Enter Solinus, the Duke of Ephesus, with Egeon the*
Merchant of Syracuse, Jailer, and other attendants

EGEON

Proceed, Solinus, to procure my fall,
And by the doom of death end woes and all.

DUKE

Merchant of Syracusa, plead no more.
I am not partial to infringe our laws.
The enmity and discord which of late   5
Sprang from the rancorous outrage of your Duke
To merchants, our well-dealing countrymen,
Who, wanting guilders to redeem their lives,
Have sealed his rigorous statutes with their bloods,
Excludes all pity from our threat'ning looks.   10

1.1.0.1 *Solinus*] COLLIER; *not in* F   *Egeon*] ROWE; *not in* F   I EGEON] ROWE; *Marchant* F (*and throughout scene, as 'Merch.' or 'Mer.'*)   6 Sprang] F (Sprung)   8 guilders] F (gilders)

1.1 Beginning with Theobald ('The Duke's palace'), editors have indicated a setting for the scene's action; e.g. 'A public place' (Capell). Malone's 'A hall in the Duke's palace' was repeated well into the twentieth century, by Kittredge, Craig, Alexander and Munro among others; Sisson returned to Theobald's less specific location. Wilson, typically, supplied a six-line scene description, followed by a three-line stage direction, both of which he retained in his second edition (1962). By that time, most editors were omitting specifications of place (Foakes, Jorgensen, Wells and others). Levin (1965) revived Capell's 'public place', and most productions suggest an outdoor setting, with houses and streets; the BBC TV text (1984), while reprinting Alexander's location, adds 'Exterior. The Mart.' in the margin.

0.1–2 'Solinus' is supplied from line 1, its only occurrence. 'Other attendants' often become townspeople in production, as directors supply stage audiences to react to Egeon's narrative.

1 **Solinus** Rowe, working from F4, had 'Salinus', and editors from Pope to Johnson followed suit.

4 **partial** inclined

6 **Sprang** Although *sprung* is sometimes still used for the past tense of *spring*, *sprang* is more common. The risk of mistaking *sprung* as the past participle in this complex, six-line sentence is avoided by adopting the usual modern form.

7 **well-dealing** honest, proper in their business dealings

8 **guilders** (Dutch *gulden*) Dutch coins. The word occurs twice in *Errors*, and nowhere else in Shakespeare. It means 'money' in general, both here and at 4.1.4.

10 **Excludes** The subject is 'enmity and discord' in l. 5. Disagreement or 'false concord' between subject and verb was permissible in Elizabethan English and is common in Shakespeare (Abbott, §§333–4).

For since the mortal and intestine jars
'Twixt thy seditious countrymen and us,
It hath in solemn synods been decreed,
Both by the Syracusans and ourselves,
To admit no traffic to our adverse towns.   15
Nay, more: if any born at Ephesus
Be seen at Syracusan marts and fairs;
Again, if any Syracusan born
Come to the bay of Ephesus, he dies,
His goods confiscate to the Duke's dispose,   20
Unless a thousand marks be levièd
To quit the penalty and ransom him.
Thy substance, valued at the highest rate,
Cannot amount unto a hundred marks.
Therefore by law thou art condemned to die.   25

EGEON

Yet this my comfort: when your words are done,
My woes end likewise with the evening sun.

---

14 Syracusans] POPE; *Siracusians* F *(and so throughout play)* 16–17 Nay, more ... Ephesus | Be
seen at Syracusan] This edition *(after* Oxford *and* Pope); Nay more, . . . *Ephesus* | Be seene at
any *Siracusian* F; Nay, more, | If any ... seen | At any Syracusan MALONE 22 ransom] F2; to
ransome, FI 26 comfort:] CAMBRIDGE; comfort, F; comfort; MALONE; comfort, — DYCE

---

11 **intestine** internal, civil. Presumably
because Ephesus and Syracuse were both
Greek city-states (Wells), though they are
represented in the play as independent,
each with its own ruler, 'synod', and
laws.
  jars discord, strife
12 **seditious** turbulent
13 **synods** parliaments
15 **admit . . . to** allow no commerce between
  adverse opposed, hostile
16–17 Pope's omission of 'any' in l. 17 seems
both the simplest and the most plausible
solution to the hypermetricality of the
line; it retains F's two lines and regular-
izes them, neither of which Malone's
emendation does. The latter has been
defended on rhetorical grounds: the part-
line 'Nay, more' arrests the hearer's
attention for what follows (see Abbott,
§512). But the likelihood of the compositor's looking ahead to 'if any Siracusian'
in l. 18 and, having just set 'if any borne
at' in l. 16, setting 'at any' in l. 17, is
surely too great to be dismissed. Pope's

dropping of the 'i' in 'Syracusian' here
and elsewhere, on metrical grounds, was
followed by eighteenth-century editors
(and in the present edition, in the interest
of consistency with the noun form *Syracusa*), but it was restored in the nineteenth; when elided (-*zhan*) in speech, the
two syllables become one.
20 **confiscate** forfeit. The verbal form as past
participle. The word is used twice thus in
Errors, and only four times elsewhere in
Shakespeare.
21 **a thousand marks** A mark was equal to
thirteen shillings and four pence, or two-
thirds of a pound sterling; an amount
of money, not a coin like a guilder or
a ducat. A thousand marks is the very
sum that Antipholus of Syracuse gives to
Dromio for safekeeping in the next scene
(1.2.81): a 'coincidence' that links father
and son, both strangers in Ephesus, one of
whom could so easily save the other's life,
if he knew.
23 **substance** present wealth
27 **likewise** also

DUKE

Well, Syracusan, say in brief the cause
Why thou departed'st from thy native home,
And for what cause thou cam'st to Ephesus.   30

EGEON

A heavier task could not have been imposed
Than I to speak my griefs unspeakable;
Yet, that the world may witness that my end
Was wrought by nature, not by vile offence,
I'll utter what my sorrow gives me leave.   35
In Syracusa was I born, and wed
Unto a woman happy but for me,
And by me too, had not our hap been bad.
With her I lived in joy, our wealth increased
By prosperous voyages I often made   40
To Epidamnus, till my factor's death,
And the great care of goods at random left,
Drew me from kind embracements of my spouse;
From whom my absence was not six months old
Before herself (almost at fainting under   45
The pleasing punishment that women bear)

---

38 by me too] F2; by me F1; by me happy OXFORD   41 Epidamnus] This edition; *Epidamium*
F; Epidamnium ROWE; Epidamnum POPE (*so throughout play*)   42 the] THEOBALD; he F

28–30 The Duke is cast as foil to the story-
telling Egeon, asking questions, eliciting
the exposition necessary to the action
which is to ensue. Egeon had, as he
thought, said his final words, as the
couplet in ll. 26–7 implies; he similarly
mistakenly assumes the end of the
proceedings at ll. 1–2 and 93–4.
34 **wrought . . . offence** brought about by
my love for my child, not by any crime
36 **Syracusa** The place-name is spelt thus
(though nearly always with 'i' instead
of 'y') throughout F, except at 5.1.364
where 'Syracuse' (three syllables) respects the metre.
41 **Epidamnus** Town on the eastern shore
of the Adriatic; the Romans renamed
it Dyrrachium, it became Durazzo in
the Middle Ages, and is now Durrës in
Albania. This edition departs from
previous ones in giving the Latin nomina-
tive form (from the Greek *Epidamnos*).
Pope's emendation, adopted by most edi-

tors, is a declined form which occurs in
Plautus' Argument and Prologue; in the
latter, 'Epidamnus' and 'Epidamnium'
are also found, and 'Epidamno' occurs
later in his play. Pope probably rejected
'Epidamium' on metrical grounds,
though his failure to choose 'Epidamnus'
is puzzling (see 16–17 n.); Warner used
'Epidamnum' throughout. The occurrence of the form 'Epidamium' in passages in F set by two different compositors
(B and C) suggests that that is what
Shakespeare may have written. Or perhaps he wrote 'Epidamnium'; the omission of *n* (minim error) would have been
an easy mistake (see Whitworth, p. 125).
Riverside, Bevington and Tetzeli prefer to
retain F's 'Epidamium'.
43 **Drew me** Apparently to Epidamnus, since
according to his account, Egeon and his
family seem to have sailed from there
(l. 61).
46 **pleasing . . . bear** i.e. pregnancy

Had made provision for her following me,
And soon and safe arrivèd where I was.
There had she not been long but she became
A joyful mother of two goodly sons;   50
And, which was strange, the one so like the other
As could not be distinguished but by names.
That very hour, and in the selfsame inn,
A mean young woman was deliverèd
Of such a burden, male twins, both alike.   55
Those, for their parents were exceeding poor,
I bought, and brought up to attend my sons.
My wife, not meanly proud of two such boys,
Made daily motions for our home return.
Unwilling, I agreed. Alas, too soon we came aboard!   60
A league from Epidamnus had we sailed
Before the always-wind-obeying deep
Gave any tragic instance of our harm.
But longer did we not retain much hope,
For what obscurèd light the heavens did grant   65
Did but convey unto our fearful minds
A doubtful warrant of immediate death,

54 mean young] This edition; meane F1; poore meane F2; meaner DELIUS (*conj.* S. Walker); mean-born OXFORD   55 burden, male twins,] This edition (*after* F2: burthen, Maletwins); bur-then Male, twins F1   60 Unwilling I agreed. Alas ... aboard!] This edition (*one line as* F); Unwilling ... soon! | We ... aboard. POPE; Unwilling ... soon. | We ... aboard: CAPELL; Unwilling I agreed; alas too soon | We ... aboard. FOAKES; Unwilling ... soon | We came aboard and put to sea, but scarce CUNINGHAM *conj.*

52 The twins, however, have the same name, Antipholus. See note to l. 127 below.
54 **mean young** One of several attempts to improve on F2's 'poor mean' solution to the metrically short line, this emendation is defended in Whitworth (pp. 126–7). Many modern editors, however, including Alexander, Foakes, Wells, Levin, Riverside and Bevington, leave the line as it stands in F.
55 **burden, male twins,** In preferring F2's reading, which may have been partly fortuitous rather than deliberate— 'Maletwins' leaves no room for a comma—this edition accords weight to the absence from *OED* of 'burden male' as a recognized collocation (though 'heir male', 'tail male', 'issue male' and other such legal compounds occur, as Wells

notes). It also dismisses Wilson's conjecture of a quibble on 'mail', i.e. 'baggage'; he was the first to revert to F's reading. An actor might emphasize 'such' (meaning 'just such'), with 'very' and 'selfsame' in l. 53 to convey the extraordinariness of the event.
56 **for** because
58 **not meanly** not a little
60 Only Rowe, and Sisson among modern editors, retain F's single long line. But the short line 'We came aboard' is dubiously defensible on rhetorical grounds without Pope's or Capell's repunctuation, which makes 'too soon' modify 'agreed' rather than 'came aboard'; F strongly suggests the latter.
63 **instance** sign
67 **doubtful warrant** dreadful certainty

Which though myself would gladly have embraced,
Yet the incessant weepings of my wife,
Weeping before for what she saw must come,   70
And piteous plainings of the pretty babes,
That mourned for fashion, ignorant what to fear,
Forced me to seek delays for them and me;
And this it was, for other means was none:
The sailors sought for safety by our boat,   75
And left the ship, then sinking-ripe, to us.
My wife, more careful for the latter-born,
Had fastened him unto a small spare mast
Such as seafaring men provide for storms;
To him one of the other twins was bound,   80
Whilst I had been like heedful of the other.
The children thus disposed, my wife and I,
Fixing our eyes on whom our care was fixed,
Fastened ourselves at either end the mast,
And floating straight, obedient to the stream,   85
Was carried towards Corinth, as we thought.
At length the sun, gazing upon the earth,
Dispersed those vapours that offended us,
And by the benefit of his wished light
The seas waxed calm, and we discoverèd   90
Two ships from far, making amain to us:
Of Corinth that, of Epidaurus this.

---

92 Epidaurus] F2 (*Epidaurus*); *Epidarus* F1; Epidamnus THEOBALD *conj.*

---

71 **plainings** wailings, complaints
72 **for fashion** in imitation of others
78 **small spare mast** A spare, to be used as a jury-mast in case of damage to the original one.
81 **other** i.e. the other pair of twins (unless, as Collier suggested, we should read 'others')
82–6 **my wife and I . . . Was carried** Another disagreement of subject and verb.
84 **end** end of
85 **stream** current
90 **waxed** began to become
91 **making amain** sailing at full speed
92 **Of . . . this** The actor will presumably indicate by gestures that the ships were

approaching from opposite directions; that this is what is intended is borne out by l. 99. Compare the Abbess's account at 5.1.356–60.
92 **Epidaurus** Probably the port on the Adriatic coast in Illyria, north-west of Epidamnus. The other Epidaurus, sanctuary of Asclepius, with its famous amphitheatre, was on the Peloponnesus, south-east of Corinth and thus in almost the same direction from the shipwrecked family as Corinth. But the play's geography is vague at best, as Cuningham's extensive note on this line demonstrates. Shakespeare may not have known the difference, or cared, if he did.

But ere they came—O let me say no more!
Gather the sequel by that went before.

DUKE

Nay, forward, old man; do not break off so,   95
For we may pity though not pardon thee.

EGEON

O, had the gods done so, I had not now
Worthily termed them merciless to us.
For, ere the ships could meet by twice five leagues,
We were encountered by a mighty rock,   100
Which being violently borne upon,
Our helpful ship was splitted in the midst;
So that in this unjust divorce of us,
Fortune had left to both of us alike
What to delight in, what to sorrow for.   105
Her part, poor soul, seeming as burdenèd
With lesser weight but not with lesser woe,
Was carried with more speed before the wind,
And in our sight they three were taken up
By fishermen of Corinth, as we thought.   110
At length another ship had seized on us,
And, knowing whom it was their hap to save,
Gave healthful welcome to their shipwrecked guests,
And would have reft the fishers of their prey
Had not their bark been very slow of sail;   115
And therefore homeward did they bend their course.
Thus have you heard me severed from my bliss,

101 upon] POPE; vp FI; up upon F2   115 bark] F2 (barke); backe FI; barque OXFORD

94 **that** that which
99 **twice five leagues** thirty miles (a league =
three nautical miles). More dramatic
approximation (or exaggeration): at sea,
the horizon is said to be thirteen miles distant, so Egeon could scarcely be imagined
actually to perceive and be able to identify
the two vessels at thirty miles' distance
from each other.
102 **ship** i.e. the mast to which they were tied
106 **Her part** i.e. of the now split mast
109–10 This differs somewhat from the
Abbess's version of the event at
5.1.356–60, where she says that it was
a ship from Epidamnus which rescued

her and the two infants with her,
before Corinthian fishermen kidnapped
the babies.
114 **reft** robbed (bereft)
115 **bark** The variant spelling (*barque*) preferred by Oxford usually designates, in
modern English, a three-masted sailing
vessel of any size with a particular system
of rigging (*barque-rigged*). The more general designation, current in the sixteenth
century, of any small sailing ship, including fishing and cargo vessels, applicable
here and throughout the play, is conveyed
in the simpler, older spelling (*OED sb.*[2]).

That by misfortunes was my life prolonged
To tell sad stories of my own mishaps.

DUKE

And for the sake of them thou sorrow'st for,   120
Do me the favour to dilate at full
What have befall'n of them and thee till now.

EGEON

My youngest boy, and yet my eldest care,
At eighteen years became inquisitive
After his brother, and importuned me   125
That his attendant—for his case was like,
Reft of his brother, but retained his name—
Might bear him company in the quest of him;
Whom whilst I laboured of a love to see,
I hazarded the loss of whom I loved.   130
Five summers have I spent in farthest Greece,
Roaming clean through the bounds of Asia,
And coasting homeward came to Ephesus,
Hopeless to find, yet loath to leave unsought
Or that or any place that harbours men.   135
But here must end the story of my life,
And happy were I in my timely death
Could all my travels warrant me they live.

---

122 have] F1; hath F2   thee] F2; they F1   126 for] F2; so F1

---

121 **dilate at full** tell the whole story in detail
122 **What have befall'n** 'What' is to be understood as plural, i.e. 'what things', since 'them' and 'thee' are several persons. Until the mid twentieth century, editors preferred F2's 'hath'; Alexander was the first to restore 'have'. This is not a case of false accord like those at ll. 10 and 86 and is not covered by Abbott (§§333–4).
123 **youngest boy** Egeon said at l. 77 that it was his wife who took charge of the 'latter-born'; an insignificant discrepancy, of a sort common in Shakespeare.
126 **for** *OED* does not provide examples of F's usage of 'so', although its general sense is clear; it may mean 'so much'. But 'for' is clearer still: Dromio's case was exactly like Antipholus', not 'so much' like it. The

F2 'editor' or compositor would seem not to have recognized 'so' as normal in this phrase, otherwise he would have had no reason to change it.
127 **retained his name** Shakespeare may be recalling here the Argument or the Prologue to *Menaechmi*, in both of which the grandfather is said to have renamed the surviving twin after the lost one. Earlier, Egeon said that their names were the only way of distinguishing between the twins (l. 52).
134 **unsought** unsearched, unexplored
136 **story** Both the tale he has been telling, and his life itself. One of several references by Egeon in this scene to his role as story-teller (see ll. 32, 94, 119).
137 **timely** i.e. occurring at a fitting time
138 **warrant** assure

DUKE

Hapless Egeon, whom the fates have marked
To bear the extremity of dire mishap!   140
Now trust me, were it not against our laws—
Which princes, would they, may not disannul—
Against my crown, my oath, my dignity,
My soul should sue as advocate for thee.
But though thou art adjudgèd to the death,   145
And passèd sentence may not be recalled
But to our honour's great disparagement,
Yet will I favour thee in what I can.
Therefore, merchant, I'll limit thee this day
To seek thy hope by beneficial help;   150
Try all the friends thou hast in Ephesus,
Beg thou or borrow to make up the sum,
And live. If no, then thou art doomed to die.
Jailer, take him to thy custody.

JAILER   I will, my lord.   155

EGEON

Hopeless and helpless doth Egeon wend,
But to procrastinate his lifeless end.   *Exeunt*

142–3 Which . . . disannul — | Against . . . dignity,] THEOBALD; Against . . . dignity, | Which
. . . disanull, F   142 princes, would they, may not] THEOBALD; Princes would they may not
F1; Princes would they may not F2   150 hope . . . help] STAUNTON (*conj.* Collier), SISSON;
helpe . . . helpe F; life . . . help ROWE 1714; help . . . means STEEVENS *conj.*; pelf . . . help CUN-
INGHAM; health . . . help WILSON; help . . . hap ALEXANDER, WILSON 1962   153 no] F; not
ROWE

142–3 Theobald's rearrangement and repunctuation of these lines are typically acute. Laws might be 'disannulled'—though Solinus, like the Duke of Venice (*Merchant* 3.3.26–31), claims not to have the right to do so—but disannulment is less clearly predicable of crowns, oaths and dignities. 'Our laws' and 'my crown, my oath, my dignity' are different orders of things; it is the inviolable 'statutes of the town' that are in question.

142 **would they** even if they wanted to
    disannul cancel, nullify
147 **disparagement** discredit
150 **hope . . . help** This much emended line

can be rendered in a variety of ways. Collier's conjecture, as defended by Sisson, namely that the compositor (C) misread *hope* as *holpe* which he then emended to *helpe* (*New Readings*, i. 89–90), is even more plausible than Wilson's (which he later abandoned, though subsequent editors have found it persuasive). 'Hope' here means 'that which is hoped for' (*OED sb.* 4c), that is, Egeon's salvation. As Collier and Sisson further point out, the Duke's injunction is echoed in Egeon's penultimate line ('Hopeless and helpless . . .').

157 **procrastinate** postpone

1.2   *Enter ⌈from the bay⌉ Antipholus of Syracuse, First*
       Merchant, and Dromio of Syracuse

FIRST MERCHANT

Therefore give out you are of Epidamnus,
Lest that your goods too soon be confiscate.
This very day a Syracusan merchant
Is apprehended for arrival here,
And, not being able to buy out his life,   5
According to the statute of the town
Dies ere the weary sun set in the west.
There is your money that I had to keep.

ANTIPHOLUS OF SYRACUSE (*to Dromio*)

Go bear it to the Centaur, where we host,
And stay there, Dromio, till I come to thee.   10
Within this hour it will be dinner-time.
Till that, I'll view the manners of the town,
Peruse the traders, gaze upon the buildings,
And then return and sleep within mine inn,

1.2.0.1 *from the bay*] OXFORD; *not in* F   *Antipholus of Syracuse*] ROWE; *Antipholis Erotes* F
0.1–2 *First Merchant*] DYCE; *a Marchant* F   0.2 *Dromio of Syracuse*] CAPELL; *Dromio* F
1, 24, 32 FIRST MERCHANT] DYCE; *Mar., E. Mar.* F; OXFORD *reads* MERCHANT OF EPHESUS (*so
throughout scene*)   4 arrival] F2 (arrivall); *a riuall* F1   9 ANTIPHOLUS OF SYRACUSE] CAPELL
(*A.S.*); *Ant.* F (*so throughout play, with few exceptions*)

1.2 All editors have followed Pope in starting
a new scene here, but not in his introduction of a further scene break at l. 33.

2 **too** There is no punctuation in F to point
to either 'your goods' or 'soon' as being
modified by 'too'. Any time would be too
soon for Antipholus to have his belong-
ings confiscated, so 'too' probably modi-
fies 'your goods', i.e. yours as well as
other unfortunate Syracusans', about
one of whom the Merchant proceeds to
tell Antipholus. The Merchant echoes the
Duke (1.1.20), one of numerous verbal
links between the two scenes.

4 **arrival** The first 'r' may have dropped out
of F1's 'a riuall'; or Compositor D, who
set column b on this page of F (H1ᵛ), may
have thought he read the equivalent of
'a rival' and believed it made sense, not
having read the first page and a half of
the play (as he was setting his copy from

H3ᵛ back toward the beginning), where
Egeon is indeed said to have been arrested
for merely 'arriving' in Ephesus.

9 **Centaur** Name of the inn. First of a series
of exotic animal names borne by
dwellings and other buildings in Ephesus;
others are Phoenix, Tiger and Porcupine.
Shakespeare used some of the same
names again, but for ships (*Phoenix*,
Tiger), in *Twelfth Night*, a play with many
affinities with *Errors*, and Sebastian's inn
in that play is the Elephant.
   host lodge. Used as a verb only elsewhere in Shakespeare (*All's Well* 3.5.95;
compare 'Your goods that lay at host',
Errors 5.1.412).

11 The first of many reminders of the passing
hours, and hence of Egeon's doom.
Dinner-time in Elizabethan England
would be between 11 a.m. and noon.

13 **Peruse** observe, survey

For with long travel I am stiff and weary.   15
Get thee away.

DROMIO OF SYRACUSE
Many a man would take you at your word,
And go indeed, having so good a means.   *Exit*

ANTIPHOLUS OF SYRACUSE
A trusty villain, sir, that very oft,
When I am dull with care and melancholy,   20
Lightens my humour with his merry jests.
What, will you walk with me about the town,
And then go to my inn and dine with me?

FIRST MERCHANT
I am invited, sir, to certain merchants'
Of whom I hope to make much benefit.   25
I crave your pardon. Soon at five o'clock,
Please you, I'll meet with you upon the mart,
And afterward consort you till bedtime.
My present business calls me from you now.

ANTIPHOLUS OF SYRACUSE
Farewell till then. I will go lose myself,   30
And wander up and down to view the city.

---

15 travel] F4; trauaile F1   17 DROMIO OF SYRACUSE] CAPELL (*D.S.*); *Dro.* F (*so throughout play*)
18 means] F2 (meanes); meane F1   23 my inn] F1 (my Inne); the Inne F2   24 merchants']
This edition; Marchants F   26 o'clock] THEOBALD; a clocke F

15 **travel** F4's form may reflect a change in usage, which by the late seventeenth century was distinguishing between modern *travel* and *travail*. Since Rowe, editors have been content with the obvious primary sense: Antipholus is weary from his journey. Compare 1.1.138 and 5.1.402, where F reads 'trauells' and 'trauaile' respectively.

18 **means** i.e. the money

19 **villain** Originally, a lowborn rustic, or a serf; here used playfully, even affectionately, with no strongly derogatory connotation. This is *OED*'s earliest instance of this usage.

23 **my inn** Shakespeare's writing (if it was he) 'my inn' here but 'mine inn' at l. 14 (and 'mine own' at l. 33) seems to have perplexed the F2 compositor. *OED* says that *mine* before vowels and *h* was the rule in England from the thirteenth to the eighteenth century. Abbott (§237) confirms that Shakespeare used both forms before vowels and offers a speculative rule for their use: 'Mine' is used when the possessive adjective is not being stressed, and 'my' when it is; it is not always an easy distinction. What, for example, of ll. 33 and 61 ('thine own')? Here 'mine' might have made too jingling a compound of assonance and alliteration.

26 **Soon ... o'clock** 'Soon at' seems to have meant 'about' or 'towards'. 'Five o'clock' is 'gradually established as the hour at which the action will be resolved' (Wells).

28 **consort you** keep you company

30 **lose myself** i.e. 'wander up and down'. But when repeated in l. 40, the expression acquires a deeper meaning.

FIRST MERCHANT

Sir, I commend you to your own content.   *Exit*

ANTIPHOLUS OF SYRACUSE

He that commends me to mine own content

Commends me to the thing I cannot get.

I to the world am like a drop of water   35

That in the ocean seeks another drop,

Who, failing there to find his fellow forth,

Unseen, inquisitive, confounds himself.

So I, to find a mother and a brother,

In quest of them unhappy, lose myself.   40

    Enter Dromio of Ephesus

Here comes the almanac of my true date.

What now? How chance thou art returned so soon?

DROMIO OF EPHESUS

Returned so soon? Rather approached too late.

The capon burns, the pig falls from the spit;

The clock hath strucken twelve upon the bell,   45

---

32 *Exit*] ROWE (*Exit Mer.*); *Exeunt* F   33 mine] FI; my F2   37 failing] This edition (*conj.*
B. Field *in* Cambridge); falling F   40 them unhappy,] WELLS; them (vnhappie a) FI; him
(unhappie) F2; him, unhappy ROWE 1709; them, unhappy, ROWE 1714; them, unhappier
CAMBRIDGE *conj.*; them (unhappy), ah, RIVERSIDE; them—unhappy, ah— TETZELI

35–40 Shakespeare turns the proverbial
expression of inconsequence, 'like a drop
of water in the sea' (Tilley, D613; Dent,
p. 96), into a striking simile of the
insignificance of an individual amid the
anonymous mass of humanity. Antipholus is not truly himself, not whole, with-
out his search, and his father's, for that necessary reunion are
the play's central romance motif. Egeon's
literal account of loss at sea is transposed
into the figurative mode here. Adriana
uses the same image in a different context
at 2.2.128–32.

37 **failing** This reading, apparently proposed
by Barron Field (1786–1846), was first
recorded by Clark and Glover in their
Cambridge edition. Once entertained, it
is hard to dismiss. The water drop in
Antipholus' image is not a raindrop
falling into the ocean, but one drop of
water *in* the ocean, seeking there and failing to find another drop. Only if we read
'failing' here, does the parallel drawn by
Antipholus with his own predicament in
ll. 39–40 hold: he, like the water drop,

fails—is 'unhappy'—in his quest, to find
his mother and brother, one lone, particular human being in the huge world
seeking and not finding other particular
ones. Tilley (D613) and Dent (p. 96) quote
'As lost as a drop of water in the sea' with
reference to this passage and to 2.2.129.
'Failing' was adopted in the Hull–Kemble
prompt-book text (1811); discussed in
Whitworth, p. 131.

37 **find . . . forth** find out, locate. Hull reads
'find . . . out'.

40 **unhappy** unsuccessful, disappointed

41 **almanac . . . date** calendar or astronomi-
cal table by which I know my own exact
age. Compare 5.1.406 ('calendars of their
nativity'); Shakespeare appears to consider 'calendar' and 'almanac' as virtual
synonyms, as at *Dream* 3.1.48. Though
this is not the person he thinks it is,
Antipholus' observation is nevertheless
true. He is thus the first victim, and the
first unwitting beneficiary, of the provi-
dential circumstances upon which the
play's action turns.

45 **strucken** struck

My mistress made it one upon my cheek.
She is so hot because the meat is cold,
The meat is cold because you come not home,
You come not home because you have no stomach,
You have no stomach, having broke your fast;   50
But we that know what 'tis to fast and pray
Are penitent for your default today.

ANTIPHOLUS OF SYRACUSE
Stop in your wind, sir. Tell me this, I pray:
Where have you left the money that I gave you?

DROMIO OF EPHESUS
O, sixpence that I had o' Wednesday last   55
To pay the saddler for my mistress' crupper?
The saddler had it, sir; I kept it not.

ANTIPHOLUS OF SYRACUSE
I am not in a sportive humour now.
Tell me, and dally not: where is the money?
We being strangers here, how dar'st thou trust   60
So great a charge from thine own custody?

DROMIO OF EPHESUS
I pray you, jest, sir, as you sit at dinner.
I from my mistress come to you in post;
If I return I shall be post indeed,
For she will score your fault upon my pate.   65

---

55 o' Wednesday] STEEVENS; a wensday F1; a *Wednesday* F4; o' we'nsday CAPELL   59 not:]
OXFORD; not, F   65 score] ROWE; scoure F

---

49 **stomach** appetite

51-2 **But we . . . today** We who haven't had
breakfast are obliged to do penance (continue fasting) for your sin (not coming
home to dinner on time).

53 **Stop . . . wind** shut up. The verb is 'stop
in', that is, 'block', 'hold back'.

56 **crupper** A leather strap fastened to the
rear of a saddle in such a way as to prevent it sliding forward on the horse.

63 **in post** in haste

64-5 **post . . . score** The second line makes
clear the primary sense of Dromio's pun
on 'post' and supports Rowe's modernization to 'score'. Dromio likens himself to
a doorpost (or any post), as in a tavern,
upon which a customer's orders were
chalked up (scored) until the final tally

was made. Compare 'Score a pint of bastard in the Half-moon' and 'Here's no
scoring but upon the pate' (*1 Henry IV*
2.5.26-7, 5.3.31); a secondary sense in
the latter of those passages, as in the present one, is to mark or cut as with a
weapon or whip. The collocation 'scouring faults' occurs at *Henry V* 1.1.35,
where 'scouring' obviously means
'cleansing'. Dromio is repeating, with a
new metaphor, his complaint (50-2)
that his master's fault is debited to his,
Dromio's, account. If there is a *double
entendre* with 'scour', meaning 'to beat' or
'punish', it is as audible with 'score' as
with 'scour', but the construction 'scour
x upon *y*' is not recorded in *OED*.

Methinks your maw, like mine, should be your clock,
And strike you home without a messenger.

ANTIPHOLUS OF SYRACUSE

Come, Dromio, come, these jests are out of season.
Reserve them till a merrier hour than this.
Where is the gold I gave in charge to thee?   70

DROMIO OF EPHESUS

To me, sir? Why, you gave no gold to me.

ANTIPHOLUS OF SYRACUSE

Come on, sir knave, have done your foolishness,
And tell me how thou hast disposed thy charge.

DROMIO OF EPHESUS

My charge was but to fetch you from the mart
Home to your house, the Phoenix, sir, to dinner.   75
My mistress and her sister stays for you.

ANTIPHOLUS OF SYRACUSE

Now, as I am a Christian, answer me
In what safe place you have bestowed my money,
Or I shall break that merry sconce of yours
That stands on tricks when I am undisposed.   80
Where is the thousand marks thou hadst of me?

DROMIO OF EPHESUS

I have some marks of yours upon my pate,
Some of my mistress' marks upon my shoulders,
But not a thousand marks between you both.
If I should pay your worship those again,   85
Perchance you will not bear them patiently.

ANTIPHOLUS OF SYRACUSE

Thy mistress' marks? What mistress, slave, hast thou?

---

66 clock] POPE; cooke F   76 stays] F (staies), CAPELL (mistress, and her sister, stays); stay ROWE

66 **maw ... clock** Similar to such expressions as Tilley's 'The belly is the truest clock' (B287a) and 'My stomach has struck twelve' (S872), but predating most examples, most of which also are verbally unlike these two entry forms, as Dent notes (p. 219).
   maw stomach
68 **out of season** untimely
76 **stays** Editors were slow to follow Capell's lead in restoring F's apparently non-agreeing verb. His punctuation makes

'and her sister' parenthetical, justifying 'stays' with the singular 'My mistress'. We are informed, casually, of the existence of the sister with whom Antipholus of Syracuse will fall in love.
79 **sconce** head (jocularly). Compare 2.2.35–9.
80 **stands on** practises, engages in. *OED*'s earliest occurrence in this sense (*stand*, v. 74e).
81 **thousand marks** Just the sum required by Egeon for his ransom (1.1.19–22).

DROMIO OF EPHESUS

Your worship's wife, my mistress, at the Phoenix;
She that doth fast till you come home to dinner,
And prays that you will hie you home to dinner.   90

ANTIPHOLUS OF SYRACUSE

What, wilt thou flout me thus unto my face,
Being forbid? There, take you that, sir knave!
    He beats Dromio

DROMIO OF EPHESUS

What mean you, sir? For God's sake, hold your hands!
Nay, an you will not, sir, I'll take my heels.   *Exit*

ANTIPHOLUS OF SYRACUSE

Upon my life, by some device or other   95
The villain is o'er-raught of all my money.
They say this town is full of cozenage,
As nimble jugglers that deceive the eye,
Dark-working sorcerers that change the mind,
Soul-killing witches that deform the body,   100
Disguisèd cheaters, prating mountebanks,
And many suchlike libertines of sin.

92.1 *He beats Dromio*] WILSON (*subs.*); *Striking him* COLLIER; *not in* F   93 God's] HANMER; God F   94 an] POPE; and F   *Exit*] F2; *Exeunt.* F1   96 o'er-raught] HANMER; ore-wrought F1; o're wrought F4; o'er-wrought ROWE   102 libertines] HANMER; liberties F

89–90 **doth fast . . . prays** Dromio resumes his metaphor from 50–2.

91–2 **thou . . . you** Antipholus' change from the more habitual master-to-servant pronoun to the other is explained thus by Abbott: 'When the appellate "sir" is used, even in anger, *thou* generally gives place to *you*' (§232). This would account for similar occurrences in ll. 53 and 72, but not those in 54 and 78–9, where unusual seriousness or deliberateness may be the reason.

91 **flout** mock, insult

94 **an** if
   take my heels i.e. take to my heels, leave. Foakes points out the opposition between 'hold your hands' and 'take my heels'.

96 **o'er-raught** overreached, cheated, outwitted

97–102 Recalls *Menaechmi* 2.1.33–8, where Messenio warns his master against the 'ribalds, parasites, drunkards, catchpoles, coneycatchers, and sycophants' of Epidamnus, but is in spirit nearer St Paul's description of Ephesus in Acts 19. Shakespeare emphasizes sorcery and sinful deception rather than Plautus' 'riot and lasciviousness'. Shakespeare may however have recalled the latter's wordplay on 'Epidamnus': *sine damno*, 'without being damned'.

102 **libertines** Johnson found Hanmer's emendation persuasive; 'Sir T. Hanmer reads, *Libertines*, which, as the author has been enumerating not acts but persons, seems right'. Other editors cite Hanmer, but none except Collier 1858 and Oxford have emended the text. Johnson's argument is strong, and is strengthened by 'suchlike', but Cuningham thinks that because Shakespeare used an abstract—'cozenage'—instead of 'cozeners', he may also therefore have used 'liberties' in place of 'libertines'; no such usage is recorded in *OED*. The religious meaning of 'liberty' is 'freedom from sin' (*OED* 1b), and the sense of 'licence' or 'lack of restraint in behaviour' is strained here,

If it prove so, I will be gone the sooner.
I'll to the Centaur to go seek this slave.
I greatly fear my money is not safe.   *Exit*   105

2.1   *Enter ⌐from the Phoenix⌐ Adriana, wife of Antipholus*
        of Ephesus, with Luciana, her sister

ADRIANA

Neither my husband nor the slave returned
That in such haste I sent to seek his master?
Sure, Luciana, it is two o'clock.

LUCIANA

Perhaps some merchant hath invited him,
And from the mart he's somewhere gone to dinner.   5
Good sister, let us dine, and never fret.
A man is master of his liberty.
Time is their master, and when they see time
They'll go or come. If so, be patient, sister.

ADRIANA

Why should their liberty than ours be more?   10

2.1.0.1 *from the Phoenix*] OXFORD; *not in* F; *Adriana and Luciana come forth* WILSON   0.1–2 *of Antipholus of Ephesus*] COLLIER; *to Antipholis Sereptus* F   8 master] F; mistress OXFORD ('M^rs' *Original-Spelling Edition*)

while 'libertine' (*OED* 2a) was in use from the mid-sixteenth century to refer to certain antinomian sects and, more generally, to religious free-thinkers, those of loose, unorthodox opinions. Several of *OED*'s early examples are reminiscent of this one: e.g. in 1589 the Privy Council noted, no doubt with disapproval, that 'In those Lowe Countryes there are Sectaryes, as Annabaptystes, Lybertines, and soche lyke'. 'Libertines', like 'soul-killing' and 'sin', belongs to the fabric of religious, specifically Christian, allusion, as other words and phrases in this passage—'deceive the eye', 'Dark-working sorcerers that change the mind', 'Disguisèd', 'mountebanks'—belong to the connected fabric of superstitious, false 'supernatural' allusion in the play, and it reinforces Shakespeare's substitution of Paul's Ephesus for Plautus' Epidamnus.

2.1.0.1 On a classical-style set, Adriana and Luciana would enter from the house and play their scene 'outdoors', before it;

some productions place them at an upstairs window or on a balcony. In Adrian Noble's 1983 RSC production, they stood in a cradle suspended above the set (see Fig. 6).

1 **slave** In *Menaechmi* Messenio is a slave; he receives his freedom at the end, having already been 'freed' by the wrong Menaechmus earlier. Egeon bought the Dromios to be servants to his sons, so they too are ostensibly slaves, though the term is frequently used in a general sense, like 'villain' (1.2.19); compare 1.2.104, where the epithet was applied to the other Dromio.

8 **master** Oxford's emendation seems unnecessary. While the compositor 'may have misexpanded an abbreviated form in his copy' (*TC*, p. 267), there seems no compelling reason to assume that he must have done so. 'Master' occurs several other times in the dialogue between the sisters in the first part of the scene.

LUCIANA
Because their business still lies out o' door.
ADRIANA
Look when I serve him so, he takes it ill.
LUCIANA
O, know he is the bridle of your will.
ADRIANA
There's none but asses will be bridled so.
LUCIANA
Why, headstrong liberty is lashed with woe.　　　15
There's nothing situate under heaven's eye
But hath his bound in earth, in sea, in sky.
The beasts, the fishes, and the wingèd fowls
Are their males' subjects and at their controls.
Man, more divine, the master of all these,　　　20
Lord of the wide world and wild wat'ry seas,
Indued with intellectual sense and souls,
Of more pre-eminence than fish and fowls,
Are masters to their females, and their lords.
Then let your will attend on their accords.　　　25
ADRIANA
This servitude makes you to keep unwed.
LUCIANA
Not this, but troubles of the marriage bed.
ADRIANA
But were you wedded, you would bear some sway.
LUCIANA
Ere I learn love, I'll practise to obey.

---

12 ill] F2; thus F1   20–1 Man . . . master . . . Lord] F; Men . . . masters . . . Lords HANMER
21 wild] F1 (wilde); wide F2   22 souls] F1 (soules); soule F2   23 fowls] F1 (fowles); fowle F2

11 **still . . . door** often takes them away from home
12 **Look when** whenever
15 **lashed** punished
18–19, 22–3 **fowls . . . controls . . . souls . . . fowls** Cercignani notes these among a number of other similar rhymes (pp. 224–6). The sentiments expressed by Luciana recall those of Katherine's famous long speech at the end of *Shrew* (5.2.141–84).

20–1 Hanmer and those who followed him were no doubt influenced by 'Are masters' in l. 24, but as Sisson observes, it is 'man' (= mankind) that is in question rather than individual men (*New Readings*, i. 90). The collective noun correctly takes the plural verb.
22 **Indued** invested, endowed
25 **accords** assent
26 **servitude** servility

ADRIANA

How if your husband start some otherwhere?   30

LUCIANA

Till he come home again, I would forbear.

ADRIANA

Patience unmoved! No marvel though she pause:
They can be meek that have no other cause.
A wretched soul, bruised with adversity,
We bid be quiet when we hear it cry.   35
But were we burdened with like weight of pain,
As much or more we should ourselves complain.
So thou, that hast no unkind mate to grieve thee,
With urging helpless patience would relieve me.
But if thou live to see like right bereft,   40
This fool-begged patience in thee will be left.

LUCIANA

Well, I will marry one day, but to try.
        Enter Dromio of Ephesus
Here comes your man. Now is your husband nigh.

ADRIANA

Say, is your tardy master now at hand?

DROMIO OF EPHESUS Nay, he's at two hands with me, and   45
that my two ears can witness.

ADRIANA

Say, didst thou speak with him? Know'st thou his
        mind?

DROMIO OF EPHESUS I? Ay, he told his mind upon mine ear.
Beshrew his hand, I scarce could understand it.

42.1 *Enter Dromio* . . .] OXFORD; *after l.* 43 F (*Enter Dromio Eph.*)   48–9] *as prose* HARNESS; *as verse* F   48 I? Ay] WELLS; I, I F; Ay, ay ROWE

30 **start some otherwhere** goes off in another
   direction, i.e. in pursuit of another
   woman
32 **pause** hesitate (before marrying)
40 **to . . . bereft** to experience a similar
   betrayal of your marriage
41 **fool-begged** foolishly urged
45 **he's . . . me** he has been beating me with
   both hands
48–9 It is hard to be sure when editors have
   set this speech by Dromio as prose, as
   ll. 45–6 are, because the line-break in
   many editions comes between 'ear' and
   'Beshrew', as it would if the lines were set

   as verse; only when 'beshrew' is not
   capitalized (as in Knight) is it clear. But
   Harness's edition is the earliest in which
   prose is obviously intended. Dromio
   breaks into the scene with prose, which
   Luciana (50–1), but not Adriana, adopts;
   Dromio then switches to verse for his
   patter-routine (61–75).
48 **told . . . ear** made it clear what he wanted
   me to know by beating me about the ears
49 **Beshrew** curse
   I . . . it Dromio puns on 'understand',
   meaning both 'comprehend', and 'stand
   up under' (the blows).

LUCIANA Spake he so doubtfully thou couldst not feel his 50
meaning?

DROMIO OF EPHESUS Nay, he struck so plainly I could too well
feel his blows, and withal so doubtfully that I could scarce
understand them.

ADRIANA

But say, I prithee, is he coming home? 55
It seems he hath great care to please his wife.

DROMIO OF EPHESUS

Why, mistress, sure my master is horn-mad.

ADRIANA Horn-mad, thou villain?

DROMIO OF EPHESUS I mean not cuckold-mad, but sure he is
stark mad. 60
When I desired him to come home to dinner,
He asked me for a thousand marks in gold.
' 'Tis dinner-time,' quoth I. 'My gold,' quoth he.
'Your meat doth burn,' quoth I. 'My gold,' quoth he.
'Will you come home?' quoth I. 'My gold,' quoth he; 65
'Where is the thousand marks I gave thee, villain?'
'The pig', quoth I, 'is burned.' 'My gold!' quoth he.
'My mistress, sir—' quoth I. 'Hang up thy mistress!
I know thy mistress not. Out on thy mistress!'

LUCIANA Quoth who? 70

DROMIO OF EPHESUS Quoth my master.
'I know', quoth he, 'no house, no wife, no mistress.'

50–4] *as prose* F; *as verse* CAPELL (. . . feel | His . . . I | Could . . . [there]withal | So . . . them);
50–1 *as verse*, 52–4 *as prose* OXFORD   59–60] *as prose (or one line)* COLLIER 1858; *as verse* F (. . .
Cuckold mad, | But . . .)   62 a thousand] F2 (a 1000); a hundred F1   65 come home]
THEOBALD; come F   69 I know thy mistress not] CUNINGHAM (*conj.* Seymour); ~~not thy mis-
tresse F; ~~not of thy mistress CAPELL; ~~no mistress STEEVENS *conj.*; Thy mistress I know not
HANMER   Out on thy mistress] F; out upon thy mistress STEEVENS *conj.*   72–5] *as verse* POPE; *as
prose* F

50 **doubtfully** ambiguously, uncertainly
53 **doubtfully** dreadfully. See Eagleson–
   Onions, p. 81, where the meaning here is
   distinguished from that in l. 50; compare
   'doubtful' at 1.1.67. *OED* lists no such
   meaning for the adverb.
54 **understand** he repeats his pun of l. 49.
57 **horn-mad** (of a horned beast) enraged so
   as to be ready to attack with its horns;
   also, angry at being made a cuckold, the
   sense in which Adriana takes it. Compare
   Merry Wives 1.4.46 and 3.5.140, where
   Ford refers to the expression as proverbial

(Tilley, H628; Dent, p. 140).
62 **thousand** F's error is obvious; compare
   1.2.81 and l. 66 below.
69 Foakes defends F's order by pointing out
   the echoing series of phrases ending
   in 'mistress'; there is also a jolt as 'my
   master' breaks the series. The price is a
   clumsy line, with the stresses falling
   awkwardly throughout.
71–5 **Quoth . . . there** This passage, near
   the bottom of column b (sig. H2), is set as
   prose by Compositor C, who was apparently cramped for space; Compositor D

So that my errand, due unto my tongue,
I thank him, I bore home upon my shoulders;
For, in conclusion, he did beat me there.   75

ADRIANA
Go back again, thou slave, and fetch him home.

DROMIO OF EPHESUS
Go back again and be new-beaten home?
For God's sake, send some other messenger.

ADRIANA
Back, slave, or I will break thy pate across.

DROMIO OF EPHESUS
An he will bless that cross with other beating,   80
Between you I shall have a holy head.

ADRIANA
Hence, prating peasant. Fetch thy master home.
        She beats Dromio

DROMIO OF EPHESUS
Am I so round with you as you with me,
That like a football you do spurn me thus?
You spurn me hence, and he will spurn me hither.   85
If I last in this service, you must case me in leather.   *Exit*

LUCIANA (*to Adriana*)
Fie, how impatience loureth in your face!

ADRIANA
His company must do his minions grace,
Whilst I at home starve for a merry look.

---

74 bore] F (bare); bear STEEVENS 1778   80 An ... beating,] WELLS; And ... beating: F
82.1 *She beats Dromio*] WILSON (*subs.*); *not in* F   86.1 *Exit*] F2; *not in* F1

was rather generous with space around
the '*Actus Secundus*' heading in column a
of the same page, and C had already set
H2ᵛ himself, so had to fit his remaining
copy into H2b. He saved a line by setting it
as prose.

74 **bore** The modern spelling of the past tense
of the verb *bear*. Both *bare* and *bore* occur
in the Folio.
75 **there** i.e. upon my shoulders
80 **An ... beating** Wells considers the alter-
native, based on F, and adopted by most
editors (p. 135); Oxford follows Wells.
83 **round** uncompromising, outspoken.

Dromio is of course punning, as the next
line makes clear.
84 **football** One of only two occurrences of
the word in Shakespeare. The other is in
The Tragedy of King Lear, 1.4.84–5: 'you
base football player'.
  spurn kick; also, treat contemptuously
87 **loureth** frowns, looks sullen. An unusual
usage, 'impatience' being personified as
residing in Adriana's face and frowning,
rather than herself simply frowning.
88 **do ... grace** do honour to his mistresses;
with the further implication of enhan-
cing their quality, making them show to
advantage by his presence.

Hath homely age th'alluring beauty took   90
From my poor cheek? Then he hath wasted it.
Are my discourses dull? Barren my wit?
If voluble and sharp discourse be marred,
Unkindness blunts it more than marble hard.
Do their gay vestments his affections bait?   95
That's not my fault: he's master of my state.
What ruins are in me that can be found
By him not ruined? Then is he the ground
Of my defeatures. My decayèd fair
A sunny look of his would soon repair.   100
But, too unruly deer, he breaks the pale,
And feeds from home. Poor I am but his stale.

LUCIANA
Self-harming jealousy! Fie, beat it hence.

ADRIANA
Unfeeling fools can with such wrongs dispense.
I know his eye doth homage otherwhere,   105
Or else what lets it but he would be here?
Sister, you know he promised me a chain.

92 wit?] POPE; wit, F

90 **homely age** age, which makes me homely, no longer beautiful. *OED*'s first recorded occurrence of *homely* in this sense.
93 **voluble** fluent
   sharp acute, sagacious
95 **their** i.e. his minions'
   bait entice
96 **That's . . . state** it is my husband's fault if I am not so well dressed as they, since he is the one who provides for me
98 **ground** cause
99 **defeatures** disfigurement, defacement. Used also by Egeon at 5.1.299; the only two occurrences in Shakespeare. The singular occurs only in *Venus and Adonis* 735–6: 'To mingle beauty with infirmities, | And pure perfection with impure defeature'. *OED* cites 5.1.299 and *Venus and Adonis* as the two earliest occurrences in this sense (*sb.* 2).
   fair i.e. fairness, beauty
101 **pale** fence, enclosure
102 **stale** dupe, laughing-stock. In her jealous state of mind, Adriana imagines herself become a mere mistress (one of many) to her husband, and a butt of amusement among her rivals for her futile devotion to him. Both *OED sb.*[3] 6 and Eagleson–Onions (p. 264) cite this passage. The implied association with deer is obscure; perhaps it is just that, having been abandoned by her 'unruly deer', Adriana feels ridiculous.
104 **with . . . dispense** put up with such wrongs
106 **what . . . here** what prevents him from being here
107 **chain** In *Menaechmi* the husband steals a cloak from his wife and gives it to a courtesan, who then gives it to the husband's twin, the stranger; at the same time she gives him a chain, also previously stolen by the husband from his wife. Shakespeare omits the cloak but keeps the chain, ordered from the goldsmith by Antipholus of Ephesus for Adriana and first mentioned here. It will contribute further to the confusion over the brothers' identity, but will also help members of the audience to distinguish between the Antipholuses.

Would that alone, alas, he would detain,
So he would keep fair quarter with his bed.
I see the jewel best enamellèd   110
Will lose his beauty; and though gold bides still
That others touch, yet often touching will
Wear gold, and so no man that hath a name
But falsehood and corruption doth it shame.
Since that my beauty cannot please his eye,   115
I'll weep what's left away, and weeping die.

LUCIANA
How many fond fools serve mad jealousy!
                        ⌐*Exeunt into the Phoenix*⌐

2.2   *Enter Antipholus of Syracuse*
ANTIPHOLUS OF SYRACUSE
    The gold I gave to Dromio is laid up

108 alone, alas,] HANMER; ~a loue F1; ~alone F2; ~o'loue CUNINGHAM *conj.*; ~a toy FOAKES (*conj.* Kellner) 111 his] F; her OXFORD (hir, *Original-Spelling Edition*) and though] HANMER; yet the F; and the THEOBALD; yet though COLLIER 112 yet] THEOBALD; and F will↓] THEOBALD; will, F 113 Wear] THEOBALD; Where F so no man] THEOBALD; no man F; yet no man OXFORD 114 But] THEOBALD; By F 117.1 *Exeunt . . . Phoenix*] OXFORD; *Exit.* F
    2.2] CAPELL (Scene II); *no scene indication in* F 0.1 *Enter . . . Syracuse*] F (*Enter Antipholis Errotis*)

108 **Would . . . detain** However one emends F's 'alone, a loue', the sense is reasonably clear: Adriana would gladly forgo the gift her husband has promised her, if only he would remain faithful. Cuningham's conjecture, 'o' [= of] love', i.e. either qualifying 'that'—the chain (the token or aspect of love)—or an interjection—'for love's sake', 'in the name of love'—has been adopted by some modern editors (Wilson, Tetzeli, Oxford).
109 **keep . . . bed** deal fairly with me, his legitimate bedfellow
110–14 This is the most debated crux in the play. Theobald's typically intelligent emendations have been very largely followed by editors; they are recorded in the collations. Among the many attempts to explicate the passage are those, with useful commentaries, by Foakes (pp. 25–6) and Wells (p. 137), Cuningham's Appendix I (pp. 125–7), and the discussions by Sisson, *New Readings*, i. 91; S. A. Tannenbaum, p. 113; and Gary Taylor, 'Textual and Sexual Criticism: A Crux in *The Comedy of*

Errors', *Renaissance Drama*, NS 19 (1988), 195–225. In performance, it will make little difference which words an actress utters in this speech, so long as she conveys with conviction Adriana's anguish at both her husband's imagined infidelity and his apparent unconcern about his sullied reputation. But directors may prefer to follow Komisarjevsky's example and simply cut the lines. Paul's admonition to husbands and wives in Ephesians 5: 22–33 stands immediately behind the passage.
111 **his** its (Abbott, §228)
    bides abides, endures
112–13 Proverbial, if Theobald's 'Wear' is correct (Tilley, I92; Dent, p. 144). Testing the quality of gold by means of a touchstone involves taking a sample of the metal, thus scratching the object slightly. If it is often tested, it will become worn and thus diminished in value, however pure it may be.
113 **name** reputation
114 **doth it shame** do bring discredit upon it

Safe at the Centaur, and the heedful slave
Is wandered forth in care to seek me out.
By computation and mine host's report,
I could not speak with Dromio since at first   5
I sent him from the mart. See, here he comes.
    Enter Dromio of Syracuse
How now, sir, is your merry humour altered?
As you love strokes, so jest with me again.
You know no Centaur? You received no gold?
Your mistress sent to have me home to dinner?   10
My house was at the Phoenix?—Wast thou mad,
That thus so madly thou didst answer me?

DROMIO OF SYRACUSE
What answer, sir? When spake I such a word?

ANTIPHOLUS OF SYRACUSE
Even now, even here, not half an hour since.

DROMIO OF SYRACUSE
I did not see you since you sent me hence   15
Home to the Centaur with the gold you gave me.

ANTIPHOLUS OF SYRACUSE
Villain, thou didst deny the gold's receipt,
And told'st me of a mistress and a dinner,
For which I hope thou felt'st I was displeased.

DROMIO OF SYRACUSE
I am glad to see you in this merry vein.   20
What means this jest? I pray you, master, tell me.

---

3 out.] ROWE; out‸ F   4 report,] ROWE; report. F

2.2.2 **heedful** attentive, mindful. May be either affectionate ('He is worried and has gone to look for me') or ironic ('He has disobeyed me and left the inn where I told him to wait for me'; 1.2.9–10).

3–6 Rowe's repunctuation of ll. 3–4 improves the sense. How would Antipholus know that Dromio is 'computing' where to find him, and how could the Host have reported anything to Dromio, not knowing where Antipholus was? Furthermore, Antipholus' statement in l. 5 would be patently false since as far as

he knows he *has* spoken with Dromio (1.2.42–94) since he sent him from the mart (1.2.9–16). It is rather that, by his own calculation and what the Host has told him of Dromio's arrival at the inn with the money, Antipholus is puzzled that there should have been time for him to meet Dromio again—another in the sequence of inexplicable happenings. The ensuing encounter compounds his perplexity, and adds Dromio of Syracuse to the list of bewildered persons.

3 **in care to** with the purpose of

ANTIPHOLUS OF SYRACUSE
 Yea, dost thou jeer and flout me in the teeth?
 Think'st thou I jest? Hold, take thou that, and that.
   He beats Dromio
DROMIO OF SYRACUSE
 Hold, sir, for God's sake—now your jest is earnest!
 Upon what bargain do you give it me?   25
ANTIPHOLUS OF SYRACUSE
 Because that I familiarly sometimes
 Do use you for my fool, and chat with you,
 Your sauciness will jest upon my love,
 And make a common of my serious hours.
 When the sun shines, let foolish gnats make sport,   30
 But creep in crannies when he hides his beams.
 If you will jest with me, know my aspect,
 And fashion your demeanour to my looks,
 Or I will beat this method in your sconce.
DROMIO OF SYRACUSE 'Sconce' call you it? So you would   35
 leave battering, I had rather have it a head. An you use
 these blows long, I must get a sconce for my head, and
 ensconce it too, or else I shall seek my wit in my shoul-
 ders. But I pray, sir, why am I beaten?
ANTIPHOLUS OF SYRACUSE Dost thou not know?   40
DROMIO OF SYRACUSE Nothing, sir, but that I am beaten.
ANTIPHOLUS OF SYRACUSE Shall I tell you why?
DROMIO OF SYRACUSE Ay, sir, and wherefore; for they say
 every why hath a wherefore.
ANTIPHOLUS OF SYRACUSE
 'Why' first: for flouting me; and then 'wherefore':   45

45–6] *as verse* CAPELL; *as prose* F

22 **flout** mock
27 **fool** jester
29 **make . . . hours** intrude upon my private time as if it were common land, open to anyone
32 **aspect** appearance of a heavenly body as observed from earth. Pursuing his metaphorical representation of himself as the sun, Antipholus warns Dromio to read his mood in his appearance ('looks') and behave accordingly.

34 **sconce** head
35–9 **'Sconce' . . . shoulders** Dromio changes the meaning of 'sconce', saying he will need to put up a protective structure, like a small fort, around his head, lest it be driven down into his shoulders, along with the 'wit' it contains, by his master's battering.
38 **ensconce** fortify by enclosing
44 **every . . . wherefore** Proverbial (Tilley, W331; Dent, p. 248).

For urging it the second time to me.

DROMIO OF SYRACUSE

Was there ever any man thus beaten out of season,
When in the why and the wherefore is neither rhyme
          nor reason?—
Well, sir, I thank you.

ANTIPHOLUS OF SYRACUSE Thank me, sir, for what?

DROMIO OF SYRACUSE Marry, sir, for this something that you   50
gave me for nothing.

ANTIPHOLUS OF SYRACUSE I'll make you amends next, to
give you nothing for something. But say, sir, is it dinner-
time?

DROMIO OF SYRACUSE No, sir, I think the meat wants that   55
I have.

ANTIPHOLUS OF SYRACUSE In good time, sir. What's that?

DROMIO OF SYRACUSE Basting.

ANTIPHOLUS OF SYRACUSE Well, sir, then 'twill be dry.

DROMIO OF SYRACUSE If it be, sir, I pray you eat none of it.   60

ANTIPHOLUS OF SYRACUSE Your reason?

DROMIO OF SYRACUSE Lest it make you choleric and purchase
me another dry basting.

ANTIPHOLUS OF SYRACUSE Well, sir, learn to jest in good time.
There's a time for all things.   65

DROMIO OF SYRACUSE I durst have denied that before you
were so choleric.

ANTIPHOLUS OF SYRACUSE By what rule, sir?

47–8] *as verse* ROWE 1714; *as prose* F

47–8 Compositor C, over-generous with spacing around the stage direction at 2.2.111 (H3a), recovered a bit by squeezing these verse lines in as prose.

48 **neither . . . reason** Proverbial (Tilley, R98; Dent, p. 201).

55 **wants** lacks

57 **In good time** indeed, to be sure (ironic). A now obsolete meaning of the expression (*OED, time, sb.* 42c (*d*)), which is, however, still current in other senses (compare l. 64 below).

58 **Basting** Dromio is punning again: cooking meat is basted, moistened, to prevent its drying out; he is basted, i.e. beaten.

62 **choleric** irascible, wrathful. One of the four humours, choler was thought to be composed of hot and dry elements, and to be induced by eating dry, overcooked meat (compare *Shrew* 4.1.156–61).

63 **dry basting** harsh beating

64 **in good time** in the proper season, at the right time. *OED sb.* 42c (*c*) cites this line; compare l. 57 above.

65 **There's . . . things** Proverbial (Tilley, T314; Dent, p. 232). From Ecclesiastes 3 : 1.

68 **rule** Refers to the rules of logic or rhetoric, which should govern formal disputation and philosophical argument.

DROMIO OF SYRACUSE Marry, sir, by a rule as plain as the
plain bald pate of Father Time himself.   70
ANTIPHOLUS OF SYRACUSE Let's hear it.
DROMIO OF SYRACUSE There's no time for a man to recover
his hair that grows bald by nature.
ANTIPHOLUS OF SYRACUSE May he not do it by fine and
recovery?   75
DROMIO OF SYRACUSE Yes, to pay a fine for a periwig, and
recover the lost hair of another man.
ANTIPHOLUS OF SYRACUSE Why is Time such a niggard of
hair, being, as it is, so plentiful an excrement?
DROMIO OF SYRACUSE Because it is a blessing that he bestows   80
on beasts, and what he hath scanted men in hair he hath
given them in wit.
ANTIPHOLUS OF SYRACUSE Why, but there's many a man
hath more hair than wit.
DROMIO OF SYRACUSE Not a man of those but he hath the wit   85
to lose his hair.
ANTIPHOLUS OF SYRACUSE Why, thou didst conclude hairy
men plain dealers, without wit.
DROMIO OF SYRACUSE The plainer dealer, the sooner lost. Yet
he loseth it in a kind of policy.   90

81 men] POPE 1728; them F   90 policy] CUNINGHAM (*conj.* Staunton); iollitie F

69–70 **plain . . . Time** Time, a prominent motif throughout the play, is here personified and given its common description as an old bald man (or sometimes woman) (Tilley, T311; Dent, p. 231).
74–5 **fine and recovery** Legal process (or legal fiction) allowing someone to dispose freely of inherited property which the terms of his inheritance were designed to prevent his doing (i.e. 'entailed' property intended to be kept in the family). One of a number of legal expressions in the play, adding weight to the hypothesis that it was written expressly for a special event such as the Gray's Inn Christmas revels of 1594 (see Introduction, pp. 1–5).
76–7 **periwig . . . man** The best wigs were and are made from genuine human hair.
79 **excrement** outgrowth
85–90 There is strong bawdy innuendo in this passage, as Dromio alludes to a common symptom of venereal disease, loss of hair.

88 **plain dealers** straightforward, candid persons, hence 'without wit' to be devious or guileful. 'Plain dealing' is proverbial (Dent, pp. 193–4). William Wycherley's comedy *The Plain Dealer* (1675) is an adaptation of Molière's *Le Misanthrope* (1666); in both, the main character speaks his mind bluntly and unequivocally.
89 **plainer . . . lost** Dromio deliberately gives 'plain dealing' another sense, i.e. as in sexual relations between man and woman. A man who deals 'plainly' with a woman will contract venereal disease and thus lose his hair more quickly than one who does not.
90 **in . . . policy** with some purpose in mind. Staunton's conjecture is persuasive (Cuningham's note elaborates, p. 36), and makes better sense of the next ten lines, especially Antipholus' next question and Dromio's two 'reasons' (98–100). The specific meaning of 'jollity'

ANTIPHOLUS OF SYRACUSE For what reason?

DROMIO OF SYRACUSE For two, and sound ones too.

ANTIPHOLUS OF SYRACUSE Nay, not sound, I pray you.

DROMIO OF SYRACUSE Sure ones, then.

ANTIPHOLUS OF SYRACUSE Nay, not sure, in a thing falsing.   95

DROMIO OF SYRACUSE Certain ones, then.

ANTIPHOLUS OF SYRACUSE Name them.

DROMIO OF SYRACUSE The one, to save the money that he
spends in tiring; the other, that at dinner they should not
drop in his porridge.   100

ANTIPHOLUS OF SYRACUSE You would all this time have
proved there is no time for all things.

DROMIO OF SYRACUSE Marry, and did, sir: namely, e'en no
time to recover hair lost by nature.

ANTIPHOLUS OF SYRACUSE But your reason was not substan-   105
tial, why there is no time to recover.

DROMIO OF SYRACUSE Thus I mend it: Time himself is
bald, and therefore to the world's end will have bald
followers.

ANTIPHOLUS OF SYRACUSE I knew 'twould be a bald   110
conclusion.

     Enter ⌐*from the Phoenix*⌐ *Adriana,* ⌐*beckoning,*⌐ *and*
     Luciana

But soft—who wafts us yonder?

95 falsing] F; falling WHITE   99 tiring] POPE; trying F   103 e'en no] MALONE (*conj.* Capell);
in no F1; no F2   111.1 *Enter . . . Luciana (after l.112 in* F) *from the Phoenix*] OXFORD; *not in* F
beckoning] This edition; *not in* F

required for F's reading, i.e. sexual pleasure particularly of an illicit kind, or
promiscuity, common in late medieval
English, was still current in Shakespeare's
day, though this would have been the
only time he used the word in that sense.
Substitution of this kind, of a word which
means something quite different but still
makes some sense, would be typical of
Compositor C who set this page (H2^v),
and whose errors tend to be both more
serious and more subtle than Compositor
D's (O'Connor, p. 65). That tendency
encourages an editor to emend in such
cases.

95 **falsing** deceptive, unreliable. A Shake-

spearian coinage. This is the only occurrence in his works or anywhere else
apparently; it is unrecorded in *OED*,
which may support White's emendation.

99 **tiring** attiring, i.e. dressing his hair

100 **porridge** soup

105–6 **substantial** solid, firmly established.
Part of the semi-legalistic or self-
consciously rhetorical and debate-like
character of this passage (compare
'rule', l. 68).

108–10 **bald . . . bald . . . bald** Father Time
is usually represented as a bald old man
(l. 70). Those who 'follow' Time will
themselves become old and bald.
Antipholus finds this a threadbare,
unconvincing conclusion.

ADRIANA

    Ay, ay, Antipholus, look strange and frown:
    Some other mistress hath thy sweet aspects.
    I am not Adriana, nor thy wife.   115
    The time was once when thou unurged wouldst vow
    That never words were music to thine ear,
    That never object pleasing in thine eye,
    That never touch well welcome to thy hand,
    That never meat sweet-savoured in thy taste,   120
    Unless I spake, or looked, or touched, or carved to thee.
    How comes it now, my husband, O how comes it
    That thou art then estrangèd from thyself?
    Thy 'self' I call it, being strange to me
    That, undividable, incorporate,   125
    Am better than thy dear self's better part.
    Ah, do not tear away thyself from me;
    For know, my love, as easy mayst thou fall
    A drop of water in the breaking gulf,
    And take unmingled thence that drop again   130
    Without addition or diminishing,
    As take from me thyself, and not me too.
    How dearly would it touch thee to the quick
    Shouldst thou but hear I were licentious,
    And that this body, consecrate to thee,   135
    By ruffian lust should be contaminate?
    Wouldst thou not spit at me, and spurn at me,
    And hurl the name of 'husband' in my face,
    And tear the stained skin of my harlot brow,

139 of] F; off HANMER

121 Some editors have followed Steevens in omitting the first two 'or's', to make a pentameter. But hexameters occur from time to time in Shakespeare's dramatic blank verse, and Compositor C who set this column (H3a) and who often regularized to iambic pentameter, probably set what he saw in his copy this time.

128–32 Adriana employs the same image as Antipholus of Syracuse in 1.2.35–40. Her speech, serious, even moving, in itself, is unavoidably comical in the context, as she addresses it so earnestly to the wrong man.

133–49 This passage reiterates, to her supposed husband, the theme of Adriana's speech at 2.1.104–14, and reinforces the reading of the corrupt passages there as referring to his honour and reputation rather than hers. The present speech is a passionate argument by analogy, grounded in the biblical doctrine that man and wife are one flesh (Ephesians 5: 31, quoting Genesis 2: 24). If that is so, argues Adriana, her husband's corruption infects her as well.

139 of 'Of' could mean 'from' or 'off' in Elizabethan English, so there is no need

And from my false hand cut the wedding ring,   140
And break it with a deep-divorcing vow?
I know thou canst, and therefore see thou do it!
I am possessed with an adulterate blot;
My blood is mingled with the crime of lust.
For if we two be one, and thou play false,   145
I do digest the poison of thy flesh,
Being strumpeted by thy contagion.
Keep then fair league and truce with thy true bed,
I live unstained, thou undishonourèd.

ANTIPHOLUS OF SYRACUSE

Plead you to me, fair dame? I know you not.   150
In Ephesus I am but two hours old,
As strange unto your town as to your talk,
Who, every word by all my wit being scanned,
Wants wit in all one word to understand.

LUCIANA

Fie, brother, how the world is changed with you!   155
When were you wont to use my sister thus?
She sent for you by Dromio home to dinner.

ANTIPHOLUS OF SYRACUSE By Dromio?

DROMIO OF SYRACUSE By me?

ADRIANA

By thee; and this thou didst return from him—   160
That he did buffet thee, and in his blows
Denied my house for his, me for his wife.

ANTIPHOLUS OF SYRACUSE

Did you converse, sir, with this gentlewoman?
What is the course and drift of your compact?

DROMIO OF SYRACUSE

I, sir? I never saw her till this time.   165

ANTIPHOLUS OF SYRACUSE

Villain, thou liest! For even her very words
Didst thou deliver to me on the mart.

---

149 unstained] HANMER (*conj.* Theobald); distain'd F; undistain'd KEIGHTLEY

to change F's spelling; 'stained skin of   149 **unstained** Clearly the sense intended,
my harlot brow' makes sense in any case,   and 'distain' (Fr. *déteindre*) elsewhere in
even if 'of' is read simply as the modern   Shakespeare and in other authors, means
preposition.   'blot', 'defile', 'shame'.

DROMIO OF SYRACUSE
  I never spake with her in all my life.
ANTIPHOLUS OF SYRACUSE
  How can she thus then call us by our names?—
  Unless it be by inspiration.   170
ADRIANA
  How ill agrees it with your gravity
  To counterfeit thus grossly with your slave,
  Abetting him to thwart me in my mood!
  Be it my wrong you are from me exempt,
  But wrong not that wrong with a more contempt.   175
  Come, I will fasten on this sleeve of thine.
  Thou art an elm, my husband, I a vine,
  Whose weakness, married to thy stronger state,
  Makes me with thy strength to communicate.
  If aught possess thee from me, it is dross,   180
  Usurping ivy, brier, or idle moss,
  Who, all for want of pruning, with intrusion
  Infect thy sap, and live on thy confusion.
ANTIPHOLUS OF SYRACUSE (*aside*)
  To me she speaks; she moves me for her theme.
  What, was I married to her in my dream?   185
  Or sleep I now, and think I hear all this?
  What error drives our eyes and ears amiss?

174 wrong_∧] MALONE; wrong, F   178 stronger] F3; stranger F1

170 **inspiration** divination, clairvoyance
172–3 **counterfeit . . . mood** conspire with Dromio to deceive and provoke me in my anger
174–205 The shift to rhyme in this passage (resumed at 214) emphasizes first Adriana's use of proverbial imagery, then the mood of bewitchment and wonder (215–19).
174 F's comma after 'wrong' is slightly misleading. Adriana is saying 'Let me suffer, if I must, your estrangement from me, but do not compound that suffering by inflicting another, greater wrong upon me also, by behaving contemptuously towards me (as you are doing now)'.
  exempt cut off, separated; as in *As You Like It* 2.1.15: 'this our life, exempt from public haunt'.
177 **Thou . . . vine** A biblical, proverbial and Ovidian metaphor, which Adriana extends in 180–3. Arthur Golding's translation (1567) of Ovid's *Metamorphoses*, xiv. 665–6, reads: '. . . if that the vine which runs upon the elm had nat | The tree to lean unto, it should upon the ground lie flat'. Compare Tilley, V61 (Dent, p. 241) and Psalm 128: 3 ('Thy wife shall be as a fruitful vine by the sides of thine house').
179 **with . . . communicate** partake of your (the tree's) strength
180 **from** besides, other than
181 **Usurping . . . moss** Unlike the fruitful vine.
183 **confusion** ruin
184 **moves . . . theme** is attempting to persuade me

Until I know this sure uncertainty,
I'll entertain the offered fallacy.

LUCIANA
Dromio, go bid the servants spread for dinner.   190

DROMIO OF SYRACUSE (*aside*)
O, for my beads! I cross me for a sinner.
This is the fairy land. O spite of spites,
We talk with goblins, owls, and elves, and sprites.
If we obey them not, this will ensue:
They'll suck our breath or pinch us black and blue.   195

LUCIANA
Why prat'st thou to thyself, and answer'st not?
Dromio, thou Dromio, thou snail, thou slug, thou sot.

DROMIO OF SYRACUSE
I am transformèd, master, am not I?

ANTIPHOLUS OF SYRACUSE
I think thou art in mind, and so am I.

DROMIO OF SYRACUSE
Nay, master, both in mind and in my shape.   200

---

189 offered] CAPELL; free'd F; proffered SINGER *conj.*; sured WALKER *conj.*   193 goblins, owls, and elves, and] This edition (Hudson *subs.*); Goblins, Owles and FI; Goblins, Owles and Elves F2; goblins, owls and elvish POPE; goblins, ouphs and THEOBALD; none but goblins, owls and DYCE 1866; fairies, goblins, elves and CUNINGHAM; goblins, oafs, and OXFORD   197 thou Dromio] F; thou drone THEOBALD; thou drumble RIVERSIDE   198 am not I] THEOBALD; am I not F

---

189 **entertain . . . fallacy** play along with the patently false proposition she is making
190 **spread** set the table
191 **beads** prayer beads, rosary
  cross me make the sign of the cross. One of many passages in which the time and setting are Christianized by Shakespeare from the pagan world of his Plautine sources.
193 **goblins . . . sprites** This line is a metric foot short as it stands in F. The 'editors' of F2 realized there was a problem, and their successors have offered a variety of solutions. This emendation is based on the hypothesis of haplography, that is, that the compositor (D) conflated 'oules and elues and', or something like it in his copy, to 'Owles and'. Dromio's feverish imagination coins monsters pell-mell. There is no need to change the 'owls' to

'ouphs' or 'oafs', as Gareth Roberts has shown ('*The Comedy of Errors* II.ii.190: "owls" or "elves"?', *N&Q* 232 (NS 34) (1987), 202–4); discussed also in Whitworth, p. 128.
195 **suck . . . blue** Witches, in owl-shapes, might suck the breath out of their victims (see Roberts, above). Fairies and pinching are elsewhere associated in Shakespeare, as in *Merry Wives* where Falstaff is pinched by children disguised as fairies as punishment for his lechery.
197 Here as elsewhere in the text, 'Dromio' is disyllabic (*drom-yo*). Greek etymology (*dromeos*, a runner) discovers a little joke in Luciana's nomination of Dromio as 'a dromio': that epithet sorts oddly with the characteristic slowness of slugs and snails.

ANTIPHOLUS OF SYRACUSE
  Thou hast thine own form.
DROMIO OF SYRACUSE   No, I am an ape.
LUCIANA
  If thou art changed to aught, 'tis to an ass.
DROMIO OF SYRACUSE
  'Tis true: she rides me, and I long for grass.
  'Tis so, I am an ass; else it could never be
  But I should know her as well as she knows me.   205
ADRIANA
  Come, come, no longer will I be a fool,
  To put the finger in the eye and weep
  Whilst man and master laughs my woes to scorn.
  (*To Antipholus*) Come, sir, to dinner.—Dromio, keep
        the gate.—
  Husband, I'll dine above with you today,   210
  And shrive you of a thousand idle pranks.—
  Sirrah, if any ask you for your master,
  Say he dines forth, and let no creature enter.—
  Come, sister.—Dromio, play the porter well.
ANTIPHOLUS OF SYRACUSE (*aside*)
  Am I in earth, in heaven, or in hell?   215
  Sleeping or waking? Mad or well advised?
  Known unto these, and to myself disguised?
  I'll say as they say, and persever so,
  And in this mist at all adventures go.
DROMIO OF SYRACUSE
  Master, shall I be porter at the gate?   220
ADRIANA
  Ay, and let none enter, lest I break your pate.
LUCIANA
  Come, come, Antipholus, we dine too late.
                           Exeunt ⌐into the Phoenix⌐

222.1 *Exeunt . . . Phoenix*] OXFORD; *Exeunt* ROWE 1714; F *omits*

210 **above** i.e. in private quarters, not in the
    main hall or dining room
215–19 Compare   Sebastian's   similar
    response to another such misdirected
    invitation, from Olivia, in *Twelfth Night*,
    4.1.59–62.
216 **well advised** in my right wits

218 **persever so** continue in this course of
    action. As always in Shakespeare, and
    until the late seventeenth century gener-
    ally, the accent is on the second syllable of
    'persevere'; this is reflected in the Folio
    spelling 'persever', here retained.
219 **at all adventures** whatever happens

3.1   *Enter Antipholus of Ephesus, his man Dromio, Angelo*
       the goldsmith, and Balthasar the merchant

ANTIPHOLUS OF EPHESUS

   Good Signor Angelo, you must excuse us all;
   My wife is shrewish when I keep not hours.
   Say that I lingered with you at your shop
   To see the making of her carcanet,
   And that tomorrow you will bring it home.—   5
   But here's a villain that would face me down
   He met me on the mart, and that I beat him,
   And charged him with a thousand marks in gold,
   And that I did deny my wife and house.
   Thou drunkard, thou, what didst thou mean by this?   10

DROMIO OF EPHESUS

   Say what you will, sir, but I know what I know—
   That you beat me at the mart I have your hand to show.
   If the skin were parchment, and the blows you gave
        were ink,
   Your own handwriting would tell you what I think.

ANTIPHOLUS OF EPHESUS

   I think thou art an ass.

DROMIO OF EPHESUS   Marry, so it doth appear   15
   By the wrongs I suffer and the blows I bear.
   I should kick being kicked, and, being at that pass,
   You would keep from my heels, and beware of an ass.

ANTIPHOLUS OF EPHESUS

   You're sad, Signor Balthasar. Pray God our cheer
   May answer my good will, and your good welcome
        here.   20

BALTHASAR

   I hold your dainties cheap, sir, and your welcome dear.

ANTIPHOLUS OF EPHESUS

   O, Signor Balthasar, either at flesh or fish
   A table full of welcome makes scarce one dainty dish.

3.1.4 **carcanet** collar or necklace (usually
   in gold or silver, and ornamented with
   precious stones)
6 **face me down** insist to my face
12 **your hand** the mark of your hand on
   me
15–18 It is now the turn of Dromio of
   Ephesus to admit to feeling that he is

truly an ass, following his twin's similar
   complaint in the previous scene.
19 **sad** solemn, serious
21–6 Dent (p. 246) cites 'Welcome is the best
   cheer' (Tilley, W258) as a proverbial
   analogue for this passage.
22 **either . . . fish** whether one is to eat meat,
   or fish as at fasting times

BALTHASAR
  Good meat, sir, is common; that every churl affords.
ANTIPHOLUS OF EPHESUS
  And welcome more common, for that's nothing but
    words.   25
BALTHASAR
  Small cheer and great welcome makes a merry feast.
ANTIPHOLUS OF EPHESUS
  Ay, to a niggardly host and more sparing guest.
  But though my cates be mean, take them in good part.
  Better cheer may you have, but not with better heart.
  But soft, my door is locked. (*To Dromio*) Go bid them let
    us in.   30
DROMIO OF EPHESUS (*at the door of the Phoenix, calling*)
  Maud, Bridget, Marian, Cicely, Gillian, Ginn!
    ⌜*Enter Dromio of Syracuse within the Phoenix*⌝
DROMIO OF SYRACUSE (*within the Phoenix*)
  Mome, malt-horse, capon, coxcomb, idiot, patch!
  Either get thee from the door or sit down at the hatch.
  Dost thou conjure for wenches, that thou call'st for
    such store
  When one is one too many? Go, get thee from the
    door.   35

3.1.31 *at . . . calling*] This edition; *calling* OXFORD; *not in* F   31.1 *Enter . . . Phoenix*] OXFORD;
not in F   32 *within . . . Phoenix*] OXFORD; *within* ROWE; *not in* F (*so throughout scene*)

---

24 **churl** knave, simple person
28 **cates** food, dainties
31.1 Dromio of Syracuse must be visible as
     well as audible in this scene. F provides
     entrances for Luce and Adriana later in
     the scene, and Dromio is clearly 'within'
     the house, as they are, teaming up with
     Luce at 48–61 to bait Antipholus and
     Dromio of Ephesus.
32 **Mome** blockhead, dolt. Shakespeare's
     sole use of the term.
     malt-horse A heavy workhorse used by
     maltsters; here, a term of abuse.
     capon A castrated cock, hence a eunuch;
     also implying dullness.
     coxcomb fool, simpleton
     patch clown, dolt

33 **Either . . . hatch** A hatch is the lower half
     of a divided door, or a small gate or
     wicket, perhaps set into a larger door or
     gate, or standing out in front of a build-
     ing, at the entrance to a garden or yard,
     for example, and thus at a distance from
     the door itself. The sense of the line is
     unclear; perhaps Dromio is telling the
     other Dromio to move away from the
     house at least, and/or to sit down (quiet-
     ly) before the door. The collocation of
     'door' and 'hatch' may be vaguely related
     to the proverb 'It is good to have a hatch
     before the door' (Tilley, H207), meaning
     'it is good to keep silent, or to think before
     speaking'.

DROMIO OF EPHESUS

  What patch is made our porter? My master stays in
    the street.

DROMIO OF SYRACUSE (*within the Phoenix*)

  Let him walk from whence he came, lest he catch cold
    on's feet.

ANTIPHOLUS OF EPHESUS

  Who talks within there? Ho, open the door!

DROMIO OF SYRACUSE (*within the Phoenix*)

  Right, sir, I'll tell you when, an you'll tell me wherefore.

ANTIPHOLUS OF EPHESUS

  Wherefore? For my dinner—I have not dined today.   40

DROMIO OF SYRACUSE (*within the Phoenix*)

  Nor today here you must not. Come again when you
    may.

ANTIPHOLUS OF EPHESUS

  What art thou that keep'st me out from the house I
    owe?

DROMIO OF SYRACUSE (*within the Phoenix*)

  The porter for this time, sir, and my name is Dromio.

DROMIO OF EPHESUS

  O villain, thou hast stol'n both mine office and my
    name!

---

37 **catch . . . feet** Proverbial (Tilley, F579a;
  Dent, p. 115). The only occurrence in
  Shakespeare.

39 **an** if. Dromio of Syracuse may here be
  glancing back at his duologue. with
  Antipholus on 'why' and 'wherefore' in
  2.2.

41 **when you may** when you are invited

42 **owe** own

44–7 In F, the column break on page H3ᵛ
  comes after line 46, the long fifteen-
  syllable line 47 and its weak rhyme, coming at the top of column b. This break may
  have distracted Compositor D, who set
  both columns; he sometimes added or
  substituted words in verse passages and
  may have done so here. This edition
  assumes that he mistook 'place' for 'face'
  in l. 47: Dromio's point is about his name
  and his place, usurped by someone claim-
  ing the same name and place ('office').
  Pursuing his own line of thought about

the 'little credit' and 'mickle blame' his
place and name have earned him, he
recalls the treatment he has received from
both his real and his supposed masters
and Adriana and Luciana, telling his
namesake that he would have been glad
to give up that place and its pains on
account of that name which he now nevertheless lays claim to, with the 'blame'
attached to it. He unwittingly hits upon
another link in his identical twinship with
the Dromio inside the house, namely that
both of them have recently been called
'ass' by their superiors. The uncertain
rhyme—'place'/'ass'—is accounted for
on etymological grounds by Cercignani,
citing this instance (p. 176). The repetition of the word *nomen* (name) in the first
scene of *Amphitruo*, the source for this
scene, may strengthen the case for 'name'
twice here.

The one ne'er got me credit, the other mickle blame.   ~ 45
If thou hadst been Dromio today in my place,
Thou wouldst have changed thy place for a name, or
        thy name for an ass.
        Enter Luce within the Phoenix
LUCE (*within the Phoenix*)
    What a coil is there, Dromio? Who are those at the
        gate?
DROMIO OF EPHESUS
    Let my master in, Luce.
LUCE (*within the Phoenix*)   Faith no, he comes too late;
    And so tell your master.
DROMIO OF EPHESUS   O Lord, I must laugh.   50
    Have at you with a proverb: 'Shall I set in my staff?'
LUCE (*within the Phoenix*)
    Have at you with another—that's 'When? Can you
        tell?'
DROMIO OF SYRACUSE (*within the Phoenix*)
    If thy name be called Luce, Luce, thou hast answered
        him well.
ANTIPHOLUS OF EPHESUS (*to Luce*)
    Do you hear, you minion? You'll let us in, I hope?
    ⌈   ⌉   55

---

47 place] This edition (*conj.* Gould); face F; office FOAKES; pate OXFORD   a name] F; an aim
WILSON, OXFORD   an ass] F; a face COLLIER   54 hope] F; trow THEOBALD   55] This edition
(*conj.* Malone); *missing line at l.* 54 OXFORD (*conj.* Malone)

---

45 **mickle** much. A Middle English word,
rather archaic by the late sixteenth
century.

47.1 *Luce* This character, named eleven
times in this passage in stage directions,
speech prefixes and dialogue, appears to
be the person referred to by Dromio of
Syracuse in the next scene (3.2.111) as
'Nell', the sole occurrence of that name
in the play. He there describes her as 'the
kitchen wench', and it is the kitchen-
maid who is said at 4.4.75–6 to have
railed, taunted and scorned Antipholus
of Ephesus when he sought to enter his
house, a clear reference to Luce in the
present scene. Evidence that Shakespeare
changed his mind and decided after
writing 3.1 to call the character 'Nell' is
scant indeed, and she does not reappear
in the play (although productions some-

times make her the Messenger of
5.1.168). See commentary on 3.2.111
below, and Whitworth, pp. 123–5.

48 **coil** commotion

51 'Shall . . . staff?' Proverbial (Tilley,
S804; Dent, p. 216). 'To set in (or up)
one's staff' means 'to take up one's
abode'; here an ironic way for Dromio
of Ephesus to ask to be let into his own
house. Probably also—and usually played
so explicitly—a bawdy *double entendre*
on 'staff' as penis. The only occurrence
of the expression in Shakespeare.

52 'When . . . tell?' Proverbial (Tilley, T88;
Dent, p. 227).

54–5 Theobald's emendation to 'trow' in l.
54 would make a triple rhyme, of which
there are several others in this passage
(64–6, 67–9, 76–8), but makes no more
sense of the following half-lines by Luce

LUCE (*within the Phoenix*)
    I thought to have asked you.
DROMIO OF SYRACUSE (*within the Phoenix*) And you said no.
DROMIO OF EPHESUS
    So, come help.
            ⌜*He and Antipholus beat the door*⌝
                    Well struck! There was blow for blow.
ANTIPHOLUS OF EPHESUS (*to Luce*)
    Thou baggage, let me in.
LUCE (*within the Phoenix*)   Can you tell for whose sake?
DROMIO OF EPHESUS
    Master, knock the door hard.
LUCE (*within the Phoenix*)   Let him knock till it ache.
ANTIPHOLUS OF EPHESUS
    You'll cry for this, minion, if I beat the door down.   60
LUCE (*within the Phoenix*)
    What needs all that, and a pair of stocks in the town?
            Enter Adriana within the Phoenix
ADRIANA (*within the Phoenix*)
    Who is that at the door that keeps all this noise?
DROMIO OF SYRACUSE (*within the Phoenix*)
    By my troth, your town is troubled with unruly boys.
ANTIPHOLUS OF EPHESUS (*to Adriana*)
    Are you there, wife? You might have come before.
ADRIANA (*within the Phoenix*)
    Your wife, sir knave? Go, get you from the door.   65
                        Exeunt Adriana and Luce
DROMIO OF EPHESUS (*to Antipholus*)
    If you went in pain, master, this 'knave' would go sore.

---

57 *He . . . door*] OXFORD; *not in* F   65.1 *Exeunt . . . Luce*] This edition; *Exit with Nell* OXFORD; *not in* F

and Dromio of Syracuse. Malone's conjecture that a line has dropped out,
though still dismissed by many editors
who nevertheless do not follow Theobald,
is accepted by the Oxford editors; they,
however, place the lacuna after l. 53. This
edition places it rather after l. 54 and
assumes that it took the interrogative
form, eliciting Luce's reply in l. 56: 'rope'
is the most likely rhyme-word (see *TC*,
p. 267). It probably was spoken by
Antipholus or Dromio of Ephesus. It is

possible that more than one line was lost.
The addressee of Dromio's half-line and
what 'no' he is referring to remain
obscure.

57 *He . . . door* Some action is obviously
    called for to account for Dromio's line.
61 *and . . . stocks* when there is a pair of
    stocks available for punishing such
    trouble-makers
66 *If . . . sore* Bevington plausibly reads
    'knave' as referring to Antipholus of

ANGELO (*to Antipholus*)

    Here is neither cheer, sir, nor welcome; we would fain
      have either.

BALTHASAR

    In debating which was best, we shall part with neither.

DROMIO OF EPHESUS (*to Antipholus*)

    They stand at the door, master. Bid them welcome
      hither.

ANTIPHOLUS OF EPHESUS

    There is something in the wind, that we cannot get in.   70

DROMIO OF EPHESUS

    You would say so, master, if your garments were thin.
    Your cake here is warm within: you stand here in the
      cold.
    It would make a man mad as a buck to be so bought and
      sold.

ANTIPHOLUS OF EPHESUS

    Go fetch me something. I'll break ope the gate.

DROMIO OF SYRACUSE (*within the Phoenix*)

    Break any breaking here, and I'll break your knave's
      pate.   75

DROMIO OF EPHESUS

    A man may break a word with you, sir, and words are
      but wind;
    Ay, and break it in your face, so he break it not behind.

DROMIO OF SYRACUSE (*within the Phoenix*)

    It seems thou want'st breaking. Out upon thee, hind!

DROMIO OF EPHESUS

    Here's too much 'Out upon thee!' I pray thee, let me in.

Ephesus. Dromio is just repeating, in a cheeky but oblique way, Adriana's unwitting insult to her husband, his master.

68 **part** depart

70 **There . . . wind** Proverbial (Tilley, S621; Dent, p. 214). The only occurrence in Shakespeare.

72 **Your . . . within** Apparently not proverbial, though it sounds as if it might be. Dromio presumably points to the house on 'here'; 'cake' just means his meal.

73 **mad as a buck** Proverbial. A variant of

Tilley's 'wild as a buck' (B692; Dent, p. 66).

73 **bought and sold** deceived. Proverbial (Tilley, B787; Dent, p. 68).

76–7 **A man . . . behind** In modern productions, these lines are often the occasion for a farting 'duel', or some such coarse business, between the Dromios on either side of the door ('words . . . wind . . . break it . . . behind').

76 **words . . . wind** Proverbial (Tilley, W833: 'words are but wind'; Dent, p. 258).

78 **Out upon thee** (a curse)
    hind slave, menial

DROMIO OF SYRACUSE (*within the Phoenix*)
  Ay when fowls have no feathers, and fish have no fin.   80
ANTIPHOLUS OF EPHESUS
  Well, I'll break in.—Go borrow me a crow.
DROMIO OF EPHESUS
  A crow without feather? Master, mean you so?
  For a fish without a fin, there's a fowl without a feather.
  (*To Dromio of Syracuse*)
  If a crow help us in, sirrah, we'll pluck a crow together.
ANTIPHOLUS OF EPHESUS
  Go, get thee gone. Fetch me an iron crow.   85
BALTHASAR
  Have patience, sir. O, let it not be so!
  Herein you war against your reputation,
  And draw within the compass of suspect
  Th'unviolated honour of your wife.
  Once this: your long experience of her wisdom,   90
  Her sober virtue, years, and modesty,
  Plead on her part some cause to you unknown;
  And doubt not, sir, but she will well excuse
  Why at this time the doors are made against you.
  Be ruled by me. Depart in patience,   95
  And let us to the Tiger all to dinner,
  And about evening come yourself alone
  To know the reason of this strange restraint.
  If by strong hand you offer to break in
  Now in the stirring passage of the day,   100
  A vulgar comment will be made of it,
  And that supposèd by the common rout
  Against your yet ungallèd estimation,
  That may with foul intrusion enter in
  And dwell upon your grave when you are dead.   105

90, 92 her] ROWE; your F

81 **crow** crowbar
84 **pluck . . . together** continue our dispute. Proverbial (Tilley, C855; Dent, p. 81).
88 **compass of suspect** realm of suspicion
90 **Once this** to sum up

100 **stirring . . . day** busy time of day, when many people are about
103 **ungallèd estimation** unsullied reputation

For slander lives upon succession,
For ever housèd where it gets possession.
ANTIPHOLUS OF EPHESUS
You have prevailed. I will depart in quiet,
And in despite of mirth mean to be merry.
I know a wench of excellent discourse,   110
Pretty and witty; wild, and yet, too, gentle.
There will we dine. This woman that I mean,
My wife—but, I protest, without desert—
Hath oftentimes upbraided me withal.
To her will we to dinner. (*To Angelo*) Get you home   115
And fetch the chain. By this, I know, 'tis made.
Bring it, I pray you, to the Porcupine,
For there's the house. That chain will I bestow—
Be it for nothing but to spite my wife—
Upon mine hostess there. Good sir, make haste: 120
Since mine own doors refuse to entertain me,
I'll knock elsewhere, to see if they'll disdain me.

---

107 housèd] This edition; hows'd F   where it gets] F1; where it once gets F2; where once it gets OXFORD   117 Porcupine] F (*Porpentine*)

106 **lives upon succession** survives from one generation to the next
112–14 **This woman . . . withal** Antipholus here pointedly denies any illicit relationship with the Courtesan, whose role Shakespeare diminished considerably from its original, that of Erotium in *Menaechmi*. Antipholus need scarcely have concealed such a liaison from male companions, if it existed, and we are probably meant to take him at his word. This is in keeping with Shakespeare's treatment of the domestic comedy, and anticipates the reconciliation between husband and wife at the end, at marked variance from Plautus' play, where Menaechmus the Citizen (of Epidamnus) boasts of having stolen clothes and jewellery from his wife to give to the 'wench' and of enjoying the latter's favours, lies blatantly to his wife about the thefts, and at the end, agrees with Messenio's proposal to offer his wife for sale at auction along with his house and possessions. See Introduction, p. 20, and Wells's commentary, pp. 18–19, 151–2.

116 **By this** by this time

117 **Porcupine** The modern spelling of the word, adopted by Rowe and retained by editors until the Cambridge edition of 1864 reverted to the archaic form. It then prevailed until the Oxford editors remodernized it in 1986. Shakespeare seems to have used only the spelling 'porpentine'; five of the word's eight occurrences in his works are in *Errors*, where it is of course a proper name.

118 **For . . . house** This line may well be accompanied by an indicative gesture if the Porcupine is one of the houses represented on stage, as in a classical comedy set, or in Komisarjevsky's and many other modern productions. At the end of the scene, those outside the Phoenix, except for Angelo, would cross to the Porcupine, and Dromio of Syracuse would withdraw into—if he was not already seen to be 'in'—the Phoenix, or withdraw 'within' it from the scene, as in the Oxford stage direction.

ANGELO

I'll meet you at that place some hour hence.

ANTIPHOLUS OF EPHESUS

Do so.   ⌜*Exit Angelo*⌝

This jest shall cost me some expense.

Exeunt ⌜*Dromio of Syracuse within the Phoenix,*
and the others into the Porcupine⌝

3.2   *Enter* ⌜*from the Phoenix*⌝ *Luciana with Antipholus of*
Syracuse

LUCIANA

And may it be that you have quite forgot
    A husband's office? Shall, Antipholus,
Even in the spring of love thy love-springs rot?
    Shall love, in building, grow so ruinous?
If you did wed my sister for her wealth,   5
    Then for her wealth's sake use her with more
        kindness;
Or if you like elsewhere, do it by stealth:
    Muffle your false love with some show of blindness.
Let not my sister read it in your eye.
    Be not thy tongue thy own shame's orator.   10
Look sweet, speak fair, become disloyalty;
    Apparel vice like virtue's harbinger.
Bear a fair presence, though your heart be tainted:
    Teach sin the carriage of a holy saint.
Be secret-false. What need she be acquainted?   15
    What simple thief brags of his own attaint?
'Tis double wrong to truant with your bed,
    And let her read it in thy looks at board.
Shame hath a bastard fame, well managèd;
    Ill deeds is doubled with an evil word.   20

124 *Exit Angelo*] OXFORD; *not in* F   124.1–2 *Exeunt . . . Porcupine*] *after* OXFORD; *Exeunt.* F
3.2] POPE (Scene 2); *not in* F   0.1 *from the Phoenix*] OXFORD; *not in* F   *Luciana*] F2; *Iuliana* F1
I LUCIANA] ROWE; *Iulia.* F   4 building] THEOBALD; buildings F ruinous] CAPELL (*conj.*
Theobald); ruinate F   16 attaint] ROWE; attaine F

3.2.3 **love-springs** tender shoots of love
10 **Be . . . orator** do not betray yourself by
speaking such shameful thoughts
11 **become disloyalty** make infidelity seem
becoming, i.e. put on a show of honesty

14 **carriage** bearing, behaviour
19 **Shame . . . managèd** if you are clever
enough about it, dishonour can be made
to appear its opposite, and your reputation be enhanced

Alas, poor women, make us but believe—
    Being compact of credit—that you love us.
Though others have the arm, show us the sleeve.
    We in your motion turn, and you may move us.
Then, gentle brother, get you in again.   25
    Comfort my sister, cheer her, call her wife:
'Tis holy sport to be a little vain
    When the sweet breath of flattery conquers strife.

ANTIPHOLUS OF SYRACUSE

Sweet mistress—what your name is else I know not,
    Nor by what wonder you do hit of mine—   30
Less in your knowledge and your grace you show not
    Than our earth's wonder, more than earth divine.
Teach me, dear creature, how to think and speak.
    Lay open to my earthy gross conceit,
Smothered in errors, feeble, shallow, weak,   35
    The folded meaning of your words' deceit.
Against my soul's pure truth why labour you
    To make it wander in an unknown field?
Are you a god? Would you create me new?
    Transform me, then, and to your power I'll yield.   40
But if that I am I, then well I know
    Your weeping sister is no wife of mine,
Nor to her bed no homage do I owe.
    Far more, far more, to you do I decline.
O, train me not, sweet mermaid, with thy note   45
    To drown me in thy sister's flood of tears.
Sing, siren, for thyself, and I will dote.
    Spread o'er the silver waves thy golden hairs,

---

21 but] THEOBALD; not F   26 wife] F2; wise F1   46 sister's] F2 (sisters); sister F1

22 **Being . . . credit** being made so that we
are inclined to believe
23 **arm . . . sleeve** maintain an outward
show of fidelity (to your wife), even if
someone else has your love. The expression sounds proverbial, but is unrecorded
in Tilley, *ODEP*, and Dent.
24 **We . . . turn** we are influenced by your
motion, move in your orbit (with allusion
to the motion of the heavenly bodies)
29 **what . . . else** what your name is, other
than 'sweet mistress'
30 **of** upon
34 **earthy . . . conceit** merely human, and
thus limited, understanding
36 **folded** hidden
44 **decline** incline
45–52 **mermaid . . . drown . . . siren . . .
waves . . . drownèd . . . sink** In this
passage, Antipholus returns to the sea
imagery he had used earlier (1.2.33–40)
where it was also associated with loss of
one's identity, dissolution and oblivion.
45 **train** entice

And as a bed I'll take them, and there lie,
       And in that glorious supposition think   50
He gains by death that hath such means to die.
       Let love, being light, be drownèd if she sink.
LUCIANA
   What, are you mad, that you do reason so?
ANTIPHOLUS OF SYRACUSE
   Not mad, but mated—how, I do not know.
LUCIANA
   It is a fault that springeth from your eye.   55
ANTIPHOLUS OF SYRACUSE
   For gazing on your beams, fair sun, being by.
LUCIANA
   Gaze where you should, and that will clear your sight.
ANTIPHOLUS OF SYRACUSE
   As good to wink, sweet love, as look on night.
LUCIANA
   Why call you me 'love'? Call my sister so.
ANTIPHOLUS OF SYRACUSE
   Thy sister's sister.
LUCIANA   That's my sister.
ANTIPHOLUS OF SYRACUSE   No,   60
   It is thyself, mine own self's better part,
   Mine eye's clear eye, my dear heart's dearer heart,
   My food, my fortune, and my sweet hope's aim,
   My sole earth's heaven, and my heaven's claim.
LUCIANA
   All this my sister is, or else should be.   65
ANTIPHOLUS OF SYRACUSE
   Call thyself 'sister', sweet, for I aim thee.
   Thee will I love, and with thee lead my life.

---

49 bed] F2; bud FI   them] CAPELL; thee F   52 she] F; he CAPELL   57 where] ROWE 1709;
when F   60–1 sister. . . . That's my sister. . . . No, | It] POPE; sister. | . . . That's my sister. |
. . . No: it F   66 aim] CAPELL; am F; mean ROWE 1709; claim CUNINGHAM *conj.*

54 **mated** confounded, amazed
58 **wink** close the eyes
   night Adriana, his alleged wife, is as night
   to Antipholus, the opposite of Luciana's
   'fair sun'.
64 **My . . . claim** my only heaven on earth,

and my hope of heaven hereafter
66 **aim** intend, direct one's course toward.
   Capell's emendation is borne out by the
   following lines, where Antipholus insists
   that she, Luciana, and not her sister, is
   the object of his affection.

Thou hast no husband yet, nor I no wife.
Give me thy hand.

LUCIANA   O soft, sir, hold you still;
I'll fetch my sister to get her good will.   70

> *Exit ⌈into the Phoenix⌉*
> *Enter Dromio of Syracuse ⌈from the Phoenix⌉*

ANTIPHOLUS OF SYRACUSE Why, how now, Dromio! Where
runn'st thou so fast?

DROMIO OF SYRACUSE Do you know me, sir? Am I Dromio?
Am I your man? Am I myself?

ANTIPHOLUS OF SYRACUSE Thou art Dromio, thou art my   75
man, thou art thyself.

DROMIO OF SYRACUSE I am an ass, I am a woman's man, and
besides myself.

ANTIPHOLUS OF SYRACUSE What woman's man? And how
besides thyself?   80

DROMIO OF SYRACUSE Marry, sir, besides myself I am due to
a woman: one that claims me, one that haunts me, one
that will have me.

ANTIPHOLUS OF SYRACUSE What claim lays she to thee?

DROMIO OF SYRACUSE Marry, sir, such claim as you would   85
lay to your horse; and she would have me as a beast—not
that, I being a beast, she would have me, but that she,
being a very beastly creature, lays claim to me.

ANTIPHOLUS OF SYRACUSE What is she?

DROMIO OF SYRACUSE A very reverend body; ay, such a one   90
as a man may not speak of without he say 'sir-reverence'.
I have but lean luck in the match, and yet is she a
wondrous fat marriage.

ANTIPHOLUS OF SYRACUSE How dost thou mean, a 'fat
marriage'?   95

DROMIO OF SYRACUSE Marry, sir, she's the kitchen wench,
and all grease; and I know not what use to put her to but
to make a lamp of her, and run from her by her own light.

70.1 *into the Phoenix*] OXFORD; *not in* F   70.2 *from the Phoenix*] OXFORD; *not in* F

---

78 **besides myself** beside myself, out of my
mind. Dromio goes on to pun on his own
words in l. 81.

91 **sir-reverence** Abbreviation and corrup-

tion of 'saving reverence', a formulaic
apology for any possible indecorum. Just
to speak of this woman, says Dromio,
calls for an apology, she is so beastly.

I warrant her rags and the tallow in them will burn a
Poland winter. If she lives till doomsday, she'll burn a   100
week longer than the whole world.

ANTIPHOLUS OF SYRACUSE What complexion is she of?

DROMIO OF SYRACUSE Swart like my shoe, but her face
nothing like so clean kept. For why? She sweats a man
may go overshoes in the grime of it.   105

ANTIPHOLUS OF SYRACUSE That's a fault that water will
mend.

DROMIO OF SYRACUSE No, sir, 'tis in grain. Noah's flood
could not do it.

ANTIPHOLUS OF SYRACUSE What's her name?   110

DROMIO OF SYRACUSE Nell, sir. But her name and three-
quarters—that's an ell and three-quarters—will not
measure her from hip to hip.

ANTIPHOLUS OF SYRACUSE Then she bears some breadth?

DROMIO OF SYRACUSE No longer from head to foot than   115
from hip to hip. She is spherical, like a globe. I could
find out countries in her.

104 For why?] F; for why DYCE   111 and] THEOBALD; is F

99–100 **a Poland winter** as long as winter
lasts in Poland. That country appears to
have had associations of long, dark and
very cold winters for the Elizabethans.

102–44 Such burlesques of the courtly *blason* of the female body date from long
before Shakespeare's time, e.g. John
Skelton's *Elinor Rumming* (*c*.1520) and
Thomas Hoccleve's 'Of my lady well me
rejoice I may' (early 15th century).
Grotesque exaggeration is essential to
such set-pieces. Directors should resist
the temptation to bring 'Nell' on stage, or
to make Luce fit Dromio's description.
Philip Sidney's 'What tongue can her
perfections tell' from *Arcadia* is the most
famous Elizabethan *blason* and was often
imitated; that in Thomas Lodge's prose
romance, *Forbonius and Prisceria* (1584),
I2–I3ᵛ, part of a collection dedicated
to Sidney, is just one of many such
imitations.

103 **Swart** dark (German *schwartz*, black)
104 **sweats a man** sweats so much a man
108 **in grain** inherent. Literally, with reference to a colour that is ingrained in a
fabric.
   Noah's flood Another sea/water image, in

this burlesque counterpart to Antipholus'
romantic wooing of Luciana, with its sea
imagery, earlier in the scene.

111 **Nell** The only occurrence of this name
in the play. An ad hoc coinage by Dromio
for the sake of his pun on 'ell'. The ro-
tund kitchen wench described here—assuming only one such creature employed
in the Ephesian household—is identified
at 4.4.75 as the one who taunted and in-
sulted her master in 3.1, that is, Luce.
Dromio also calls her 'Dowsabel' at
4.1.110, and she is the 'fat friend' of
5.1.416. There is no basis for postulating
two characters. See commentary on
3.1.47.1.

112 **ell** A unit of linear measure, equal to 45
inches (1.143 metres) in England (vari-
able elsewhere). Dromio's 'spherical' Nell
is thus some two metres (six and a half
feet) in diameter. When inventing her on
Dromio's behalf, Shakespeare may have
recalled Plautus' geometrically-named
cook Cylindrus in *Menaechmi*.

116 **globe** Globes had been known since
1541, when Mercator's appeared. A new
one, by Emory Molyneux, was produced
in 1592.

ANTIPHOLUS OF SYRACUSE In what part of her body stands
  Ireland?
DROMIO OF SYRACUSE Marry, sir, in her buttocks. I found it   120
  out by the bogs.
ANTIPHOLUS OF SYRACUSE Where Scotland?
DROMIO OF SYRACUSE I found it by the barrenness, hard in
  the palm of her hand.
ANTIPHOLUS OF SYRACUSE Where France?   125
DROMIO OF SYRACUSE In her forehead, armed and reverted,
  making war against her hair.
ANTIPHOLUS OF SYRACUSE Where England?
DROMIO OF SYRACUSE I looked for the chalky cliffs, but I
  could find no whiteness in them. But I guess it stood   130

---

124 her] ROWE; the F   127 hair] F2 (haire); heire F1

121 **bogs** Probably related, in view of its association here with 'buttocks', to the vulgar
term 'bog' (privy, toilet) although that
slang term is unrecorded so early. 'Bog'
does not appear until the 18th century
(short for 'bog-house', first recorded in
1666), but 'boggard' was current in
the 16th. This sense, if present here, is
secondary and allusive. In Dromio's
catalogue of anatomico-geographical
features characteristic of particular countries, Ireland's famous bogs are represented by the spongy, wobbly flesh of
'Nell's' backside.

123 **barrenness** A conventional English slur
upon the alleged unfruitfulness and
poverty of Scotland. It is not clear that
Scots were renowned for thriftiness at this
time. Wilson saw an implication of hard-
ness, caused by callouses, in the kitchen-
maid's hands, but 'hard', as Cuningham
observed, could simply mean 'directly' or
'exactly'. Foakes compares Tilley H86: 'A
moist hand argues an amorous nature' or
'argues fruitfulness'.

126 **reverted** turned backward or facing
the wrong way. This is *OED*'s first cited
occurrence, and one of only two in
Shakespeare. Here the literal meaning is
strained; it is difficult to picture what sort
of forehead Dromio has in mind (Johnson
imagined incipient baldness due to venereal disease). The pertinence of the image
to France lies in its apparent allusion to

the armed resistance of the Catholic
League to the Protestant Henri de Bourbon, King of Navarre, designated by
Henri III as his heir, and who, as Henri IV,
succeeded Henri III to the French throne
on the latter's death in 1589. The League
proclaimed Cardinal Charles de Bourbon
king, as Charles X, but he died in 1590. A
series of battles ensued, most of which
were won by Henri IV, but not until he
abjured Protestantism and returned to
the Catholic faith (1593) was he recognized by the largely Catholic nobility and
the church, and crowned in Paris (1594).

127 **hair** This edition prefers F2's 'hair',
which keeps to the pattern established in
this passage of cataloguing parts of the
anatomy explicitly, with jokes or puns
being implied. In performance, the actor
need not make such an either/or choice
and can easily convey the 'hair'/'heir'
pun orally. These lines have been cited
frequently in discussions of the play's
likely date: Henri IV might have been considered to be heir to the French throne
between the years 1589 and 1594, when
he was finally crowned (see previous
note). But to attach much significance
to a single word in Dromio's bravura
routine, especially as he puns and draws
tenuous parallels given the remotest
opportunity, would be misguided.

129 **chalky cliffs** (of Dover); i.e. her teeth

in her chin, by the salt rheum that ran between France
and it.

ANTIPHOLUS OF SYRACUSE Where Spain?

DROMIO OF SYRACUSE Faith, I saw it not, but I felt it hot in her
breath.   135

ANTIPHOLUS OF SYRACUSE Where America, the Indies?

DROMIO OF SYRACUSE O, sir, upon her nose, all o'er
embellished with rubies, carbuncles, sapphires, declining their rich aspect to the hot breath of Spain, who
sent whole armadas of carracks to be ballast at her   140
nose.

ANTIPHOLUS OF SYRACUSE Where stood Belgia, the Netherlands?

DROMIO OF SYRACUSE O, sir, I did not look so low. To conclude, this drudge or diviner laid claim to me, called me   145
Dromio, swore I was assured to her, told me what privy
marks I had about me—as the mark of my shoulder, the

---

140 armadas] F (Armadoes)   carracks] F (Carrects)

131 **rheum** watery secretion as from the eyes
or nose. Sometimes (and often in Shakespeare), tears. Here, given that France is
in her forehead, England in her chin, she
works in the kitchen and is fat, perhaps
just perspiration: 'She sweats' (104).
Compare 'salt and sorry rheum' (*Othello*
3.4.51).

136 **America** The only occurrence of the
place-name in Shakespeare.
the Indies Originally a general name for
most of the lands in the Western Hemi-
sphere discovered by Europeans during
the fifteenth and sixteenth centuries,
thought at first to be parts of India; later
they were distinguished as the East and
the West Indies, a distinction recognized
by Shakespeare, e.g. in *Merry Wives*:
'They shall be my East and West Indies,
and I will trade to them both' (1.3.63–5).
Here a looser connotation applies: those
parts of the world from which Spanish
treasure ships returned laden with fabu-
lous riches.

138 **carbuncles** Both precious stones, usually
red like rubies and garnets, and inflamed
spots or pimples on the skin.

138–41 **declining . . . nose** America and the
Indies offering their riches to Spain (her
nose, hideously covered with bumps,

boils, pustules, etc., curving down
towards her mouth).

140 **armadas** fleets. It is not clear that the
'armadas' correspond to any part of
'Nell's' physiognomy; Dromio is carried
away by his own invention.
carracks large cargo ships, which could
also be armed; galleons. F's spelling looks
like one of many variants, but *OED* omits
it, while listing 29 other forms. This line is
nevertheless quoted, with F's spelling of
the word. In its only other occurrence in
F, it is spelt 'carract' (*Othello* 1.2.50).
ballast (past participle) ballasted, loaded,
i.e. with jewels

144 **low** Netherlands = Low Countries. Such
coy avoidance of specific mention of the
private parts is a feature of many *blasons*.
Compare 'Loath, I must leave his
[Cupid's] chief resort. | For such an use
the world hath gotten, | The best things
still must be forgotten', from Sidney's
'What tongue can her perfections tell'
(ll. 84–6).

145 **drudge** slave, menial worker
diviner one who practises divination;
here, a sorcerer or witch. Only occurrence of the word in Shakespeare.

146 **assured** engaged

mole in my neck, the great wart on my left arm—that I,
    amazed, ran from her as a witch.
And I think if my breast had not been made of faith, and
    my heart of steel,   150
She had transformed me to a curtal dog, and made me
    turn i'th' wheel.

ANTIPHOLUS OF SYRACUSE
Go, hie thee presently. Post to the road.
An if the wind blow any way from shore,
I will not harbour in this town tonight.
If any bark put forth, come to the mart,   155
Where I will walk till thou return to me.
If everyone knows us, and we know none,
'Tis time, I think, to trudge, pack, and be gone.

DROMIO OF SYRACUSE
As from a bear a man would run for life,
So fly I from her that would be my wife.   160

                              Exit ⌜to the bay⌝

ANTIPHOLUS OF SYRACUSE
There's none but witches do inhabit here,
And therefore 'tis high time that I were hence.
She that doth call me husband, even my soul

150–1] *as verse* KNIGHT; *as prose* F   160.1 *to the bay*] OXFORD; *not in* F

---

149 **as a witch** believing her to be a witch
150–1 On bibliographical grounds, there
would appear to be no reason for Compositor B to have recast verse lines in his
copy as prose: there is plenty of white
space showing in the second column of
this page in the Folio (H4ᵛ), where a
new act heading falls, so he was not
cramped for room. Yet these lines so
obviously are a couplet in fourteeners
that it seems obstinate not to print them
as such. Doing so draws attention too
to the frequent sudden switches from
one medium to the other in the play, an
aspect of its hectic movement and bewil-
dering action, in tension with its classical
form.
150 **breast . . . faith . . . heart . . . steel**
Echoes proverbial 'heart of steel' image
(Dent, H310.1); compare 'true as steel'
(Tilley, S840), and also Ephesians 6:
14–17, where Paul exhorts Christians to
put on the armour of Christ, which

includes the breastplate of righteousness
and the shield of faith (Appendix D).
151 **curtal . . . wheel** a dog, with its tail
docked (curtailed), harnessed to a turn-
stile attached to a spit
152 **presently** immediately
    road roadstead, harbour
153 **An if** if
158 **trudge** depart, be off
159–60 Dromio's fearful flight from the
woman who has designs on him provides
the final comic contrast to his master's
vows of desire and devotion in ll. 66–9
above. His evocation of the nightmarish
prospect of being attacked by a bear, even
as he heads for the port to find a ship to
carry them to safety, anticipates, if only
dimly, Shakespeare's vivid representation
years later of that beastly terror and of
the equally deadly perils of a sea-voyage,
in *Winter's Tale* 3.3. The same two mortal
dangers are strikingly evoked by Lear (*The
Tragedy of King Lear* 3.4.9–11).

Doth for a wife abhor. But her fair sister,
Possessed with such a gentle, sovereign grace,   165
Of such enchanting presence and discourse,
Hath almost made me traitor to myself.
But lest myself be guilty of self-wrong,
I'll stop mine ears against the mermaid's song.
        Enter Angelo with the chain
ANGELO
  Master Antipholus.
ANTIPHOLUS OF SYRACUSE Ay, that's my name.   170
ANGELO
  I know it well, sir. Lo, here's the chain.
  I thought to have ta'en you at the Porcupine.
  The chain unfinished made me stay thus long.
ANTIPHOLUS OF SYRACUSE (*taking the chain*)
  What is your will that I shall do with this?
ANGELO
  What please yourself, sir. I have made it for you.   175
ANTIPHOLUS OF SYRACUSE
  Made it for me, sir? I bespoke it not.
ANGELO
  Not once, nor twice, but twenty times you have.
  Go home with it, and please your wife withal,
  And soon at supper-time I'll visit you,
  And then receive my money for the chain.   180
ANTIPHOLUS OF SYRACUSE
  I pray you, sir, receive the money now,
  For fear you ne'er see chain nor money more.
ANGELO
  You are a merry man, sir. Fare you well.   *Exit*
ANTIPHOLUS OF SYRACUSE
  What I should think of this I cannot tell.
  But this I think: there's no man is so vain   185

168 of] POPE; to F

168 **of** Compositor B probably repeated 'to selfe', having set 'to my selfe' in the preceding line.
179 **soon at supper-time** at about supper-time, i.e. late afternoon (five o'clock). Another of the many reminders of the time of day in the play, and thus of the approach of Egeon's doom. See 1.2.26 and commentary. Angelo repeats that he is to be paid for the chain at five o'clock at 4.1.10–11.

That would refuse so fair an offered chain.
I see a man here needs not live by shifts,
When in the streets he meets such golden gifts.
I'll to the mart, and there for Dromio stay.
If any ship put out, then straight away!   *Exit*   190

4.1   *Enter Second Merchant, Angelo the goldsmith,*
       and an Officer
SECOND MERCHANT (*to Angelo*)
You know since Pentecost the sum is due,
And since I have not much importuned you;
Nor now I had not, but that I am bound
To Persia, and want guilders for my voyage.
Therefore make present satisfaction,   5
Or I'll attach you by this officer.
ANGELO
Even just the sum that I do owe to you
Is growing to me by Antipholus,
And in the instant that I met with you
He had of me a chain. At five o'clock   10

4.1.0.1 *Second Merchant*] DYCE; *a Merchant* F (*so throughout scene*)

187 **shifts** expedients, devices
4.1.0.1 *Second Merchant* Most editors
    have adopted Dyce's distinction between
    this character, the goldsmith's creditor,
    and the First Merchant, who appears in
    only the brief scene with Antipholus of
    Syracuse, 1.2. This merchant is clearly
    a stranger to Ephesus and has never
    seen either Antipholus; the former one
    befriends Antipholus of Syracuse and
    does not mistake him for his Ephesian
    twin, so he may not be local, but he seems
    to know his way about the town and what
    is going on there. While such vagueness
    is usually considered characteristic of
    authorial first-draft copy, it is conceivable
    that very minor inconsistencies of this
    kind would remain even in a script revised
    by the dramatist.
  1 **Pentecost** Whitsun (seven weeks after
    Easter). One of several explicitly Christian
    references in the play, and to one of the
    major feasts in the church calendar; also,
    inevitably by association, to the famous
    event recorded in Acts 2, the visitation

of the Holy Spirit bringing the gift of
tongues to the apostles. It may not be
irrelevant to note that Paul's first letter to
the Corinthians was written from Ephesus
(*c.*AD 54), and that at the end of it he
writes: 'I will tarry at Ephesus until
Pentecost. For a great door and effectual
is opened unto me, but there are many
adversaries' (1 Corinthians 16: 8–9;
Geneva Bible), although the Pentecost
mentioned by Paul is perhaps the Jewish
Feast of Weeks which occurred at more or
less the same time of year as the later
Christian feast, that is, in late spring.
This passage, containing as it does explicit mention of Ephesus, could have
prompted Shakespeare's otherwise gratuitous allusion to Pentecost.
  2 **since** since then
  4 **guilders** See commentary at 1.1.8.
  6 **attach** arrest
  8 **growing** owing, accruing
 10 **five o'clock** The second time that hour is
    mentioned (see 1.2.26). Obviously the
    same time as 'supper-time' at 3.2.179.

I shall receive the money for the same.
Pleaseth you walk with me down to his house,
I will discharge my bond, and thank you too.
    Enter Antipholus of Ephesus and Dromio of Ephesus
    from the Courtesan's house (*the Porcupine*)

OFFICER
That labour may you save. See where he comes.

ANTIPHOLUS OF EPHESUS (*to Dromio*)
While I go to the goldsmith's house, go thou   15
And buy a rope's end. That will I bestow
Among my wife and her confederates
For locking me out of my doors by day.
But soft, I see the goldsmith. Get thee gone.
Buy thou a rope, and bring it home to me.   20

DROMIO OF EPHESUS
I buy a thousand pound a year, I buy a rope.   *Exit*

ANTIPHOLUS OF EPHESUS (*to Angelo*)
A man is well holp up that trusts to you!
You promisèd your presence and the chain,
But neither chain nor goldsmith came to me.
Belike you thought our love would last too long   25
If it were chained together, and therefore came not.

ANGELO
Saving your merry humour, here's the note
How much your chain weighs to the utmost carat,
The fineness of the gold, and chargeful fashion,
Which doth amount to three odd ducats more   30

17 her] ROWE; their F   12.2 *Courtesan's . . . Porcupine*)] OXFORD; *Courtizans* F   23 You] DYCE
1866; I F   promisèd] WILSON; promised F; promised me COLLIER *conj.*   28 carat] POPE;
charect F

12 **Pleaseth you** if you please
13.2 The Folio s.d. leaves open the possibility
    that 'the Courtesan's' may be 'off', like
    the Centaur and the bay.
16 **rope's end** the end of a rope, especially as
    used as an instrument of punishment.
    That is clearly Antipholus' intention here
    in sending Dromio for one. See 4.1.98.
21 **I . . . rope** Not satisfactorily explained.
    The line has twelve syllables, and may
    possibly be corrupt. Perhaps best under-
    stood (and played) as an exclamation,
    of resignation, incomprehension or ex-
    asperation, and delivered with a shrug

and a beseeching or helpless glance to
the audience.
22 **holp up** helped out, served. Shakespeare
    frequently abbreviates the old past par-
    ticiple, *holpen* (Abbott, §343).
27 **Saving** with respect for
29 **chargeful fashion** expensive workman-
    ship. *OED* cites this line in its entries for
    both words.
30 **ducats** One of several apparently specific
    sums or species of money mentioned in
    the play (see also *guilders*, *marks*). 'Ducat'
    was the name of a gold coin current in
    several European countries, worth ap-

Than I stand debted to this gentleman.
I pray you see him presently discharged,
For he is bound to sea, and stays but for it.
ANTIPHOLUS OF EPHESUS
  I am not furnished with the present money.
  Besides, I have some business in the town.   35
  Good signor, take the stranger to my house,
  And with you take the chain, and bid my wife
  Disburse the sum on the receipt thereof.
  Perchance I will be there as soon as you.
ANGELO
  Then you will bring the chain to her yourself?   40
ANTIPHOLUS OF EPHESUS
  No, bear it with you, lest I come not time enough.
ANGELO
  Well, sir, I will. Have you the chain about you?
ANTIPHOLUS OF EPHESUS
  An if I have not, sir, I hope you have;
  Or else you may return without your money.
ANGELO
  Nay, come, I pray you, sir, give me the chain.   45
  Both wind and tide stays for this gentleman,
  And I, to blame, have held him here too long.
ANTIPHOLUS OF EPHESUS
  Good Lord! You use this dalliance to excuse
  Your breach of promise to the Porcupine.
  I should have chid you for not bringing it,   50

---

40 yourself?] THEOBALD; your selfe. F   47 to blame] F3; too blame F1

proximately forty-seven pence, also a silver coin in Italy of lesser value. The word occurs ten times in *Errors* (but only in Acts 4 and 5), more than in any other play except *The Merchant of Venice*.

32 **discharged** paid off
34 **I . . . money** I do not have the money on me now
46 **Both . . . gentleman** The proverb affirms the contrary, that wind (or time) and tide stay for no man (Tilley, T323).
  stays The common singular verb with plural subject (Abbott, §336).
47 **to blame** Some editors retain F's 'too', which would make 'blame' an adjective

meaning 'blameworthy'; *OED* has no such entry for the word. As *OED* explains (*blame*, v. 6), this was a common 16th- and early 17th-century misunderstanding of the dative infinitive 'to blame'. The 'misunderstanding' was no longer current by the time of F3 (1663). Foakes cites *OED*, and gives another Shakespearian example, 'too wilful blame', from *1 Henry IV* (p. 63).
50–1 **I . . . brawl** Possibly proverbial (Tilley, C579), though Dent is doubtful (p. 78). Compare *Richard III* 1.3.322: 'I do the wrong, and first begin to brawl'.
50 **chid** chided, upbraided

But like a shrew you first begin to brawl.

SECOND MERCHANT (*to Angelo*)
The hour steals on. I pray you, sir, dispatch.

ANGELO (*to Antipholus*)
You hear how he importunes me. The chain!

ANTIPHOLUS OF EPHESUS
Why, give it to my wife, and fetch your money.

ANGELO
Come, come, you know I gave it you even now.   55
Either send the chain, or send me by some token.

ANTIPHOLUS OF EPHESUS
Fie, now you run this humour out of breath.
Come, where's the chain? I pray you let me see it.

SECOND MERCHANT
My business cannot brook this dalliance.
Good sir, say whe'er you'll answer me or no.   60
If not, I'll leave him to the officer.

ANTIPHOLUS OF EPHESUS
I answer you? What should I answer you?

ANGELO
The money that you owe me for the chain.

ANTIPHOLUS OF EPHESUS
I owe you none till I receive the chain.

ANGELO
You know I gave it you half an hour since.   65

ANTIPHOLUS OF EPHESUS
You gave me none. You wrong me much to say so.

ANGELO
You wrong me more, sir, in denying it.
Consider how it stands upon my credit.

56 me by] F; by me SINGER

51 **brawl** scold, chide
56 **send me ... token** give me some piece
   of evidence to show your wife that I am
   entitled to be paid
   by with
57 **you ... breath** you are wearing out this
   joke. Proverbial (Tilley, B641; Dent, p.
   65).
59 **brook** tolerate
60 **whe'er** (whe'r F) whether
61 **him** i.e. Angelo

65 **half an hour since** In performance, when
   the interval is taken between Acts 3 and
   4 as it often is (and there may well have
   been act intervals at the indoor, night-
   time performances at Gray's Inn in 1594
   and at Court in 1604), it will have been
   very nearly half an hour since Angelo
   gave the chain to Antipholus (3.2.171 ff.).
68 **it ... credit** this matter threatens my
   business reputation

SECOND MERCHANT
    Well, officer, arrest him at my suit.
OFFICER (*to Angelo*)
    I do, and charge you in the Duke's name to obey me.   70
ANGELO (*to Antipholus*)
    This touches me in reputation.
    Either consent to pay this sum for me,
    Or I attach you by this officer.
ANTIPHOLUS OF EPHESUS
    Consent to pay thee that I never had?
    Arrest me, foolish fellow, if thou dar'st.   75
ANGELO (*to Officer*)
    Here is thy fee: arrest him, officer.
    I would not spare my brother in this case
    If he should scorn me so apparently.
OFFICER (*to Antipholus*)
    I do arrest you, sir. You hear the suit.
ANTIPHOLUS OF EPHESUS
    I do obey thee till I give thee bail.   80
    (*To Angelo*) But, sirrah, you shall buy this sport as dear
    As all the metal in your shop will answer.
ANGELO
    Sir, sir, I shall have law in Ephesus,
    To your notorious shame, I doubt it not.
        Enter Dromio of Syracuse, from the bay
DROMIO OF SYRACUSE
    Master, there's a bark of Epidamnus   85
    That stays but till her owner comes aboard,
    And then she bears away. Our freightage, sir,
    I have conveyed aboard, and I have bought
    The oil, the balsamum, and aqua-vitae.
    The ship is in her trim, the merry wind   90

85, 94] Epidamnus] This edition; *Epidamium* F; Epidamnum POPE   87 freightage] F (fraught-tage)

---

78 **apparently** blatantly
87 **freightage** baggage. 'Modernizing' editors have clung to the old spelling until very recently.
89 **balsamum** balsam, balm. The aromatic, resinous product of certain trees, most

commonly used in making medicinal ointments to soothe pain. The only occurrence of this Latin form in Shakespeare.
89 **aqua-vitae** distilled alcoholic spirits, eau-de-vie
90 **in her trim** rigged and ready to sail

Blows fair from land. They stay for naught at all
But for their owner, master, and yourself.

ANTIPHOLUS OF EPHESUS

How now? A madman? Why, thou peevish sheep,
What ship of Epidamnus stays for me?

DROMIO OF SYRACUSE

A ship you sent me to, to hire waftage.   95

ANTIPHOLUS OF EPHESUS

Thou drunken slave, I sent thee for a rope,
And told thee to what purpose and what end.

DROMIO OF SYRACUSE

You sent me for a rope's end as soon.
You sent me to the bay, sir, for a bark.

ANTIPHOLUS OF EPHESUS

I will debate this matter at more leisure,   100
And teach your ears to list me with more heed.
To Adriana, villain, hie thee straight.
Give her this key, and tell her in the desk
That's covered o'er with Turkish tapestry
There is a purse of ducats; let her send it.   105
Tell her I am arrested in the street,
And that shall bail me. Hie thee, slave. Be gone!—
On, officer, to prison, till it come.

Exeunt all but Dromio of Syracuse

DROMIO OF SYRACUSE

To Adriana. That is where we dined,
Where Dowsabel did claim me for her husband.   110
She is too big, I hope, for me to compass.
Thither I must, although against my will;
For servants must their masters' minds fulfil.   *Exit*

108.1 *Exeunt . . . Syracuse*] OXFORD (*after* Capell); *Exeunt* F

92 **master** Possibly the ship's master (captain
of a merchant vessel), as distinct from her
owner, but more likely Dromio's address
to Antipholus. If the ship were ready to
sail, the master would already be aboard.
In F the word is capitalized and separated
by commas from the preceding and following words. See l.86.
95 **waftage** passage
98 **rope's end** whipping or, possibly, hanging. Antipholus did of course send the
other Dromio for a rope's end (ll. 15–16).

110 **Dowsabel** Fr. *douce et belle*, from Italian
dulcibella. Conventional pastoral name
(though it seems also to have been used
in real life in various forms, such as
'Dussable'; see *OED*), which came to
have comic connotations, or to be used
ironically; a floozy. Obviously the same
woman whom Dromio called 'Nell' and
described in grotesque terms in 3.2.
111 **compass** Literally, encompass, get
round, hence embrace; also undertake or
obtain.

4.2   *Enter ⸤from the Phoenix⸥ Adriana and Luciana*

ADRIANA
　Ah, Luciana, did he tempt thee so?
　　Mightst thou perceive austerely in his eye
　That he did plead in earnest, yea or no?
　　Looked he or red or pale, or sad or merrily?
　What observation mad'st thou in this case   5
　Of his heart's meteors tilting in his face?

LUCIANA
　First he denied you had in him no right.

ADRIANA
　He meant he did me none, the more my spite.

LUCIANA
　Then swore he that he was a stranger here.

ADRIANA
　And true he swore, though yet forsworn he were.   10

LUCIANA
　Then pleaded I for you.

ADRIANA   And what said he?

LUCIANA
　That love I begged for you, he begged of me.

ADRIANA
　With what persuasion did he tempt thy love?

LUCIANA
　With words that in an honest suit might move.
　First he did praise my beauty, then my speech.   15

ADRIANA
　Didst speak him fair?

LUCIANA   Have patience, I beseech.

ADRIANA
　I cannot, nor I will not, hold me still.

4.2] CAPELL (Scene 2); Scene 3 POPE; *no scene break in* F   4.2.0.1 *from the Phoenix*] OXFORD; *not in* F   5–6 case | Of] F4; case? | Of F2; case? | Oh F1

4.2.1–6 Adriana begins with a six-line stanza (*ababcc*), and the dialogue continues in
couplets. She attempts to resume the
stanza at l. 25, but is interrupted by
Dromio's bursting in. She concludes the
scene with another cross-rhymed quatrain (62–5).
　2 **austerely** soberly, strictly; i.e. 'can you

be certain that he was in earnest?'
Shakespeare's only use of the adverb in
this unusual sense.
5–6 **What . . . face?** How far were you able to
read his true feelings in the altering
expressions in his face?
　7 **no** any

My tongue, though not my heart, shall have his will.
He is deformèd, crookèd, old, and sere,
Ill-faced, worse-bodied, shapeless everywhere,   20
Vicious, ungentle, foolish, blunt, unkind,
Stigmatical in making, worse in mind.

LUCIANA
Who would be jealous, then, of such a one?
No evil lost is wailed when it is gone.

ADRIANA
Ah, but I think him better than I say,   25
    And yet would herein others' eyes were worse.
Far from her nest the lapwing cries away;
    My heart prays for him, though my tongue do curse.
        Enter Dromio of Syracuse running

DROMIO OF SYRACUSE
Here, go—the desk, the purse! Sweet—now, make
    haste!

LUCIANA
How hast thou lost thy breath?

DROMIO OF SYRACUSE   By running fast.   30

ADRIANA
Where is thy master, Dromio? Is he well?

DROMIO OF SYRACUSE
No, he's in Tartar limbo, worse than hell.
A devil in an everlasting garment hath him,
One whose hard heart is buttoned up with steel;

28.1 *running*] OXFORD; *not in* F   29 purse! Sweet—now,] This edition; purse! Sweet now,
OXFORD; purse, sweet now‸ F; purse! sweat now, WILSON   33 hath him] F; hath him by the
heel CUNINGHAM (*conj.* Spedding)

19 **sere** withered
22 **Stigmatical** deformed, ill-favoured
27 **Far . . . away** Proverbial (Tilley, L68;
   Dent, p. 150). Adriana is not revealing her
   true feelings about her husband, as the
   lapwing makes a show of pretending that
   her nest is not where it really is, thus pro-
   tecting it.
29 **Sweet—** This edition takes F's 'sweet' to
   be an interrupted oath or inappropriate
   form of address by the breathless Dromio.
32–61 This passage and that at 4.3.12–40
   are undoubtedly the most obscure in the
   play.
32 **Tartar limbo** hell or the underworld in

general (though limbo is, in medieval
Christian doctrine, a neutral region
where many good souls await the Last
Judgement). Also slang for 'prison' (see
l. 40). Tartarus is the infernal prison of
classical mythology, but there may also
be an allusion to the Tartars, believed by
the English to be a barbarous, savage
people. Dromio is obviously imagining
some horrible place, however confused he
may be about fine definitions.
33 **everlasting** Strong material, like twill,
   from which uniforms, as for law officers,
   were made. Here also with its obvious
   connotation, 'eternal'.

A fiend, a fairy, pitiless and rough;   35
A wolf, nay, worse, a fellow all in buff;
A backfriend, a shoulder-clapper, one that
    countermands
The passages of alleys, creeks, and narrow lands;
A hound that runs counter, and yet draws dryfoot well;
One that before the Judgement carries poor souls to hell.   40

ADRIANA Why, man, what is the matter?

DROMIO OF SYRACUSE

I do not know the matter, he is 'rested on the case.

ADRIANA

What, is he arrested? Tell me at whose suit.

DROMIO OF SYRACUSE

I know not at whose suit he is arrested well,
But is in a suit of buff which 'rested him, that can I tell.   45
Will you send him, mistress, redemption—the money in
    his desk?

ADRIANA

Go fetch it, sister.   *Exit Luciana ⌈into the Phoenix⌉*
    This I wonder at,

---

35 fairy] F; fury POPE 1728 *(conj.* Theobald)   38 lands] F ('lans', *some copies*); launds
OXFORD   44–6] *as verse* CAPELL; *as prose* F   47.1 *into the Phoenix*] OXFORD; *not in* F
47–8 at, | That] F2; at. | Thus F

35 **fairy** Originally, a supernatural being
believed to possess power for good or evil.
Theobald's conjecture, made when 'fairy'
had come mainly to denote benign or
harmless imaginary creatures, is thus
unnecessary.

36 **buff** ox-leather. Used in Shakespeare's
time for military and other uniforms
where a degree of protection was needed.

37 **backfriend** false friend. Here also alluding
to an officer's coming up behind someone
to apprehend him.
  shoulder-clapper Slang term for an
officer.

37–8 **countermands . . . lands** prohibits
people from escaping through alleys and
narrow passages. The exact meaning of
'lands' here is unclear; possibly the strips,
or parcels, often quite narrow, in the
open field system of cultivation, common
in medieval England but virtually non-
existent by the late sixteenth century,
though this sense appears overly technical in the context. Perhaps 'lanes' was

intended, and was emended to 'lands'
for the sake of rhyme; the spelling
'lans' in some copies of F is grounds for
doubt. Some general meaning, such as
'spaces' or 'stretches' of open land (the
sense of Oxford's 'launds'), as distinct
from 'alleys' and 'creeks', is probably
sufficient.

39 **runs counter** follows the scent of the
quarry in the wrong direction. Probably a
strained pun on the Counter, a London
prison, suggested by 'countermand';
'Counter' is capitalized in F. Dromio's
wordplay is increasingly desperate and
strained in this scene and the next.
  draws dryfoot tracks game by the mere
scent of its footprint on the trail. *OED* cites
this line *(draw, v.* 74).

40 **Judgement . . . hell** Both the Final Judgement and hell, and a verdict in a law court
and prison.

42 **on the case** A legal expression covering
arrest for things not specifically provided
for by other laws.

That he unknown to me should be in debt.
Tell me, was he arrested on a bond?

DROMIO OF SYRACUSE

Not on a bond but on a stronger thing: 50
A chain, a chain—do you not hear it ring?

ADRIANA

What, the chain?

DROMIO OF SYRACUSE

            No, no, the bell. 'Tis time that I were gone:
It was two ere I left him, and now the clock strikes one.

ADRIANA

The hours come back! That did I never hear.

DROMIO OF SYRACUSE

O yes, if any hour meet a sergeant, a turns back for very
        fear.   55

ADRIANA

As if time were in debt. How fondly dost thou reason!

DROMIO OF SYRACUSE

Time is a very bankrupt, and owes more than he's worth
        to season.
Nay, he's a thief too. Have you not heard men say
That time comes stealing on by night and day?
If a be in debt and theft, and a sergeant in the way,   60
Hath he not reason to turn back an hour in a day?
        Enter Luciana ⌈from the Phoenix⌉ with the money

49, 50 bond] ROWE; band F   60 a be] STAUNTON; I be F   61.1 *from the Phoenix*] OXFORD; *not in* F   *with the money*] OXFORD (Dyce *Subs.*); *not in* F

49, 50 **bond** The old spelling, *band*, does not convey for a modern reader the primary sense, that of being arrested for failure to pay a debt on time (like Antonio in *The Merchant of Venice*).

53 In Komisarjevsky's 1938 Stratford production, the large clock on the set had moving hands, which duly turned back an hour at this point. That Dromio says and means 'one' and not 'on' as some commentators have suggested, is clear from both Adriana's response and his own concluding lines, esp. 61. This passage recalls Dromio's earlier discourse on time (2.2), and is yet another reminder of its inexorable passage in the play's day. See Introduction, pp. 48, 57–9.

55, 60 **sergeant** Law officer charged with

carrying out the judgements of a tribunal, or with the arrest of offenders.

55 **a turns** he turns

56 **fondly** madly

57 **owes . . . season** An obscure expression, variously glossed by editors. Camille W. Slights surveys alternatives ('Time's Debt to Season: *The Comedy of Errors*, IV.ii.58', *ELN* 24 (1986), 22–5). 'Season' elsewhere in the play means appropriate or due occasion, as determined by human need or convenience. Dromio seems to be saying that time assumes greater significance than it intrinsically has, according to such convenience or exigency, i.e. 'season'.

60 **If a** if he

ADRIANA

Go, Dromio, there's the money. Bear it straight,

And bring thy master home immediately.

[Exit Dromio]

Come, sister, I am pressed down with conceit:

Conceit, my comfort and my injury.   65

Exeunt [into the Phoenix]

4.3   *Enter Antipholus of Syracuse[, wearing the chain]*

ANTIPHOLUS OF SYRACUSE

There's not a man I meet but doth salute me

As if I were their well-acquainted friend,

And everyone doth call me by my name.

Some tender money to me, some invite me,

Some other give me thanks for kindnesses.   5

Some offer me commodities to buy;

Even now a tailor called me in his shop,

And showed me silks that he had bought for me,

And therewithal took measure of my body.

Sure, these are but imaginary wiles,   10

And Lapland sorcerers inhabit here.

Enter Dromio of Syracuse with the money

DROMIO OF SYRACUSE Master, here's the gold you sent me
for. What, have you got redemption of the picture of old
Adam new-apparelled?

63.1 *Exit Dromio*] OXFORD; *not in* F   65.1 *Exeunt . . . Phoenix*] OXFORD; *Exit* F

4.3] CAPELL (Scene 3); Scene 5 POPE; *no scene break in* F   0.1 *wearing the chain*] OXFORD; *not in* F   11.1 *with the money*] OXFORD; *not in* F   13 redemption of the picture of] This edition; the picture of F; rid of the picture of THEOBALD; redemption from the picture of OXFORD

---

64 **conceit** thought, imagination. To rhyme with 'straight', ending the scene as it began, with a quatrain.

4.3.10 **imaginary wiles** tricks of the imagination

11 **Lapland sorcerers** According to Giles Fletcher, the Lapps 'for practice of witchcraft and sorcery . . . pass all nations in the world' (*Of the Russe Common Wealth*, 1591). This is the only reference to Lapland in Shakespeare. The magic–witchcraft–enchantment motif, already prominent, recurs, and will do so with increasing intensity throughout this scene and the next.

13 **redemption of the picture of** This edition

follows Oxford's lead in recalling 'redemption' from 4.2.46, but conjectures that Compositor D left out 'redemption of', his eye skipping from 'got' to the second 'of'. Compare *Measure* 5.1.29: 'You bid me seek redemption of the devil'. The entire passage to l. 33 is probably the most obscure in the play; Dromio's desperate straining for puns may just be seen as reflecting his increasingly frantic state of mind. The reader/auditor will no doubt sympathize with Antipholus: 'I understand thee not' (21).

13 **picture** image, copy

13–14 **old Adam new-apparelled** i.e. the Officer. 'Old Adam', the father of sinful man,

ANTIPHOLUS OF SYRACUSE

What gold is this? What Adam dost thou mean?   15

DROMIO OF SYRACUSE Not that Adam that kept the Paradise,
but that Adam that keeps the prison—he that goes in the
calf's skin, that was killed for the Prodigal; he that came
behind you, sir, like an evil angel, and bid you forsake
your liberty.   20

ANTIPHOLUS OF SYRACUSE I understand thee not.

DROMIO OF SYRACUSE No? Why, 'tis a plain case: he
that went like a bass viol in a case of leather; the man,
sir, that when gentlemen are tired gives them a sob
and 'rests them; he, sir, that takes pity on decayed   25
men and gives them suits of durance; he that sets up his
rest to do more exploits with his mace than a Moorish
pike.

ANTIPHOLUS OF SYRACUSE What, thou mean'st an officer?

DROMIO OF SYRACUSE Ay, sir, the sergeant of the band: he   30
that brings any man to answer it that breaks his bond;

---

27 Moorish] OXFORD; Moris F   31 bond] ROWE; Band F

was dressed in animal skins after the Fall
(Genesis 3: 21). The Officer in his suit of
buff leather is 'new-apparelled' (but
better-dressed) in the same material that
Adam wore.

16 **Paradise** Wells conjectures a punning
allusion to a public house or inn kept by
someone named Adam; the primary
reference is obvious.

18 **calf's skin . . . Prodigal** Dromio leaps
from one biblical allusion to another, here
the killing of the fatted calf in celebration
of the prodigal son's return in the parable
in Luke 15, coupling it with the one made
previously to the sergeant's or Officer's
leather garment.

19 **evil angel** Possibly, in this biblically reso-
nant passage, an oblique allusion to the
incident reported in Acts 12 where an
angel came to awaken Peter and set him
free from prison, an evil angel presumably
doing the opposite. Perhaps recalling too
a common figure in morality drama, who
would appear behind, and was thus
'invisible' to, the character being tempted
or led astray. Compare Sonnet 144, where
a good and an evil angel are evoked.

23 **bass viol . . . leather** In the 1989 Bristol

Old Vic production, designer Anthony
Ward dressed the Officer (Darren Tun-
stall) in a brown leather uniform with
jodhpurs, giving him a shape rather suggestive of a bass viol or double bass, or its
case.

24 **sob** pause, breathing space given to a
horse

25 **'rests** rests, arrests

26 **suits of durance** long prison sentences.
Compare 'everlasting garment' (4.2.33);
here, 'the suit of durance' is transferred
to the prisoner or 'decayed man' apprehended by an officer.

27 **mace** symbol of office. Dromio conflates
several distinct meanings of 'sergeant' in
this passage (and in 4.2): a police officer
who enforces judgements and carries out
orders for arrests (*OED sb.* 4a); 'sergeant
at (of) the mace', an inferior municipal
executive officer (8b); 'sergeant of a band'
(l. 30), a specific military rank in the sixteenth century.

27–8 **Moorish pike** A military weapon supposedly of Moorish origin. 'Moris' was a
common Elizabethan spelling.

31 **bond** Modernizing the spelling makes the
sense clear, but slightly obscures the pun
with 'sergeant of the band'.

one that thinks a man always going to bed, and says 'God
give you good rest.'

ANTIPHOLUS OF SYRACUSE Well, sir, there rest in your
foolery. Is there any ship puts forth tonight? May we be   35
gone?

DROMIO OF SYRACUSE Why, sir, I brought you word an hour
since that the bark *Expedition* puts forth tonight, and
then were you hindered by the sergeant to tarry for the
hoy *Delay*. Here are the angels that you sent for to deliver   40
you.

ANTIPHOLUS OF SYRACUSE
The fellow is distraught, and so am I,
And here we wander in illusions.
Some blessèd power deliver us from hence.

    Enter a Courtesan [from the Porcupine]

COURTESAN
Well met, well met, Master Antipholus.   45
I see, sir, you have found the goldsmith now.
Is that the chain you promised me today?

ANTIPHOLUS OF SYRACUSE
Satan, avoid! I charge thee, tempt me not!

DROMIO OF SYRACUSE Master, is this Mistress Satan?

ANTIPHOLUS OF SYRACUSE It is the devil.   50

DROMIO OF SYRACUSE Nay, she is worse, she is the devil's
dam; and here she comes in the habit of a light wench.
And thereof comes that the wenches say 'God damn
me'—that's as much to say 'God make me a light
wench.' It is written they appear to men like angels of   55
light. Light is an effect of fire, and fire will burn. Ergo,
light wenches will burn. Come not near her.

---

35 ship] F2; ships F1   38 puts] ROWE 1709; put F   42 distraught] OXFORD; distract F   44.1
from the Porcupine] OXFORD; *not in* F

40 **hoy** Small sailing vessel, sloop-rigged,
carrying passengers and goods.
  angels gold coins. Dromio resumes his
angel/devil deliverance theme, setting
up Antipholus' plea at l. 44 and the
entrance, not of an angel or 'some blessèd
power', but the Courtesan (see Introduction p. 56).
44.1 See notes to 3.1.118 and 4.1.13.2.
48 Compare Matthew 4.10: 'Then said Iesus

unto him, "Avoid, Satan!"' (Geneva).
52 **dam** mother. Proverbial (Tilley, D225;
Dent, p. 90). Opprobrious term for a
woman.
52–7 **light wench . . . burn** A 'light wench',
i.e. a woman of loose morals, or a pros-
titute, will 'burn' a man with venereal
disease.
56 **Ergo** therefore (as in the conclusion to a
logical syllogism)

COURTESAN
>Your man and you are marvellous merry, sir.
>Will you go with me? We'll mend our dinner here.

DROMIO OF SYRACUSE Master, if you do, expect spoon-meat, 60
>and bespeak a long spoon.

ANTIPHOLUS OF SYRACUSE Why, Dromio?

DROMIO OF SYRACUSE Marry, he must have a long spoon that
>must eat with the devil.

ANTIPHOLUS OF SYRACUSE (*to Courtesan*)
>Avoid, thou fiend! What tell'st thou me of supping? 65
>Thou art, as you are all, a sorceress.
>I conjure thee to leave me and be gone.

COURTESAN
>Give me the ring of mine you had at dinner,
>Or for my diamond the chain you promised,
>And I'll be gone, sir, and not trouble you. 70

DROMIO OF SYRACUSE Some devils ask but the parings of
>one's nail, a rush, a hair, a drop of blood, a pin, a nut, a
>cherry-stone; but she, more covetous, would have a
>chain. Master, be wise; an if you give it her, the devil will
>shake her chain, and fright us with it. 75

COURTESAN (*to Antipholus*)
>I pray you, sir, my ring, or else the chain.
>I hope you do not mean to cheat me so?

ANTIPHOLUS OF SYRACUSE
>Avaunt, thou witch!—Come, Dromio, let us go.

---

60 you do] F2; do F1 61 and] WHITE (*conj.* Ritson); or F 65 thou fiend] F4; then fiend F1
71–5] *as prose* F; *as verse* CAPELL

---

59 **mend** complete, make up. We are to suppose that the dinner at the Porcupine, where Antipholus of Ephesus went at the end of 3.1 and from where he re-entered in 4.1, was interrupted when Angelo failed to come with the chain at the agreed hour, and Antipholus left to seek him. The Courtesan probably indicates her house on 'here'.

60 **spoon-meat** Soft or liquid food, suitable for eating with a spoon, as for infants or

invalids. Dromio may be saying that Antipholus deserves to be treated like a child or an idiot if he is so foolish as to accept the Courtesan's invitation; or he may just be setting up another laboured joke.

63–4 **long spoon . . . devil** Proverbial (Tilley, S771; Dent, p. 216). In Shakespeare, only here and in *The Tempest* at 2.2.97–8.

74 **an if** if

78 **Avaunt** Go away

DROMIO OF SYRACUSE

'Fly pride' says the peacock. Mistress, that you know.

                Exeunt Antipholus of Syracuse

                  and Dromio of Syracuse

COURTESAN

Now, out of doubt, Antipholus is mad;   80

Else would he never so demean himself.

A ring he hath of mine worth forty ducats,

And for the same he promised me a chain.

Both one and other he denies me now.

The reason that I gather he is mad,   85

Besides this present instance of his rage,

Is a mad tale he told today at dinner

Of his own doors being shut against his entrance.

Belike his wife, acquainted with his fits,

On purpose shut the doors against his way.   90

My way is now to hie home to his house,

And tell his wife that, being lunatic,

He rushed into my house, and took perforce

My ring away. This course I fittest choose,

For forty ducats is too much to lose.   *Exit*   95

4.4   *Enter Antipholus of Ephesus with the Officer*

ANTIPHOLUS OF EPHESUS

Fear me not, man, I will not break away.

I'll give thee ere I leave thee so much money

To warrant thee as I am 'rested for.

My wife is in a wayward mood today,

And will not lightly trust the messenger.   5

79.1 *Exeunt . . . Dromio of Syracuse*] CAPELL; *Exit.* F   95 *Exit*] F2; *not in* F1
    4.4] CAPELL; Scene 8 POPE; *no scene break in* F   0.1 *the Officer*] CAPELL; *a Iailor* F   5–6 messenger. | . . . Ephesus—] This edition; Messenger, | . . . *Ephesus*, F1; Messenger; | . . . Ephesus, F4; Messenger. | . . . Ephesus, ROWE; messenger, | . . . Ephesus: CAPELL

79 **pride . . . peacock** The peacock is a proverbial emblem of pride (Tilley, P157; Dent, p. 190). Dromio implies that it is as ironical for the Courtesan to accuse them of cheating her as for a peacock to denounce pride in others.

4.4.5–6 This edition reverts to the earlier editorial tradition, deriving from F4 and Rowe, in pointing these lines; F's commas at the ends of both leave the sense ambiguous. Here, 'That I should be attached in Ephesus' is an exclamation and that is the incredible news that will 'sound harshly' in Adriana's ears.

That I should be attached in Ephesus—
I tell you 'twill sound harshly in her ears.
> *Enter Dromio of Ephesus with a rope's end*
Here comes my man. I think he brings the money.—
How now, sir? Have you that I sent you for?

DROMIO OF EPHESUS

Here's that, I warrant you, will pay them all.   10

ANTIPHOLUS OF EPHESUS But where's the money?

DROMIO OF EPHESUS

Why, sir, I gave the money for the rope.

ANTIPHOLUS OF EPHESUS

Five hundred ducats, villain, for a rope?

DROMIO OF EPHESUS

I'll serve you, sir, five hundred at the rate.

ANTIPHOLUS OF EPHESUS

To what end did I bid thee hie thee home?   15

DROMIO OF EPHESUS To a rope's end, sir, and to that end am
I returned.

ANTIPHOLUS OF EPHESUS

And to that end, sir, I will welcome you.
> *He beats Dromio*

OFFICER Good sir, be patient.

DROMIO OF EPHESUS Nay, 'tis for me to be patient: I am in   20
adversity.

OFFICER Good now, hold thy tongue.

DROMIO OF EPHESUS Nay, rather persuade *him* to hold his
hands.

ANTIPHOLUS OF EPHESUS Thou whoreson, senseless villain!   25

DROMIO OF EPHESUS I would I were senseless, sir, that I
might not feel your blows.

ANTIPHOLUS OF EPHESUS Thou art sensible in nothing but
blows, and so is an ass.

18.1 *He beats Dromio*] OXFORD; *Beats Dro.* POPE; *Beating him* CAPELL; *not in* F

---

6 **attached** arrested.
14 **I'll . . . rate** I'll buy you five hundred ropes
for five hundred ducats
21 **adversity** Dromio's more immediate

concern is with the fact that he is being
beaten yet again, rather than with his
and his master's being under arrest.
22 **Good now** An expression of entreaty.

DROMIO OF EPHESUS I am an ass indeed. You may prove it   30
by my long ears.—I have served him from the hour of
my nativity to this instant, and have nothing at his hands
for my service but blows. When I am cold, he heats me
with beating. When I am warm, he cools me with beating. I am waked with it when I sleep, raised with it when   35
I sit, driven out of doors with it when I go from home,
welcomed home with it when I return. Nay, I bear it on
my shoulders, as a beggar wont her brat, and I think
when he hath lamed me I shall beg with it from door to
door.   40

> *Enter Adriana, Luciana, Courtesan, and a schoolmaster*
> *called Pinch*

ANTIPHOLUS OF EPHESUS
Come, go along. My wife is coming yonder.

DROMIO OF EPHESUS (*to Adriana*) Mistress, *respice finem*—
respect your end—or rather, to prophesy like the parrot,
'Beware the rope's end'.

ANTIPHOLUS OF EPHESUS Wilt thou still talk?   45

> *He beats Dromio*

---

31 ears.—] OXFORD; eares. F   43 to prophesy] DYCE; the prophesie F

30–1 Dromio now claims to have been metamorphosed, repeating, more emphatically, the view of himself expressed at 3.1.15–18.

31 **ears** Probably with an aural pun on 'years', as the following lines suggest. He presumably speaks the remainder of the speech to the audience, since he refers to Antipholus in the third person throughout; Oxford's punctuation makes clear the change of addressee.

38 **wont** is accustomed to do with

40.1 *schoolmaster* Why schoolmaster? Pinch's subsequent behaviour is that of a charlatan healer, not a pedant (Shakespeare's usual comic characterization of schoolmasters, such as Holofernes in *Love's Labour's Lost* and Parson Evans in *Merry Wives*); Pinch, for example, speaks no Latin. The Pedant in *Shrew*, however, is an impostor, like Pinch. Adriana addresses Pinch (l. 48) as 'Doctor' and 'a conjurer', and he later prescribes the standard treatment for madness.

There is no implication that he is also a clergyman, as Sir Hugh Evans is; 'Doctor' Rat, in *Gammer Gurton's Needle* (1575) is, however, the parish curate. In *Love's Labour's Lost*, 'Sir' Nathaniel, the curate, is a different character from Holofernes the schoolmaster; neither is called 'Doctor', and Doctor Caius in *Merry Wives* is simply a physician. Schoolmasters, priests and physicians received more or less the same basic university education in Tudor England. The stage direction may well preserve Shakespeare's first thought, dropped when it came to writing out the dialogue for the Pinch episode.

43 Dyce's emendation is certainly right. Dromio provides the translation of his Latin admonition. Parrots, it seems, used to be taught to say 'rope' among other witticisms (the allusion being to hanging); Dromio refers to the rope's end he has brought and which he expects to be used upon Adriana.

COURTESAN (*to Adriana*)
How say you now? Is not your husband mad?
ADRIANA
His incivility confirms no less.—
Good Doctor Pinch, you are a conjurer.
Establish him in his true sense again,
And I will please you what you will demand. 50
LUCIANA
Alas, how fiery and how sharp he looks!
COURTESAN
Mark how he trembles in his ecstasy.
PINCH (*to Antipholus*)
Give me your hand, and let me feel your pulse.
ANTIPHOLUS OF EPHESUS
There is my hand, and let it feel your ear.
He strikes Pinch
PINCH
I charge thee, Satan, housed within this man, 55
To yield possession to my holy prayers,
And to thy state of darkness hie thee straight:
I conjure thee by all the saints in heaven.
ANTIPHOLUS OF EPHESUS
Peace, doting wizard, peace! I am not mad.
ADRIANA
O that thou wert not, poor distressèd soul. 60
ANTIPHOLUS OF EPHESUS
You minion, you, are these your customers?
Did this companion with the saffron face
Revel and feast it at my house today,
Whilst upon me the guilty doors were shut,
And I denied to enter in my house? 65

54.1 *He strikes Pinch*] OXFORD (Dyce *subs.*); *not in* F

52 **ecstasy** mad fit
55–8 The stakes are raised now, as witches, goblins, mermaids and other such figments of the fevered imagination give way to a struggle between no less than divine and satanic forces, though Pinch's pretension to powers of exorcism is as vain as all the previous allegations and fears of madness, bewitchment and possession by spirits.
62 **saffron** Literally orange-red, the colour of saffron. Probably, when applied to 'face', synonymous with *sallow*, i.e. having a sickly yellowish complexion, like one who suffers from jaundice. Food cooked with saffron is characteristically yellow.

ADRIANA

O husband, God doth know you dined at home,
Where would you had remained until this time,
Free from these slanders and this open shame.

ANTIPHOLUS OF EPHESUS

Dined at home? (*To Dromio*) Thou villain, what sayst
    thou?

DROMIO OF EPHESUS

Sir, sooth to say, you did not dine at home.   70

ANTIPHOLUS OF EPHESUS

Were not my doors locked up, and I shut out?

DROMIO OF EPHESUS

Pardie, your doors were locked, and you shut out.

ANTIPHOLUS OF EPHESUS

And did not she herself revile me there?

DROMIO OF EPHESUS

Sans fable, she herself reviled you there.

ANTIPHOLUS OF EPHESUS

Did not her kitchen-maid rail, taunt, and scorn me?   75

DROMIO OF EPHESUS

Certes she did. The kitchen vestal scorned you.

ANTIPHOLUS OF EPHESUS

And did not I in rage depart from thence?

DROMIO OF EPHESUS

In verity you did.—My bones bears witness,
That since have felt the vigour of his rage.

ADRIANA (*aside to Pinch*)

Is't good to soothe him in these contraries?   80

---

78 did.— My] This edition; did, my F

72 **Pardie** by God, truly (Fr. *par Dieu*)
74 **Sans fable** (Fr.) without 'fabling' or lying.
One of a series of asseverations by Dromio
('sooth to say', 'Pardie', 'Certes', 'In
verity').
75 **kitchen-maid** Dromio's affirmative reply
to Antipholus' question confirms that
Luce, who 'railed, taunted and scorned'
her master in 3.1, and the kitchen-maid
anatomized and called 'Nell' by Dromio of
Syracuse in 3.2 are one and the same
(though she assumed exaggeratedly grotesque proportions and features in his
burlesque set-piece). See commentary on

3.1.47.1 and 3.2.111.
76 **Certes** certainly (Fr. *certes*). Disyllabic in
English.
vestal By Shakespeare's time, the sub-
stantive (orig. *vestal virgin*) meant 'a
chaste woman'. Humorously appropriate
here in its original connection with the
priestesses who had charge of the sacred
fire in the temple of Vesta at Rome. Vesta
was goddess of the family hearth and of
the home.
80 **soothe . . . contraries** humour him when
he makes these inaccurate claims

PINCH (*aside to Adriana*)
　　It is no shame. The fellow finds his vein,
　　And, yielding to him, humours well his frenzy.
ANTIPHOLUS OF EPHESUS (*to Adriana*)
　　Thou hast suborned the goldsmith to arrest me.
ADRIANA
　　Alas, I sent you money to redeem you,
　　By Dromio here, who came in haste for it.   85
DROMIO OF EPHESUS
　　Money by me? Heart and good will you might,
　　But surely, master, not a rag of money.
ANTIPHOLUS OF EPHESUS
　　Went'st not thou to her for a purse of ducats?
ADRIANA
　　He came to me, and I delivered it.
LUCIANA
　　And I am witness with her that she did.   90
DROMIO OF EPHESUS
　　God and the ropemaker bear me witness
　　That I was sent for nothing but a rope.
PINCH (*aside to Adriana*)
　　Mistress, both man and master is possessed.
　　I know it by their pale and deadly looks.
　　They must be bound and laid in some dark room.   95
ANTIPHOLUS OF EPHESUS (*to Adriana*)
　　Say wherefore didst thou lock me forth today,
　　(*To Dromio*) And why dost thou deny the bag of gold?
ADRIANA
　　I did not, gentle husband, lock thee forth.
DROMIO OF EPHESUS
　　And, gentle master, I received no gold.
　　But I confess, sir, that we were locked out.   100

81–2 **The fellow . . . frenzy** Pinch believes that Dromio is playing along with his master, pretending to agree with all he says. He shortly concludes (93) that Dromio too is 'possessed'.

86–7 **Heart . . . money** Apparently a conjunction of two distinct proverbs (Tilley, H338.1, R6.1; Dent, pp. 135, 199), but as they occur together in Nashe's *Four Letters Confuted* (1592) and in James Mabbes's *Celestina* (1631), as well as here,

the conjunction would seem to have been common. Foakes (p. 83) quotes Nashe ('heart and good will, but never a ragge of money'). Lodge has 'oh it is a proper man, but never a rag of money' (*Euphues' Shadow*, 1592). Dromio's first line is addressed to Adriana, the second to Antipholus.

87 **rag** a scrap, trifling amount

95 **bound . . . room** Common treatment for madness; compare Malvolio's fate in *Twelfth Night*.

ADRIANA

Dissembling villain, thou speak'st false in both.

ANTIPHOLUS OF EPHESUS

Dissembling harlot, thou art false in all,
And art confederate with a damnèd pack
To make a loathsome abject scorn of me.
But with these nails I'll pluck out those false eyes, 105
That would behold in me this shameful sport.
⌈*He tries to attack Adriana*⌉

ADRIANA

O, bind him, bind him. Let him not come near me.
Enter three or four, and offer to bind him. He strives

PINCH

More company! The fiend is strong within him.

LUCIANA

Ay me, poor man, how pale and wan he looks.

ANTIPHOLUS OF EPHESUS

What, will you murder me?—Thou, jailer, thou, 110
I am thy prisoner. Wilt thou suffer them
To make a rescue?

OFFICER   Masters, let him go.
He is my prisoner, and you shall not have him.

PINCH

Go, bind his man, for he is frantic too.
They bind Dromio

ADRIANA

What wilt thou do, thou peevish officer? 115
Hast thou delight to see a wretched man

---

105 those] ROWE; these F   106.1 *He . . . Adriana*] This edition (Capell *subs.*); *not in* F   107.1
Enter . . . strives] This edition; *after l.* 106 F; *after l.* 108 DYCE   110–13] *as verse* POPE; *as prose* F
114 his] WELLS (*conj.* Tannenbaum); this F   114.1 *They bind Dromio*] OXFORD (Cambridge
subs.); *not in* F

---

101 **false in both** Adriana unwittingly hits
upon Dromio's dual identity: he received
no gold, it was given to Dromio of
Syracuse; he was, as himself, Dromio of
Ephesus, locked out. For her, he both
received the gold *and* dined at home.
107.1 The imprecise F direction suggests
authorial copy, not yet made concrete in
the playhouse, where 'three or four'
would necessarily become *either* 'three' *or*
'four'. *Menaechmi* specifies 'four porters'.

108 **More company** Pinch calls for more
help when Antipholus 'strives', but there
is no indication that anyone else enters.
Dyce's solution may be the best. Any production will arrange suitable business
for the struggle that is obviously going
on.
114 **his** F's *this* is conceivably right; Pinch
could point to Dromio as he says it.
115 **peevish** obstinate

Do outrage and displeasure to himself?
OFFICER
    He is my prisoner. If I let him go,
    The debt he owes will be required of me.
ADRIANA
    I will discharge thee ere I go from thee.   120
    Bear me forthwith unto his creditor,
    And, knowing how the debt grows, I will pay it.—
    Good Master Doctor, see him safe conveyed
    Home to my house. O most unhappy day!
ANTIPHOLUS OF EPHESUS O most unhappy strumpet!   125
DROMIO OF EPHESUS
    Master, I am here entered in bond for you.
ANTIPHOLUS OF EPHESUS
    Out on thee, villain! Wherefore dost thou mad me?
DROMIO OF EPHESUS
    Will you be bound for nothing? Be mad, good master—
    Cry, 'The devil!'
LUCIANA
    God help, poor souls, how idly do they talk!   130
ADRIANA
    Go bear him hence.—Sister, go you with me.
        Exeunt ⌈into the Phoenix⌉, Pinch and others carrying
        off Antipholus of Ephesus and Dromio of Ephesus. The
        Officer, Adriana, Luciana, and the Courtesan remain
    (*To the Officer*) Say now, whose suit is he arrested at?
OFFICER
    One Angelo, a goldsmith. Do you know him?
ADRIANA
    I know the man. What is the sum he owes?
OFFICER
    Two hundred ducats.
ADRIANA   Say, how grows it due?   135
OFFICER
    Due for a chain your husband had of him.
ADRIANA
    He did bespeak a chain for me, but had it not.

131.1–3 *Exeunt . . . remain*] OXFORD (Capell *subs.*); *Exeunt. Manet Offic. Adri. Luci. Courtesan* F
(after 132)

158

COURTESAN

Whenas your husband all in rage today
Came to my house, and took away my ring—
The ring I saw upon his finger now—   140
Straight after did I meet him with a chain.

ADRIANA

It may be so, but I did never see it.—
Come, jailer, bring me where the goldsmith is.
I long to know the truth hereof at large.

> *Enter Antipholus of Syracuse (wearing the chain) and*
> *Dromio of Syracuse with their rapiers drawn*

LUCIANA

God, for thy mercy, they are loose again!   145

ADRIANA

And come with naked swords. Let's call more help
To have them bound again.

OFFICER   Away, they'll kill us!

> *Exeunt all but Antipholus and Dromio, as fast as may*
> *be, frighted*

144.1–2 *Enter . . . drawn*] DYCE (*subs.*); *Enter Antipholus Siracusia with his Rapier drawne, and Dromio Sirac.* F   146–7 *And . . . help* | *To . . . us*] STEEVENS 1778; *And . . . swords,* | *Let's . . . againe.* | *Runne all out.* | *Off. Away . . . vs.* F   147.1 *Exeunt . . . Dromio*] This edition (Oxford *subs.*); *Exeunt omnes* F

146 The plural 'swords' justifies Dyce's emendation to the plural in the preceding stage direction, though conceivably only the master might have worn a rapier. Dromio perhaps brandished a dagger or other weapon.

147.1–2 The F stage direction here is an expanded repetition of the one printed at the bottom right of column a (H6ᵛ), following the line 'Let's call more helpe to have them bound againe'. Most unusually, that direction, '*Runne all out.*', is printed in the cue-space, normally left blank in 'a' columns; nowhere else in the Folio is anything printed in that space (in 'b' columns it is used for catchwords and signatures; see Werstine, ' "Foul Papers" and "Prompt Books" '). Foakes conjectures (pp. xiv–xv, 86 n.) that the original direction '*Run all out* | *as fast as may be, frighted*' was thus divided in the manuscript, and the compositor (B) was misled into thinking '*Run all out*' was all there was to it. When he came to set the remaining clause, he prefixed '*Exeunt*

omnes' to make sense of it, thus making two directions of what had been only one. But that highly unusual placing of the direction in column a suggests other difficulties, involving, if Steevens was right, the mislineation of 146–7. Had B set the half-line 'To have them bound again' correctly and completed it with the Officer's half-line, he would have been faced with an exit direction to begin the second column. This was against standard practice, and is done nowhere in F, although numerous '*Enter*' and other directions are placed at the top of 'b' columns. I suggest that B, still thinking '*Run all out*' to be the complete stage direction, squeezed it into the cue-space in column a, having deliberately mislined 146–7 to leave himself the Officer's half-line with which to begin column b. Supposing his problem solved, he returned to his copy, found the remainder of the direction (perhaps on the following sheet), and made up a new first clause for it, satisfied that it would not now violate the taboo against starting a

ANTIPHOLUS OF SYRACUSE

    I see these witches are afraid of swords.

DROMIO OF SYRACUSE

    She that would be your wife now ran from you.

ANTIPHOLUS OF SYRACUSE

    Come to the Centaur. Fetch our stuff from thence.   150

    I long that we were safe and sound aboard.

DROMIO OF SYRACUSE Faith, stay here this night. They will

    surely do us no harm. You saw they speak us fair, give

    us gold. Methinks they are such a gentle nation that, but

    for the mountain of mad flesh that claims marriage of   155

    me, I could find in my heart to stay here still, and turn

    witch.

ANTIPHOLUS OF SYRACUSE

    I will not stay tonight for all the town.

    Therefore away, to get our stuff aboard.   *Exeunt*

5.1   *Enter Second Merchant and Angelo the goldsmith*

ANGELO

    I am sorry, sir, that I have hindered you,

    But I protest he had the chain of me,

    Though most dishonestly he doth deny it.

SECOND MERCHANT

    How is the man esteemed here in the city?

ANGELO

    Of very reverend reputation, sir,   5

    Of credit infinite, highly beloved,

    Second to none that lives here in the city.

    His word might bear my wealth at any time.

5.1.0.1 *Second Merchant*] DYCE; *the Merchant* F (*so throughout scene*)

'b' column with an exit direction. Compare r4ᵛ in *Richard III* where B split a direction between columns, but where it lent itself to such a procedure more readily than the present one, dividing between '*Exeunt*' and '*Mane[n]t*'. The Oxford editors find Greg's hypothesis of some annotations relating to performance, including a second stage direction here, having been made in the manuscript more plausible than that of such compositorial intervention as is suggested here (*TC*, p. 266: 'an unparalleled and remarkably stupid interpolation by the compositor'). But this is an 'unparalleled' occurrence in F, and the apparent conjunction of circumstances, coupled with Compositor B's known free (not necessarily stupid) way with his copy on occasion, seems to call for an unusual hypothesis.

5.1.0.1 *Second Merchant* See note at 4.1.0.1.
8 **bear my wealth** suffice for me to engage all I am worth upon it

SECOND MERCHANT
  Speak softly. Yonder, as I think, he walks.

  Enter Antipholus of Syracuse, wearing the chain, and
  Dromio of Syracuse again

ANGELO
  'Tis so, and that self chain about his neck   10
  Which he forswore most monstrously to have.
  Good sir, draw near to me. I'll speak to him.—
  Signor Antipholus, I wonder much
  That you would put me to this shame and trouble,
  And not without some scandal to yourself,   15
  With circumstance and oaths so to deny
  This chain, which now you wear so openly.
  Beside the charge, the shame, imprisonment,
  You have done wrong to this my honest friend,
  Who, but for staying on our controversy,   20
  Had hoisted sail and put to sea today.
  This chain you had of me. Can you deny it?

ANTIPHOLUS OF SYRACUSE
  I think I had. I never did deny it.

SECOND MERCHANT
  Yes, that you did, sir, and forswore it too.

ANTIPHOLUS OF SYRACUSE
  Who heard me to deny it or forswear it?   25

SECOND MERCHANT
  These ears of mine, thou knowest, did hear thee.
  Fie on thee, wretch! 'Tis pity that thou liv'st
  To walk where any honest men resort.

9.1 *wearing the chain*] OXFORD; *not in* F   26 knowest] POPE; knowst F

9.1–2 **Enter ... again** It may be inferred from this re-entry direction—'*again*'—that an act break was not originally planned here and that the action was continuous. The act divisions in *Errors* may have been added at the time of printing, but they are unusually appropriately placed and may well reflect preparation for a special Inns of Court or Court indoor performance where intervals for refreshment and for trimming of the lamps would have been taken, if not the actual composition of the play with such a venue in mind. See Introduction, p. 12, and *TC*, p. 266.

10 **self** same

16 **circumstance** excuses

26 **knowest** The syllable added by Pope makes the line scan, and may find added justification in the fact that it is a long line, running right out to the margin; to save space, the compositor (B) omitted even the apostrophe, which, however, he was careful to include elsewhere (e.g. ll. 27, 31).

ANTIPHOLUS OF SYRACUSE

Thou art a villain to impeach me thus.

I'll prove mine honour and mine honesty   30

Against thee presently, if thou dar'st stand.

SECOND MERCHANT

I dare, and do defy thee for a villain.

> *Antipholus and the Merchant draw. Enter Adriana,*
> *Luciana, Courtesan, and others ⌈from the Phoenix⌉*

ADRIANA

Hold, hurt him not, for God's sake; he is mad.

Some get within him, take his sword away.

Bind Dromio too, and bear them to my house.   35

DROMIO OF SYRACUSE

Run, master, run! For God's sake take a house.

This is some priory—in, or we are spoiled.

> *Exeunt Antipholus of Syracuse and*
> *Dromio of Syracuse to the priory*
> *Enter ⌈from the priory⌉ the Lady Abbess*

ABBESS

Be quiet, people. Wherefore throng you hither?

ADRIANA

To fetch my poor distracted husband hence.

Let us come in, that we may bind him fast,   40

And bear him home for his recovery.

ANGELO

I knew he was not in his perfect wits.

32.1 *Antipholus . . . draw*] This edition; *They draw* F   32.2 *from the Phoenix*] OXFORD; *not in* F
37.1–2 *Exeunt Antipholus of Syracuse . . . Dromio of Syracuse . . . priory*] OXFORD (Capell *subs.*);
Exeunt to the Priorie. F   37.3 *from the priory*] OXFORD; *not in* F

---

29 **impeach** accuse
31 **presently** immediately
34 **within him** within his guard, inside the
    effective reach of his weapon
37 **This . . . priory** The priory, or abbey,
    must face the open space, the 'mart', and
    have a door, unused till this moment. This
    is the sole occurrence of the word *priory*
    in Shakespeare. Elsewhere in the play
    (eight times), it is called 'abbey', and its
    location on the set is always indicated:
    'the abbey here', 'these abbey walls'. It
    may be imagined to be against the city
    wall, with waste land behind it where exe-
    cutions took place (see below, ll. 120–2:

'the melancholy vale . . . behind the
ditches of the abbey here'). In *The Two
Gentlemen of Verona*, 'the postern by the
abbey wall', i.e. a small back door, leading
to a forest beyond, is a way to slip out of
the town without being seen (5.1.9). The
insistence in *Errors* upon the kind of insti-
tution is further evidence of the deliberate
christianizing of the play's world; Apollonius' wife was a priestess in the temple of
Diana at Ephesus. Abbeys and priories
(generally smaller establishments, often
founded as dependencies of the larger
abbeys) had of course been suppressed in
England in the 1530s, under Henry VIII.

SECOND MERCHANT

   I am sorry now that I did draw on him.

ABBESS

   How long hath this possession held the man?

ADRIANA

   This week he hath been heavy, sour, sad,   45

   And much, much different from the man he was.

   But till this afternoon his passion

   Ne'er broke into extremity of rage.

ABBESS

   Hath he not lost much wealth by wreck at sea?

   Buried some dear friend? Hath not else his eye   50

   Strayed his affection in unlawful love—

   A sin prevailing much in youthful men,

   Who give their eyes the liberty of gazing?

   Which of these sorrows is he subject to?

ADRIANA

   To none of these, except it be the last,   55

   Namely some love that drew him oft from home.

ABBESS

   You should for that have reprehended him.

ADRIANA

   Why, so I did.

ABBESS   Ay, but not rough enough.

ADRIANA

   As roughly as my modesty would let me.

ABBESS

   Haply in private.

ADRIANA   And in assemblies too.   60

ABBESS Ay, but not enough.

ADRIANA

   It was the copy of our conference.

   In bed he slept not for my urging it;

   At board he fed not for my urging it.

---

46 much, much] F2 (much much); much F1   48 broke] F (brake)   49 at] F2; of F1   51 love—] OXFORD; loue, F   53 gazing?] OXFORD; gazing. F   58 Why . . . enough] *as one verse line* CAMBRIDGE; *as two short lines* F   60 Haply . . . too] *as one verse line* CAMBRIDGE; *as two short lines* F

62 **copy . . . conference** theme of our conversation

Alone, it was the subject of my theme;   65
In company I often glanced at it.
Still did I tell him it was vile and bad.
ABBESS
And thereof came it that the man was mad.
The venom clamours of a jealous woman
Poisons more deadly than a mad dog's tooth.   70
It seems his sleeps were hindered by thy railing,
And thereof comes it that his head is light.
Thou sayst his meat was sauced with thy upbraidings:
Unquiet meals make ill digestions.
Thereof the raging fire of fever bred,   75
And what's a fever but a fit of madness?
Thou sayst his sports were hindered by thy brawls:
Sweet recreation barred, what doth ensue
But moody and dull melancholy,
Kinsman to grim and comfortless despair,   80
And at her heels a huge infectious troop
Of pale distemperatures and foes to life?
In food, in sport, and life-preserving rest
To be disturbed would mad or man or beast.
The consequence is, then, thy jealous fits   85
Hath scared thy husband from the use of wits.
LUCIANA
She never reprehended him but mildly
When he demeaned himself rough, rude, and wildly.
(*To Adriana*) Why bear you these rebukes, and answer
    not?
ADRIANA
She did betray me to my own reproof.—   90
Good people, enter, and lay hold on him.

66 glanced at it] POPE; glanced it F; glancèd it OXFORD

67 **Still** continually
69 **venom** (i.e. venomous) poisonous
79–82 Such allegorical personifications of melancholy as a monster are common in Renaissance literature, e.g. in Milton's *L'Allegro*.
79 Abbott (§484) cites this among many examples of lines lacking a syllable where diphthongs or long vowels may be read as compensating.

80 **Kinsman** Melancholy is personified by a feminine pronoun in the next line; 'kinsman' is merely generic.
82 **distemperatures** Mental or emotional disorders associated with an imbalance of 'humours' in the body, hence 'pale'. One of only three occurrences in Shakespeare; the others, in the singular, are in *Dream* and *Pericles*.

ABBESS
  No, not a creature enters in my house.

ADRIANA
  Then let your servants bring my husband forth.

ABBESS
  Neither. He took this place for sanctuary,
  And it shall privilege him from your hands   95
  Till I have brought him to his wits again,
  Or lose my labour in essaying it.

ADRIANA
  I will attend my husband, be his nurse,
  Diet his sickness, for it is my office,
  And will have no attorney but myself.   100
  And therefore let me have him home with me.

ABBESS
  Be patient, for I will not let him stir
  Till I have used the approved means I have,
  With wholesome syrups, drugs, and holy prayers
  To make of him a formal man again.   105
  It is a branch and parcel of mine oath,
  A charitable duty of my order.
  Therefore depart, and leave him here with me.

ADRIANA
  I will not hence and leave my husband here;
  And ill it doth beseem your holiness   110
  To separate the husband and the wife.

ABBESS
  Be quiet and depart. Thou shalt not have him.
                                   ⌜*Exit into the priory*⌝

LUCIANA (*to Adriana*)
  Complain unto the Duke of this indignity.

---

97 essaying] OXFORD; assaying F   112.1 *Exit . . . priory*] OXFORD; *Exit* THEOBALD; *not in* F

100 **attorney** agent, deputy. *OED* quotes this line.
102–7 The Abbess claims genuine healing skills, a practical extension of her religious vocation, in contrast to 'Doctor' Pinch's sham occult powers.
105 **formal** normal, sane. *OED* cites only this instance of the word in that par-
ticular sense.
106 **branch and parcel** component and integral part
112 The Abbess's judgement is wiser than even she is aware: Adriana must not have him because he, Antipholus of Syracuse, is not her husband.

ADRIANA

Come, go, I will fall prostrate at his feet,
And never rise until my tears and prayers   115
Have won his grace to come in person hither
And take perforce my husband from the Abbess.

⌈ANGELO⌉

By this, I think, the dial point's at five.
Anon, I'm sure, the Duke himself in person
Comes this way to the melancholy vale,   120
The place of death and sorry execution,
Behind the ditches of the abbey here.

⌈SECOND MERCHANT⌉ Upon what cause?

⌈ANGELO⌉

To see a reverend Syracusan merchant,
Who put unluckily into this bay   125
Against the laws and statutes of this town,
Beheaded publicly for his offence.

⌈SECOND MERCHANT⌉

See where they come. We will behold his death.

LUCIANA

Kneel to the Duke before he pass the abbey.

    Enter Solinus Duke of Ephesus, and Egeon the
    merchant of Syracuse, bareheaded ⌈*and bound*⌉*, with*
    the headsman and other officers

118, 124 ANGELO] This edition; *Mar⟨chant⟩*. F; *Sec⟨ond⟩*. *Mer⟨chant⟩*. DYCE   118 point's]
OXFORD (*conj.* McKerrow); points F   121 death] F3; depth FI   123, 128 SECOND MERCHANT]
This edition; *Gold⟨smith⟩*. F

118, 123–4, 128 How does the Second
Merchant, who is obviously a stranger in
Ephesus (5.1.4), know all this? Angelo
the goldsmith, on the other hand, is an
Ephesian. The vagueness of the F speech
prefixes throughout, in which both
anonymous merchants and Egeon are
designated *Mar.* or *Mer.*, suggests that
Shakespeare was not concerned at this
stage of composition to make such nice
distinctions. Dyce's designations are confirmed, as First Merchant in 1.2, unlike
Second Merchant in Acts 4 and 5, is
knowledgeable about current events in
Ephesus (the former is called '*E. Mar.*' (=
'Ephesian Merchant') in two prefixes in

1.2). This passage, like 1.2.1–8, serves to
link the two plots. This is the first we have
heard of Egeon and his fate since 1.2. The
action now opens out to embrace the
romance plot of Egeon and his lost family,
as well as the comical-farcical one of the
two pairs of twins.

118 **point's** point is. The Oxford editors adopt
McKerrow's suggestion, as a *dial* (i.e. sun-
dial) does not *point* at anything; its hand
casts a shadow whose point is now at five.
five The third explicit reference to that
hour (1.2.26, 4.1.10). It marks the end of
the working day and of Egeon's allotted
period of grace.

121 **sorry** grievous, dismal

DUKE
Yet once again proclaim it publicly:
If any friend will pay the sum for him,
He shall not die; so much we tender him.

ADRIANA (*kneeling*)
Justice, most sacred Duke, against the Abbess!

DUKE
She is a virtuous and a reverend lady.
It cannot be that she hath done thee wrong.

ADRIANA
May it please your grace, Antipholus my husband,
Who I made lord of me and all I had
At your important letters—this ill day
A most outrageous fit of madness took him,
That desp'rately he hurried through the street,
With him his bondman, all as mad as he,
Doing displeasure to the citizens
By rushing in their houses, bearing thence
Rings, jewels, anything his rage did like.
Once did I get him bound, and sent him home,
Whilst to take order for the wrongs I went
That here and there his fury had committed.
Anon, I wot not by what strong escape,
He broke from those that had the guard of him,
And with his mad attendant and himself,
Each one with ireful passion, with drawn swords,
Met us again, and, madly bent on us,
Chased us away; till, raising of more aid,
We came again to bind them. Then they fled
Into this abbey, whither we pursued them,
And here the Abbess shuts the gates on us,
And will not suffer us to fetch him out,
Nor send him forth that we may bear him hence.

130

135

140

145

150

155

136–60 The syntax of this long speech is irregular in places, suggesting Adriana's breathlessness and the confused events she is relating. Her husband gives his version of the same events in an even longer speech (214–53).
136–8 **Antipholus . . . letters** This implies, in the background, some such relationship of Adriana to the Duke as that of ward to guardian, an impression strengthened by his words at 161–4.
138 **important** importunate
146 **Whilst . . . went** whilst I went to make amends for the wrongs
152 **bent** turned

Therefore, most gracious Duke, with thy command
Let him be brought forth, and borne hence for help.   160
DUKE *(raising Adriana)*
Long since, thy husband served me in my wars,
And I to thee engaged a prince's word,
When thou didst make him master of thy bed,
To do him all the grace and good I could.—
Go, some of you, knock at the abbey gate,   165
And bid the Lady Abbess come to me.
I will determine this before I stir.
                Enter a Messenger [from the Phoenix]
MESSENGER *(to Adriana)*
O mistress, mistress, shift and save yourself!
My master and his man are both broke loose,
Beaten the maids a-row, and bound the Doctor,   170
Whose beard they have singed off with brands of fire,
And ever as it blazed they threw on him
Great pails of puddled mire to quench the hair.
My master preaches patience to him, and the while
His man with scissors nicks him like a fool;   175
And sure—unless you send some present help—
Between them they will kill the conjurer.
ADRIANA
Peace, fool. Thy master and his man are here,
And that is false thou dost report to us.
MESSENGER
Mistress, upon my life I tell you true.   180
I have not breathed almost since I did see it.

167.1 *from the Phoenix*] OXFORD; *not in* F   168 MESSENGER] F2; *not in* F1

167 **I will . . . stir** The resolution of Egeon's fate and of the tragicomic plot is suspended, while the Duke intervenes in the farcical comedy occasioned by the presence in Ephesus of the two pairs of twins. The diversion occasions the merging of the two plots and ultimately their simultaneous resolution.

170 **a-row** all in a row, one after the other

171–5 Some editors note a resemblance in this reported action to Edward II's humiliation in Marlowe's play (5.3).

173 **puddled mire** dirty, foul water (as from a muddy puddle)

174 A twelve-syllable line. Compositor B easily fitted it in by abbreviating 'master' as 'M'.

175 Dromio is reported to be cutting Pinch's hair in the style of a court fool, who went either completely shaven or tonsured like a monk.

178, 188, 257, 263 **here** The speakers must gesture towards the door of the clearly marked abbey.

He cries for you, and vows, if he can take you,
To scorch your face and to disfigure you.
        Cry within ⌈the Phoenix⌉
Hark, hark, I hear him, mistress. Fly, be gone!
DUKE (*to Adriana*)
    Come stand by me. Fear nothing.—Guard with halberds!   185
        Enter Antipholus of Ephesus and Dromio of Ephesus
        ⌈from the Phoenix⌉
ADRIANA
    Ay me, it is my husband! Witness you
    That he is borne about invisible.
    Even now we housed him in the abbey here,
    And now he's there, past thought of human reason.
ANTIPHOLUS OF EPHESUS
    Justice, most gracious Duke, O grant me justice,   190
    Even for the service that long since I did thee,
    When I bestrid thee in the wars, and took
    Deep scars to save thy life; even for the blood
    That then I lost for thee, now grant me justice!
EGEON (*aside*)
    Unless the fear of death doth make me dote,   195
    I see my son Antipholus, and Dromio.
ANTIPHOLUS OF EPHESUS
    Justice, sweet prince, against that woman there,
    She whom thou gav'st to me to be my wife,
    That hath abusèd and dishonoured me
    Even in the strength and height of injury.   200
    Beyond imagination is the wrong
    That she this day hath shameless thrown on me.

183.1 *the Phoenix*] This edition; *not in* F   185.1–2 *Enter . . . Phoenix*] OXFORD; *after 189* F
185.2 *from the Phoenix*] OXFORD; *not in* F   195 EGEON] JOHNSON; *Mar⟨chant⟩. Fat⟨her⟩.* F
195–6] *as verse* ROWE 1709; *as prose* F

183 **scorch** score, scratch, or possibly, flay. Perhaps also recalling the 'brands of fire' in 171.
185 **Guard with halberds** The Duke's guard would form a defensive ring around them, with their weapons, part spear, part long-handled axe, pointing outward.
191–4 Antipholus is more specific than the Duke was (161) about the particular service rendered.

195 Egeon is distinguished by F's prefixes in this scene from the Second Merchant (*Mar.* at 259). Subsequently he is *Fa.*, *Fath.*, *Fat.* or *Father*.
195–6 Reads as prose in F, probably because 'dote' would not fit in at the end of its verse line.
195 **make me dote** drive me mad
202 **shameless** shamelessly

DUKE

  Discover how, and thou shalt find me just.

ANTIPHOLUS OF EPHESUS

  This day, great Duke, she shut the doors upon me

  While she with harlots feasted in my house.   205

DUKE

  A grievous fault!—Say, woman, didst thou so?

ADRIANA

  No, my good lord. Myself, he, and my sister

  Today did dine together. So befall my soul

  As this is false he burdens me withal.

LUCIANA

  Ne'er may I look on day nor sleep on night   210

  But she tells to your highness simple truth.

ANGELO (*aside*)

  O perjured woman! They are both forsworn.

  In this the madman justly chargeth them.

ANTIPHOLUS OF EPHESUS

  My liege, I am advisèd what I say,

  Neither disturbed with the effect of wine,   215

  Nor heady-rash provoked with raging ire,

  Albeit my wrongs might make one wiser mad.

  This woman locked me out this day from dinner.

  That goldsmith there, were he not packed with her,

  Could witness it, for he was with me then,   220

  Who parted with me to go fetch a chain,

  Promising to bring it to the Porcupine,

  Where Balthasar and I did dine together.

  Our dinner done, and he not coming thither,

  I went to seek him. In the street I met him,   225

  And in his company that gentleman.

    He points to the Second Merchant

226.1 *He . . . Merchant*] OXFORD; *not in* F

---

203 **Discover** reveal

205 **harlots** loose persons, perhaps fornicators. The word was already at this time also applied in a more restricted sense to unchaste women or prostitutes; compare 2.2.139 and 4.4.102.

208 An alexandrine.

208 **So . . . soul** 'May the fate of my soul depend on it' (Dorsch).

214 **I . . . say** I speak deliberately, with due consideration

219 **packed with** in league with, having made a pact with

There did this perjured goldsmith swear me down
That I this day of him received the chain,
Which, God he knows, I saw not. For the which
He did arrest me with an officer.   230
I did obey, and sent my peasant home
For certain ducats; he with none returned.
Then fairly I bespoke the officer
To go in person with me to my house.
By the way, we met my wife, her sister, and a rabble more   235
Of vile confederates. Along with them
They brought one Pinch, a hungry lean-faced villain,
A mere anatomy, a mountebank,
A threadbare juggler, and a fortune-teller,
A needy, hollow-eyed, sharp-looking wretch,   240
A living dead man. This pernicious slave,
Forsooth, took on him as a conjurer,
And gazing in mine eyes, feeling my pulse,
And with no face, as 'twere, outfacing me,
Cries out I was possessed. Then all together   245
They fell upon me, bound me, bore me thence,
And in a dark and dankish vault at home
There left me and my man, both bound together,
Till, gnawing with my teeth my bonds in sunder,
I gained my freedom, and immediately   250
Ran hither to your grace, whom I beseech
To give me ample satisfaction
For these deep shames and great indignities.

ANGELO

My lord, in truth, thus far I witness with him:

245 all together] ROWE; altogether F

227 **swear me down** swear emphatically, as if
to silence me by his vehemence. Compare
'face me down' (3.1.6), cited by *OED*
(*down, adv.*, 17b).

230 **with** by

235 A fifteen-syllable line, which Compositor
B managed to squeeze in by omitting 'e' in
'the' and spaces after two commas. F's
'By' th' way' may be an attempt to make a
double contraction—'byth' way'—of 'by
the way'. Read thus, the number of syllables is reduced to fourteen.

237–41 This is thought to be an exaggerated
description of the actor John Sinclair, Sin-
cler, or Sincklo, whose physique seems to
have suited small, thin, even skeletal
characters, such as the Tailor in *Shrew*
and the Apothecary in *Romeo*. He probably joined the Chamberlain's Men upon
their formation in the spring of 1594.

242 **took on him as** pretended to be

244 **with no face** Referring to the preceding
description of Pinch: 'a mere anatomy',
'a living dead man'.

171

That he dined not at home, but was locked out.   255
DUKE
But had he such a chain of thee, or no?
ANGELO
He had, my lord, and when he ran in here
These people saw the chain about his neck.
SECOND MERCHANT (*to Antipholus*)
Besides, I will be sworn these ears of mine
Heard you confess you had the chain of him,   260
After you first forswore it on the mart,
And thereupon I drew my sword on you;
And then you fled into this abbey here,
From whence I think you are come by miracle.
ANTIPHOLUS OF EPHESUS
I never came within these abbey walls,   265
Nor ever didst thou draw thy sword on me.
I never saw the chain, so help me heaven,
And this is false you burden me withal.
DUKE
Why, what an intricate impeach is this!
I think you all have drunk of Circe's cup.   270
If here you housed him, here he would have been.
If he were mad, he would not plead so coldly.
(*To Adriana*) You say he dined at home, the goldsmith
        here
Denies that saying. (*To Dromio*) Sirrah, what say you?
DROMIO OF EPHESUS (*pointing to the Courtesan*)
Sir, he dined with her there, at the Porcupine.   275
COURTESAN
He did, and from my finger snatched that ring.
ANTIPHOLUS OF EPHESUS
'Tis true, my liege, this ring I had of her.

275 *pointing . . . Courksan*] OXFORD; *not in* F

268 Antipholus echoes Adriana's line at 209. All such accusations of falsehood will shortly be proven to be groundless.
269 **impeach** accusation, charge. This is the earliest occurrence of this particular sense cited in *OED*.
270 **Circe's cup** The enchantress Circe gave men a potion which turned them into swine in Homer's *Odyssey*, Book 10. The Duke merely means that they are all bewitched. The themes of metamorphosis and enchantment in the play reach their climax here.
272 **coldly** rationally

DUKE (*to Courtesan*)

  Saw'st thou him enter at the abbey here?

COURTESAN

  As sure, my liege, as I do see your grace.

DUKE

  Why, this is strange.—Go call the Abbess hither.   280
  I think you are all mated, or stark mad.

                    Exit one to the priory

EGEON (*coming forward*)

  Most mighty Duke, vouchsafe me speak a word.
  Haply I see a friend will save my life,
  And pay the sum that may deliver me.

DUKE

  Speak freely, Syracusan, what thou wilt.   285

EGEON (*to Antipholus*)

  Is not your name, sir, called Antipholus?
  And is not that your bondman Dromio?

DROMIO OF EPHESUS

  Within this hour I was his bondman, sir,
  But he, I thank him, gnawed in two my cords.
  Now am I Dromio, and his man, unbound.   290

EGEON

  I am sure you both of you remember me.

DROMIO OF EPHESUS

  Ourselves we do remember, sir, by you;
  For lately we were bound as you are now.
  You are not Pinch's patient, are you, sir?

EGEON

  Why look you strange on me? You know me well.   295

ANTIPHOLUS OF EPHESUS

  I never saw you in my life till now.

EGEON

  O, grief hath changed me since you saw me last,
  And careful hours with time's deformèd hand

281.1 *priory*] OXFORD; *Abbesse* F   282 *coming forward*] OXFORD; *not in* F   285, 327 Syracusan]
F2; *Siracusian* F1

281 **mated** confounded, amazed
283 **Haply** perhaps
288–90 **bondman . . . unbound** Dromio
  puns on his status as bond-slave to
  Antipholus, and their recent condition,

i.e. being 'bound', tied up. In the play
generally, Dromio of Ephesus is much less
given to punning than his twin.
298 **careful** literally, 'full of care'
  time's deformèd hand Like Father Time's

Have written strange defeatures in my face.
But tell me yet, dost thou not know my voice?   300
ANTIPHOLUS OF EPHESUS Neither.
EGEON Dromio, nor thou?
DROMIO OF EPHESUS No, trust me sir, nor I.
EGEON I am sure thou dost.
DROMIO OF EPHESUS Ay, sir, but I am sure I do not, and   305
     whatsoever a man denies, you are now bound to believe
     him.
EGEON
     Not know my voice? O time's extremity,
     Hast thou so cracked and splitted my poor tongue
     In seven short years that here my only son   310
     Knows not my feeble key of untuned cares?
     Though now this grainèd face of mine be hid
     In sap-consuming winter's drizzled snow,
     And all the conduits of my blood froze up,
     Yet hath my night of life some memory,   315
     My wasting lamps some fading glimmer left,
     My dull deaf ears a little use to hear.
     All these old witnesses, I cannot err,
     Tell me thou art my son Antipholus.

302–3] *as prose* F; *as verse* CAMBRIDGE

bald pate (2.2.70), an attribute of the chief agent of change and the mutability of nature, including human life, a central theme in the play as it is in all romance. Shakespeare went much further in *The Winter's Tale*, bringing Time on stage as Chorus in Act 4.
298 **deformèd** crooked, withered (as by age)
299 **defeatures** See note at 2.1.99.
301–7 As Foakes notes, the fact that 302–3 make up a regular verse line is probably accidental; this passage is clearly set as prose in F.
308–19 The emphasis on Egeon's age in this speech is part of the build-up to the 'rebirth' and beginning of a new life for him and his family. His 'old witnesses' of course do not err: this *is* Antipholus and Egeon's son. This is the final error of identity before the climactic moment of

discovery, the re-entry of the Abbess with the Syracusan Antipholus and Dromio at 330.
310 **seven short years** This does not, as some editors state, contradict Egeon's account of his travels in 1.1, where he says that he had left home five years earlier (l. 131). His son and Dromio had left home *before* that (123–30); he here specifies the time elapsed since that separation, and repeats it at 321–2.
311 **feeble . . . cares** the weak voice ('cracked and splitted') with which I speak my sorrows (the latter being likened by Egeon to unmelodious, harsh music)
312 **grainèd** lined, wrinkled
313 **sap-consuming . . . snow** i.e. his white beard
314 **conduits** veins
316 **lamps** eyes

ANTIPHOLUS OF EPHESUS

I never saw my father in my life.   320

EGEON

But seven years since, in Syracusa, boy,

Thou know'st we parted. But perhaps, my son,

Thou sham'st to acknowledge me in misery.

ANTIPHOLUS OF EPHESUS

The Duke, and all that know me in the city,

Can witness with me that it is not so.   325

I ne'er saw Syracusa in my life.

DUKE (*to Egeon*)

I tell thee, Syracusan, twenty years

Have I been patron to Antipholus,

During which time he ne'er saw Syracusa.

I see thy age and dangers make thee dote.   330

Enter ⌈from the priory⌉ the Abbess, with Antipholus of
Syracuse, and Dromio of Syracuse

ABBESS

Most mighty Duke, behold a man much wronged.

All gather to see them

ADRIANA

I see two husbands, or mine eyes deceive me.

DUKE

One of these men is *genius* to the other:

And so of these, which is the natural man,

And which the spirit? Who deciphers them?   335

DROMIO OF SYRACUSE

I, sir, am Dromio. Command him away.

DROMIO OF EPHESUS

I, sir, am Dromio. Pray let me stay.

---

321 Syracusa, boy] F (*subs.*); Syracusa bay ROWE, OXFORD   330.1 *from the priory*] OXFORD; *not
in* F

321 **But** only
    boy F is surely right: Egeon is understand-
    ably impatient at his son's infuriating
    refusal to recognize him. In the next line,
    he changes tack and tone.

333 *genius* Attendant or tutelary spirit
    believed in pagan antiquity to be identical
    to and to accompany a person through-
    out life. The word is italicized in F, as
    though it were foreign; it was known in

English, though still quite new in some of
its meanings, in Shakespeare's time.

334 **these** The Duke turns from the Antipho-
    lus twins ('these men') to the Dromios,
    who answer him in 336–7.

335 **deciphers** explains, interprets, or here,
    distinguishes. None of the definitions in
    OED seems quite to match the sense
    required here, and the example given of
    the nearest meaning (*v.* 3) postdates this.

ANTIPHOLUS OF SYRACUSE

Egeon, art thou not? Or else his ghost.

DROMIO OF SYRACUSE

O, my old master, who hath bound him here?

ABBESS

Whoever bound him, I will loose his bonds,   340
And gain a husband by his liberty.
Speak, old Egeon, if thou be'st the man
That hadst a wife once called Emilia,
That bore thee at a burden two fair sons.
O, if thou be'st the same Egeon, speak,   345
And speak unto the same Emilia.

DUKE

Why, here begins his morning story right:
These two Antipholus', these two so like,
And these two Dromios, one in semblance—
Besides his urging of her wreck at sea—   350
These are the parents to these children,
Which accidentally are met together.

EGEON

If I dream not, thou art Emilia.
If thou art she, tell me, where is that son
That floated with thee on the fatal raft?   355

347–52] *as in* F; *after l.* 362 CAPELL   350 his] COLLIER; her F

---

344 **at a burden** at one birth. The word *bur-den* is also used in this sense (*OED sb.* 4) at 1.1.55 and 5.1.404, a linguistic link, if only a slight one, between the beginning and the end of the play and of its romance plot.

347–52 Capell's transposition of the Duke's lines, recorded here because it was adopted (without acknowledgement) by Steevens, Malone and subsequent editors until Wilson, is intelligent. It allows Egeon to respond immediately to Emilia, without interrupting the heightened moment of recognition and its incantatory repetition of her name. The Duke's speech refers to the shipwreck which, though not 'urged' by Emilia, is elaborated upon by her in 356–62, and his addressing the wrong

Antipholus at 363 could logically follow 351–2 where he refers to the brothers' accidental meeting. But in F's arrangement of the lines, the Duke picks up quickly Emilia's reference to the twins, and recalling the beginning of Egeon's story in 1.1, makes the obvious connection. He is thinking aloud, leaping ahead to 'her wreck at sea' about which he had heard earlier in the day (Collier's emendation of 'her' to 'his' in 350 is thus defensible; 'their' might be preferable to the second 'her'). He triumphantly sums up the (correct) conclusion he has reached in 351–2, then falls victim to error, like all the others, in 363 as he attempts to resolve 'what became of them'.

ABBESS

By men of Epidamnus he and I
And the twin Dromio all were taken up.
But, by and by, rude fishermen of Corinth
By force took Dromio and my son from them,
And me they left with those of Epidamnus.   360
What then became of them I cannot tell;
I, to this fortune that you see me in.

DUKE *(to Antipholus of Syracuse)*

Antipholus, thou cam'st from Corinth first.

ANTIPHOLUS OF SYRACUSE

No, sir, not I. I came from Syracuse.

DUKE

Stay, stand apart. I know not which is which.   365

ANTIPHOLUS OF EPHESUS

I came from Corinth, my most gracious lord.

DROMIO OF EPHESUS And I with him.

ANTIPHOLUS OF EPHESUS

Brought to this town by that most famous warrior,
Duke Menaphon, your most renownèd uncle.

ADRIANA

Which of you two did dine with me today?   370

ANTIPHOLUS OF SYRACUSE I, gentle mistress.

ADRIANA And are not you my husband?

ANTIPHOLUS OF EPHESUS No, I say nay to that.

ANTIPHOLUS OF SYRACUSE

And so do I. Yet did she call me so;
And this fair gentlewoman, her sister here,   375
Did call me brother. *(To Luciana)* What I told you then

356, 360 Epidamnus] This edition; *Epidamium* F; Epidamnum POPE

356–60 Emilia's story does not exactly
match Egeon's in 1.1, but the discrepancy
is slight and goes unnoticed in performance. He had not mentioned the 'men
of Epidamnus' and their encounter with
Corinthian fishermen, but his 'as we
thought' (1.1.110) leaves room for uncertainty. The 'men of Epidamnus' here may
imperfectly recall the ship from Epidaurus
of 1.1.92; Theobald suggested emending
'Epidaurus' to 'Epidamnum' there, in the
light of the present passage. In any case,
the divergence of characters' recollection
of details of events long past is credible,

and the recollection itself only approxi-
mate, like the play's Mediterranean
geography.

369 **Duke Menaphon** A gratuitous allusion
to a person who is not in the play and
whose name is thus entirely inconsequen-
tial. The name was used by Marlowe in
Tamburlaine, Part One (c.1587) and by
Greene in his pastoral romance *Menaphon*
(1589).

376 **What . . . then** That is, in 3.2, when he
wooed her and she rejected him, thinking
him to be her sister's husband.

I hope I shall have leisure to make good,
If this be not a dream I see and hear.

ANGELO
That is the chain, sir, which you had of me.

ANTIPHOLUS OF SYRACUSE
I think it be, sir. I deny it not.   380

ANTIPHOLUS OF EPHESUS (*to Angelo*)
And you, sir, for this chain arrested me.

ANGELO
I think I did, sir. I deny it not.

ADRIANA (*to Antipholus of Ephesus*)
I sent you money, sir, to be your bail,
By Dromio, but I think he brought it not.

DROMIO OF EPHESUS No, none by me.   385

ANTIPHOLUS OF SYRACUSE (*to Adriana*)
This purse of ducats I received from you,
And Dromio my man did bring them me.
I see we still did meet each other's man,
And I was ta'en for him, and he for me,
And thereupon these errors are arose.   390

ANTIPHOLUS OF EPHESUS
These ducats pawn I for my father here.

DUKE
It shall not need. Thy father hath his life.

COURTESAN (*to Antipholus of Ephesus*)
Sir, I must have that diamond from you.

ANTIPHOLUS OF EPHESUS
There, take it, and much thanks for my good cheer.

ABBESS
Renownèd Duke, vouchsafe to take the pains   395
To go with us into the abbey here,
And hear at large discoursèd all our fortunes;
And all that are assembled in this place,
That by this sympathizèd one day's error

392 The Duke, who had imposed the sentence upon Egeon's life, now lifts it, as that tragicomic plot is resolved happily amid the various other resolutions.
393 **diamond** i.e. the ring of 4.3.68–9

399 **sympathizèd** 'compounded of corresponding parts or elements, complicated' (*OED*, citing this line); shared or undergone by all.

Have suffered wrong, go, keep us company,   400
And we shall make full satisfaction.
Thirty-three years have I but gone in travail
Of you, my sons, and till this present hour
My heavy burden ne'er deliverèd.
The Duke, my husband, and my children both,   405
And you the calendars of their nativity,
Go to a gossips' feast, and joy with me.
After so long grief, such felicity!

DUKE
With all my heart I'll gossip at this feast.
       Exeunt ⌈into the priory⌉ all but the two Dromios and two
                                        brothers Antipholus
DROMIO OF SYRACUSE (*to Antipholus of Ephesus*)
Master, shall I fetch your stuff from shipboard?   410

---

400 wrong, go] ROWE; wrong. Goe F   402 Thirty-three] F; Twenty-five THEOBALD   404
ne'er] DYCE; are F   406 nativity] F (Natiuity); maturity CLAYTON *conj.*   407 joy] RANN; go F
408 felicity] HANMER; nativity (Natiuitie) F; festivity DYCE (*conj.* Johnson)   409.1–2 *Exeunt
. . . Antipholus*] OXFORD (F *subs.*)

---

402 **Thirty-three years** The Abbess's statement has elicited much commentary. It is
one of many such imprecise or contradic-
tory temporal references in Shakespeare.
Perhaps the nativity theme in an explicitly Christian context, so pronounced
here at the play's end (whether or not F's
repetition at l. 408 is retained), and
appropriate to the Christmas season for
which the play was probably written,
suggested 'thirty-three' to Shakespeare:it
Christ was thirty-three years old when he
died. Theobald sensibly arrived at twenty-
five by adding eighteen (1.1.124) and
seven (5.1.310).
       gone in travail been in labour
404 **burden** i.e. her twin sons. See note to
l. 344 above.
406 **you . . . nativity** i.e. the Dromios, whose
birthdays are the same as those of
Emilia's own sons, and whose lives
record or mark exactly the dates of theirs.
407 **gossips' feast** celebration of a birth or
baptism. Here 'gossips' means godpar-
ents, or sponsors, family and close friends
invited to a baptism, rather than the
narrower (and later) sense of the female
friends and relations who attend a woman
during childbirth.
       joy rejoice. A common English verbal

form until the eighteenth century. The
syntax of the line leaves open the possible
reading of 'joy'—if the emendation is
accepted—as a noun, the second object of
the Abbess's invitation, 'Go . . .'. This
sense, of 'jubilant festivity', is well
attested (*OED sb.* 1c). The comma after
'feast' in F suggests the former reading,
however: a verb 'joy', for another, 'go'.
408 **felicity** Emended on the assumption that
the repetition of 'Nativity' (though with a
different spelling) is a mistake, authorial
or compositorial, an assumption that may
not be warranted, it must be admitted.
Nativity, or rebirth, is the theme and is
emphasized by the Abbess's speech which
closes the frame opened by Egeon's long,
dolorous tale in 1.1. It seems clumsy,
however, and both Johnson's and
Hanmer's emendations are thoughtful (as
is Clayton's conjecture at 406, previously
unrecorded by editors). 'Felicity' provides
stronger contrast to the 'so long grief' of
the first part of the line, and avoids the
near-repetition of 'feast' in the previous
line. Similar considerations support the
emendation of 'go' to 'joy' in 407.
410–13 A final instant of comic confusion is
allowed, now that everything is resolved.
This passage, and the recollection by

ANTIPHOLUS OF EPHESUS
  Dromio, what stuff of mine hast thou embarked?
DROMIO OF SYRACUSE
  Your goods that lay at host, sir, in the Centaur.
ANTIPHOLUS OF SYRACUSE
  He speaks to me.—I am your master, Dromio.
  Come, go with us. We'll look to that anon.
  Embrace thy brother there. Rejoice with him.   415
               Exeunt the brothers Antipholus ⌈*to the priory*⌉
DROMIO OF SYRACUSE
  There is a fat friend at your master's house,
  That kitchened me for you today at dinner.
  She now shall be my sister, not my wife.
DROMIO OF EPHESUS
  Methinks you are my glass and not my brother.
  I see by you I am a sweet-faced youth.   420
  Will you walk in to see their gossiping?
DROMIO OF SYRACUSE Not I, sir, you are my elder.
DROMIO OF EPHESUS That's a question. How shall we try it?
DROMIO OF SYRACUSE We'll draw cuts for the senior. Till
  then, lead thou first.   425
DROMIO OF EPHESUS Nay, then thus:
  We came into the world like brother and brother,
  And now let's go hand in hand, not one before another.
               Exeunt ⌈*to the priory*⌉

415.1 *Exeunt . . . priory*] This edition; *Exit* F   428.1 *Exeunt . . . priory*] OXFORD; *Exeunt.* F

Dromio of Syracuse of the 'fat friend' who
mistook him for his twin earlier in the
day (416–17), serve as a recapitulation,
recalling briefly, in a comic mode, the
massive confusion and sometimes ter-
rifying bewilderment of which everyone in the play has so recently been a
victim.

412 **at host** at the inn
417 **kitchened** entertained in the kitchen.
  OED cites only this line under the transi-
  tive verb form *to kitchen*.
419 **glass** mirror
424 **draw cuts for the senior** draw straws
  (cut to different lengths) to decide which
  of us is the elder

PROVERBIAL LANGUAGE IN *THE COMEDY OF ERRORS*

FURTHER confirmation that Shakespeare was composing at least partly in the romance vein in *The Comedy of Errors*, even while using Plautine drama for a good part of his plot material, is to be found in the relatively low frequency of proverbs and proverbial expressions, compared to other plays in the canon. This is a striking feature of the language of the late romances. A rough table based on R. W. Dent's tallies of proverbs in the plays reveals that only five of the seventeen comedies and romances, all of them much later than *Errors*, make less frequent use of proverbial language: *All's Well*, *Pericles*, *Cymbeline*, *The Winter's Tale*, *The Two Noble Kinsmen*. Only *The Tempest* among the late romances has a greater proportion.[1] Apart from *Errors* and *All's Well*, all of the other comedies, up to and including *Measure for Measure*, make more frequent use of such expressions. They occur on average once every twenty-eight lines or so in *Errors*, and once every fourteen (*Love's Labour's Lost*) to twenty-four or twenty-five lines (*Measure for Measure*, *The Tempest*) in the remaining eleven plays of the combined comedy-romance group. It is notable both that *Errors* stands well apart from the rest of the first ten comedies (up to *Twelfth Night*), and also that the plays statistically nearest to it in the table are the much later *Measure*, *All's Well*, and *The Tempest*.

The frequency in the five late comedies and romances named above which make less use of proverbial language ranges from about once every thirty lines in *All's Well* to once every forty-two lines or so in *Pericles* and *Cymbeline*, the two most nearly 'pure' romances in the canon; another in that category, *The Two Noble Kinsmen*, which is, admittedly, like *Pericles* a collaborative work, is close to these two with a figure of forty. Beyond the comedy-romance group, those nearest *Errors* in frequency are several early historical and tragical plays: *The First Part of the Contention* (*Henry VI*, Part 2), *The True Tragedy of Richard Duke of York* (*Henry VI*, Part 3), *Titus Andronicus* and *Richard III*. Significantly, all date from the period in Shakespeare's career immediately preceding the probable time of the composition of *Errors* in 1594.[2] Closest of all is *Richard III*, with the same frequency count, 1:27.8.

[1] R. W. Dent, *Shakespeare's Proverbial Language: An Index* (Berkeley, 1981), pp. 3–5. This evidence was first published in ' "Standing i' th' gaps": Telling and Showing from Egeon to Gower', p. 138 (Introduction, p. 46 n. 2).

[2] The one outstanding deviation, with by far the lowest frequency of proverb use in the canon, is *Henry VI*, Part 1, with a distribution of one only every fifty-two lines, although it is close in date and of the same or similar genre to those plays that are nearest *Errors* in frequency. This anomaly perhaps reflects the multiple authorship of *1 Henry VI*. The remaining plays with lower frequencies than *Errors* are *Julius*

Of particular note is the fact that no proverbs or proverbial expressions—according to Dent's definitions and indexes (and his exclusions from Tilley's lists)—occur in Act 1, Scene 1, or in Act 5, Scene 1, after Egeon's and the Duke's entrance at line 129. In other words, in the purely romance sections of the play, those dealing with the Egeon/Apollonius plot, which comprise a quarter of the whole work, the text is entirely free of proverbial language. This phenomenon places *Errors* in that respect with the late romances and *All's Well*, rather than with other comedies closer to it in time of composition: *The Two Gentlemen of Verona*, *The Taming of the Shrew*, *Love's Labour's Lost*, *A Midsummer Night's Dream* and *The Merchant of Venice* all have markedly greater frequencies of proverb occurrence.

TABLE OF FREQUENCY OF PROVERBS AND PROVERBIAL EXPRESSIONS IN THE SEVENTEEN COMEDIES AND ROMANCES

The following table, based on the entries for each play in Dent's index, lists the plays in *descending* order of concentration of proverbial language, expressed in terms of the average number of lines of text per occurrence of a proverbial expression; e.g. *Love's Labour's Lost* has the greatest frequency among the plays listed, with a proverbial expression every fourteen lines on average. The Oxford Shakespeare *Complete Works* was used for line counts.

Love's Labour's Lost	14.1
Twelfth Night	16.7
Much Ado About Nothing	18.2
The Merry Wives of Windsor	20.1
As You Like It	20.2
The Two Gentlemen of Verona	20.4
The Taming of the Shrew	21.1
A Midsummer Night's Dream	21.7
The Merchant of Venice	22.1
The Tempest	23.7
Measure for Measure	24.5
The Comedy of Errors	27.8
All's Well that Ends Well	29.8
The Winter's Tale	33.9
The Two Noble Kinsmen	40.1
Pericles	42.5
Cymbeline	42.8

Caesar, *Timon of Athens*, *Antony and Cleopatra* and *Coriolanus*. Romances and tragedies on classical subjects thus are the genres in which Shakespeare used the least proverb-laced language. The mean for all the plays is between twenty-three and twenty-four.

EXTRACTS FROM *GESTA GRAYORUM* (1688)

THE account of what took place at Gray's Inn on 28 December 1594, as described at the beginning of the Introduction to this edition, was not published until 1688. Its title-page ran thus:

Gesta Grayorum: | OR, THE | HISTORY | Of the High and mighty PRINCE, | HENRY | Prince of Purpoole, Arch-Duke of Stapulia and | Bernardia, Duke of High and Nether Holborn, | Marquis of St. Giles and Tottenham, Count | Palatine of Bloomsbury and Clerkenwell, Great | Lord of the Cantons of Islington, Kentish- | Town, Paddington and Knights-bridge, | Knight of the most Heroical Order of the | Helmet, and Sovereign of the Same; | Who Reigned and Died, A.D. 1594. | TOGETHER WITH | A Masque, as it was presented (by His Highness's Com- | mand) for the Entertainment of Q. ELIZABETH; | who, with the Nobles of both Courts, was present | thereat. | LONDON, Printed for W. Canning, at his Shop in | the Temple-Cloysters, MDCLXXXVIII. | Price, one Shilling.

In the following extract, spelling and punctuation are modernized from the edition by Desmond Bland, English Reprints Series (Liverpool, 1968). The extract begins on p. 29 of Bland's edition. Initial capitals are used copiously in the original; here they are reserved for proper names and titles only. The present editor's emendations and additions are enclosed in square brackets; bridging and explanatory comments are in italics. See Bland's edition for details of publication, a brief history of revels at the Inns of Court, and the remaining contents of the volume; the latter include the text of a *Masque of Proteus* by Francis Davison, an important transitional work between the earlier Tudor mummings and later Inns entertainments such as Francis Beaumont's *Masque of the Inner Temple and Gray's Inn* (1613), William Browne's *Masque of the Inner Temple* (1615), and Thomas Middleton's *Inner Temple Masque, or Masque of Heroes* (1619), as well as the lavish Jacobean and Caroline court masques of Ben Jonson, Inigo Jones and others.

A first 'Grand Evening' was held at Gray's Inn on 20 December 1594, when the elected 'Prince of Purpool', who was to preside over the Christmastide festivities of the Inn, was installed.

The next grand night was intended to be upon Innocents' Day [28 December] at night, at which time there was a great presence of lords, ladies, and worshipful personages, that did expect some notable performance at that time; which indeed had been effected, if the multitude of beholders had not been so exceeding great that thereby there was no convenient room for those that were actors. By reason whereof, very good inventions and conceits could not have opportunity to be applauded, which otherwise would have been great contentation to the beholders. Against which time, our friend the Inner Temple determined to send their Ambassador to our Prince of State, as sent from Frederick Templarius, their Emperor, who was then busied in his wars against the Turk. The Ambassador came very gallantly appointed, and attended by a great number of brave gentlemen, which arrived at our Court about nine of the clock at night. . . . He was received very kindly of the Prince, and placed in a chair besides His Highness, to the end that he might be partaker of the sports intended. But first, he made a speech to the Prince . . . [*the Ambassador from Templaria recalled the 'ancient league of amity and near kindness' between the two realms, and declared his pleasure at being present that evening to represent his master*] because our state of Graya did grace Templaria with the presence of an Ambassador about thirty years since, upon like occasion. . . .

When the Ambassador was placed as aforesaid, and that there was something to be performed for the delight of the beholders, there arose such a disordered tumult and crowd upon the stage that there was no opportunity to effect that which was intended. There came so great a number of worshipful personages upon the stage that might not be displaced, and gentlewomen, whose sex did privilege them from violence, that when the Prince and his officers had in vain a good while expected and endeavoured a reformation, at length there was no hope of redress for that present. The Lord Ambassador and his train thought that they were not so kindly entertained as was before expected, and thereupon would not stay any longer at that time, but [departed], in a sort discontented and displeased. After their departure, the throngs and tumults did somewhat cease, although so much of them continued as was able to disorder and confound any good inventions whatsoever. In regard whereof, as also for that the sports intended were especially for the gracing of the Templarians, it was thought good not to offer any thing of account, saving dancing and revelling with gentlewomen; and after such sports, a Comedy of Errors (like to Plautus his *Menaechmus*) was played by the players. So that night was begun, and continued to the end, in nothing but confusion and errors, whereupon it was ever afterwards called *The Night of Errors*.

This mischanced accident sorting so ill, to the great prejudice of the rest of our proceedings, was a great discouragement and disparagement to our whole state. Yet it gave occasion to the lawyers of the Prince's Council, the next night, after revels, to read a commission of Oyer and Terminer,[1]

---

[1] **commission of Oyer and Terminer** a writ or order, literally, 'to hear and determine' (from Fr.), issued to judges, sergeants at law, sometimes other persons of note, as commissioners, usually in cases of severe disturbance or insurrection. Those thus commissioned would constitute a special court to hear evidence and bring indictments in specific cases. Clearly a precise technical usage here, in the

directed to certain noblemen and lords of His Highness's Council, and others, that they should inquire or cause inquiry to be made of some of the great disorders and abuses lately done and committed with[in] His Highness's dominions of Purpool, especially by sorceries and enchantments, and namely, of a great witchcraft used the night before, whereby there were great disorders and misdemeanours, by hurly-burlies, crowds, errors, confusions, vain representations and shows, to the utter discredit of our state and policy.

The next night upon this occasion, we preferred judgements thick and threefold, which were read publicly by the Clerk of the Crown, being all against a sorcerer or conjurer that was supposed to be the cause of that confused inconvenience. Therein was contained how he had caused the stage to be built, and scaffolds to be reared to the top of the house, to increase expectation. Also how he had caused divers ladies and gentlewomen and others of good condition to be invited to our sports; also our dearest friend, the State of Templaria, to be disgraced, and disappointed of their kind entertainment deserved and intended. Also that he caused throngs and tumults, crowds and outrages, to disturb our whole proceedings. And lastly, that he had foisted a company of base and common fellows, to make up our disorders with a play of errors and confusions; and that that night had gained to us discredit, and itself a nickname of 'Errors'. All which were against the Crown and dignity of our Sovereign Lord, the Prince of Purpool.

Under colour of these proceedings were laid open to the view all the causes of note that were committed by our chiefest statesmen in the government of our principality, and every officer in any great place that had not performed his duty in that service was taxed hereby, from the highest to the lowest, not sparing the guard and porters, that suffered so many disordered persons to enter in at the court-gates. Upon whose aforesaid indictments, the prisoner was arraigned at the Bar, being brought thither by the Lieutenant of the Tower (for at that time the stocks were graced with that name), and the Sheriff impanelled a jury of twenty-four gentlemen that were to give their verdict upon the evidence given. The prisoner appealed to the Prince his Excellency for justice, and humbly desired that it would please His Highness to understand the truth of the matter by his supplication, which he had ready to be offered to the Master of the Requests, that he should read the petition, wherein was a disclosure of all the knavery and juggling of the Attorney and Solicitor, which had brought all this law-stuff on purpose to blind the eyes of His Excellency and all the honourable Court there, that those things which they all saw and perceived sensibly to be in very deed done and actually performed,

context of the 'great disorders and abuses lately done' during the 'Night of Errors' at the Inn.

were nothing else but vain illusions, fancies, dreams and enchantments, and to be wrought and compassed by the means of a poor harmless wretch that never had heard of such great matters in all his life. Whereas the very fault was in the negligence of the Prince's Council, lords and officers of his State, that had the rule of the roast,[2] and by whose advice the Commonwealth was so soundly misgoverned. To prove these things to be true, he brought divers instances of great absurdities committed by the greatest, and made such allegations as could not be denied. These were done by some that were touched by the Attorney and Solicitor in their former proceedings, and they used the prisoners' names for means of quittance with them in that behalf. But the Prince and Statesmen (being pinched on both sides, by both the parties) were not a little offended at the great liberty that they had taken in censuring so far of His Highness's government. And thereupon the prisoner was freed and pardoned; the Attorney, Solicitor, Master of the Requests, and those that were acquainted with the draught of the petition were all of them commanded to the Tower. So the Lieutenant took charge of them. And this was the end of our law-sports, concerning the Night of Errors.

When we were wearied with mocking thus at our own follies, at length there was a great consultation had for the recovery of our lost honour. [*Another entertainment is planned for the Templarians, on 3 January following.*]

On the 3rd of January at night, there was a most honourable presence of great and noble personages that came as invited to our Prince; as, namely, the Right Honourable the Lord Keeper, the Earls of Shrewsbury, Cumberland, Northumberland, Southampton, and Essex; the Lords Buckhurst, Windsor, Mountjoy, Sheffield, Compton, Rich, Burghley, Mounteagle, and the Lord Thomas Howard; Sir Thomas Heneage, Sir Robert Cecil, with a great number of knights, ladies and very worshipful personages, all which had convenient places, and very good entertainment, to their good liking and contentment.

When they were all thus placed and settled in very good order, the Prince came into the hall with his wonted State, and ascended his throne at the high end of the hall, under His Highness's arms; and after him came the Ambassador of Templaria . . . [*A masque of Amity was presented, with various legendary pairs of friends presenting offerings to the deity, who at first refused then graciously accepted that of the two friends Graius and Templarius.*]

Then the Arch-Flamen[3] did pronounce Graius and Templarius to be as true and perfect friends, and so familiarly united and linked with the

[2] **rule of the roast** precedence, authority (Tilley, R144). Specifically, to sit at the head of the table and to preside over the carving and serving of the meat. 'To rule the roost', as a cock in a henhouse, is a more modern variant.
[3] **Arch-Flamen** high priest

bond and league of sincere friendship and amity as ever were Theseus and Pirithous, Achilles and Patroclus[4] . . . , and therewithal did further divine that this love should be perpetual. And lastly, denounced an heavy curse on them that shall any way go about to break or weaken the same, and an happiness to them that study and labour to eternize it for ever. So with sweet and pleasant melody, the curtain was drawn, as it was at the first.

Thus was this show ended, which was devised to that end, that those that were present might understand that the unkindness which was growing betwixt the Templarians and us, by reason of the former Night of Errors, and the uncivil behaviour wherewith they were entertained, as I before have partly touched, was now clean rooted out and forgotten, and that we now were more firm friends and kind lovers than ever before we had been, contrary to the evil reports that some enviers of our happiness had sown abroad . . .

[4] Both of these pairs of legendary friends appear in later plays by Shakespeare: Theseus and Pirithous in *The Two Noble Kinsmen*, Achilles and Patroclus in *Troilus and Cressida*.

PLAUTUS, *MENAECHMI*, TRANSLATED BY WILLIAM WARNER (1595)

THE following modernized text of Warner's *Menaechmi* is based on the quarto of 1595, collated with the old-spelling text in Geoffrey Bullough's *Narrative and Dramatic Sources of Shakespeare*, vol. i (1957), 12–39, and the modern-spelling texts in Harry Levin's Signet (1965) and David Bevington's Bantam Shakespeare (1980) editions of *The Comedy of Errors*; the present text is particularly indebted to that in Bevington's edition. The Loeb Classics text of Plautus' *Menaechmi* has also been consulted. Punctuation and stage directions are emended in accordance with the principles of the Oxford Shakespeare series, as for the text of *The Comedy of Errors*. No textual apparatus is provided. Corrections of obvious errors in the quarto have been made silently; these are in some cases adopted from Bevington. Stage directions not in the quarto are mostly from Bevington's edition, frequently with modifications. In a few instances, uncertainty is indicated by broken brackets. Glosses and annotations have been kept to a minimum. See Introduction, pp. 23–5, for a discussion of the possible connections between Shakespeare's play and Warner's translation. Readers familiar with *The Comedy of Errors* will immediately recognize comparable scenes and incidents, as well as the many differences, in the two works.

The names of some characters in *Menaechmi* are those of stock 'types' in Roman comedy, rather than individual names: 'Senex' means 'old man', 'Mulier' means 'wife', 'Ancilla' means 'maid', 'Medicus' means 'doctor', etc. One or two names are more specific, e.g. 'Cylindrus', meaning in Latin a round or cylindrically shaped stone used for levelling or rolling, hence, among other things, a rolling pin, appropriate for a cook. See the note on the name 'Peniculus'.

Menaechmi

Translated by William Warner (1595)

THE PERSONS OF THE PLAY

MENAECHMUS THE CITIZEN, *a gentleman residing in Epidamnum*
MENAECHMUS THE TRAVELLER, *his twin, also called Sosicles, from Syracuse*
MESSENIO, *slave of Menaechmus the Traveller*
PENICULUS, *parasite attached to Menaechmus the Citizen*
MULIER, *wife of Menaechmus the Citizen*
EROTIUM, *a courtesan*
CYLINDRUS, *her cook*
ANCILLA, *her maid*
SENEX, *Mulier's father*
MEDICUS, *a doctor*
SAILORS
Boy (Vecio)

The Argument

Two twinborn sons a Sicil merchant had,
   Menaechmus one and Sosicles the other.
The first his father lost a little lad;
   The grandsire named the latter like his brother.
This, grown a man, long travel took to seek   5
   His brother, and to Epidamnum came
Where th'other dwelt enriched, and him so like
   That citizens there take him for the same.
Father, wife, neighbours each mistaking either,
Much pleasant error ere they meet together.   10

I.I   *Enter Peniculus, a parasite*

PENICULUS Peniculus was given me for my name when I was young,
because like a broom I swept all clean away wheresoe'er I be come,
namely, all the victuals which are set before me. Now, in my judgement men that clap iron bolts on such captives as they would keep
safe and tie those servants in chains who they think will run away,   5

I.I.O.I *Peniculus* L., literally 'little penis'; also, tail, sponge or brush.

they commit an exceeding great folly. My reason is, these poor wretches enduring one misery upon another never cease devising how, by wrenching asunder their gyves or by some subtlety or other, they may escape such cursed bonds. If then ye would keep a man without all suspicion of running away from ye, the surest way is to tie him with meat, drink, and ease; let him ever be idle, eat his bellyful, and carouse while his skin will hold, and he shall never, I warrant ye, stir a foot. These strings to tie one by the teeth pass all the bonds of iron, steel, or what metal soever, for the more slack and easy ye make them, the faster still they tie the party which is in them. I speak this upon experience of myself, who am now going for Menaechmus, there willingly to be tied to his good cheer. He is commonly so exceeding bountiful and liberal in his fare, as no marvel though such guests as myself be drawn to his table and tied there in his dishes. Now, because I have lately been a stranger there, I mean to visit him at dinner, for my stomach methinks even thrusts me into the fetters of his dainty fare. But yonder I see his door open and himself ready to come forth.

I.2   *Enter Menaechmus ⌈the Citizen⌉ from his house, talking back*
             to his wife within

MENAECHMUS THE CITIZEN If ye were not such a brabbling fool and madbrain scold as ye are, ye would never thus cross your husband in all his actions! (*To himself*) 'Tis no matter. Let her serve me thus once more, I'll send her home to her dad with a vengeance. I can never go forth a-doors but she asketh me whither I go, what I do, what business, what I fetch, what I carry, as though she were a constable or a toll-gatherer. I have pampered her too much. She hath servants about her, wool, flax, and all things necessary to busy her withal, yet she watcheth and wondereth whither I go. Well, sith it is so, she shall now have some cause. I mean to dine this day abroad with a sweet friend of mine.

PENICULUS (*aside*) Yea, marry, now comes he to the point that pricks me. This last speech galls me as much as it would do his wife. If he dine not at home, I am dressed.

MENAECHMUS THE CITIZEN (*to himself*) We that have loves abroad and wives at home are miserably hampered. Yet, would every man could tame his shrew as well as I do mine! I have now

---

8 **gyves** fetters, chains   10 **sith** since
1.2.1 **brabbling** quarrelsome   15 **dressed** done for

filched away a fine riding cloak of my wife's which I mean to
bestow upon one that I love better. Nay, if she be so wary and   20
watchful over me, I count it an alms deed to deceive her.
PENICULUS Come, what share have I in that same?
MENAECHMUS THE CITIZEN Out, alas, I am taken.
PENICULUS True, but by your friend.
MENAECHMUS THE CITIZEN What, mine own Peniculus?   25
PENICULUS Yours, i' faith, body and goods—if I had any.
MENAECHMUS THE CITIZEN Why, thou hast a body.
PENICULUS Yea, but neither goods nor good body.
MENAECHMUS THE CITIZEN Thou couldst never come fitter in all thy
life.   30
PENICULUS Tush, I ever do so to my friends. I know how to come
always in the nick. Where dine ye today?
MENAECHMUS THE CITIZEN I'll tell thee of a notable prank.
PENICULUS What, did the cook mar your meat in the dressing?
Would I might see the reversion.   35
MENAECHMUS THE CITIZEN Tell me, didst thou see a picture how
Jupiter's eagle snatched away Ganymede, or how Venus stole
away Adonis?
PENICULUS Often, but what care I for shadows? I want substance.
MENAECHMUS THE CITIZEN (*showing the cloak he has concealed*) Look   40
thee here. Look not I like such a picture?
PENICULUS Oho, what cloak have ye got here?
MENAECHMUS THE CITIZEN Prithee, say I am now a brave fellow.
PENICULUS But hark ye, where shall we dine?
MENAECHMUS THE CITIZEN Tush, say as I bid thee, man.   45
PENICULUS Out of doubt ye are a fine man.
MENAECHMUS THE CITIZEN What? Canst add nothing of thine own?
PENICULUS Ye are a most pleasant gentleman.
MENAECHMUS THE CITIZEN On, yet.
PENICULUS Nay, not a word more, unless ye tell me how you and   50
your wife be fallen out.
MENAECHMUS THE CITIZEN Nay, I have a greater secret than that to
impart to thee.
PENICULUS Say your mind.
MENAECHMUS THE CITIZEN Come farther this way from my house.   55
PENICULUS So, let me hear.
MENAECHMUS THE CITIZEN Nay, farther yet.
PENICULUS I warrant ye, man.
MENAECHMUS THE CITIZEN Nay, yet farther.

21 **alms deed** act of charity   35 **reversion** leftovers

PENICULUS 'Tis pity ye were not made a waterman, to row in a 60
wherry.

MENAECHMUS THE CITIZEN Why?

PENICULUS Because ye go one way and look another still, lest your
wife should follow ye. But what's the matter, is't not almost
dinner-time? 65

MENAECHMUS THE CITIZEN Seest thou this cloak?

PENICULUS Not yet. Well, what of it?

MENAECHMUS THE CITIZEN This same I mean to give to Erotium.

PENICULUS That's well, but what of all this?

MENAECHMUS THE CITIZEN There I mean to have a delicious dinner 70
prepared for her and me.

PENICULUS And me?

MENAECHMUS THE CITIZEN And thee.

PENICULUS O sweet word! What, shall I knock presently at her
door? 75

MENAECHMUS THE CITIZEN Ay, knock. But stay too, Peniculus, let's
not be too rash. O, see, she is in good time coming forth.

PENICULUS Ah, he now looks against the sun. How her beams
dazzle his eyes!

Enter Erotium [from her house]

EROTIUM What, mine own Menaechmus? Welcome, sweetheart. 80

PENICULUS And what, am I welcome too?

EROTIUM You, sir? Ye are out of the number of my welcome
guests.

PENICULUS I am like a voluntary soldier—out of pay.

MENAECHMUS THE CITIZEN Erotium, I have determined that here 85
shall be pitched a field this day. We mean to drink, for the heavens, and which of us performs the bravest service at his
weapon—the wine bowl—yourself as captain shall pay him his
wages according to his deserts.

EROTIUM Agreed. 90

PENICULUS I would we had the weapons, for my valour pricks me to
the battle.

MENAECHMUS THE CITIZEN Shall I tell thee, sweet mouse? I never
look upon thee but I am quite out of love with my wife.

EROTIUM Yet ye cannot choose but ye must still wear something of 95
hers. What's this same?

MENAECHMUS THE CITIZEN This? Such a spoil, sweetheart, as I took
from her to put on thee.

---

61 **wherry** taxi-boat
78 **against** toward
86 **field** i.e. of battle

93 **mouse** (a term of affection)
97 **spoil** prize

EROTIUM Mine own Menaechmus, well worthy to be my dear, of
all dearest!   100

PENICULUS (*aside*) Now she shows herself in her likeness: when she
finds him in the giving vein, she draws close to him.

MENAECHMUS THE CITIZEN I think Hercules got not the garter from
Hippolyta so hardly as I got this from my wife. Take this, and
with the same take my heart.   105
    ⌈*He gives her the cloak*⌉

PENICULUS Thus they must do that are right lovers—(*aside*) especially if they mean to be beggars with any speed.

MENAECHMUS THE CITIZEN I bought this same of late for my wife. It
stood me, I think, in some ten pound.

PENICULUS (*aside*) There's ten pound bestowed very thriftily.   110

MENAECHMUS THE CITIZEN But know ye what I would have ye do?

EROTIUM It shall be done. Your dinner shall be ready.

MENAECHMUS THE CITIZEN Let a good dinner be made for us three.
Hark ye: some oysters, a marrowbone pie or two, some arti-
chokes, and potato roots; let our other dishes be as you please.   115

EROTIUM You shall, sir.

MENAECHMUS THE CITIZEN I have a little business in this city; by
that time dinner will be prepared. Farewell till then, sweet
Erotium. Come, Peniculus.

PENICULUS Nay, I mean to follow ye. I will sooner lose my life than   120
sight of you till this dinner be done.
                Exeunt ⌈*Menaechmus and Peniculus*⌉

EROTIUM (*calling into her house*) Who's there? Call me Cylindrus
the cook hither.
    Enter Cylindrus
Cylindrus, take the handbasket, and here, there's ten shillings,
is there not?   125

CYLINDRUS 'Tis so, mistress.

EROTIUM Buy me of all the daintiest meats ye can get—ye know
what I mean—so as three may dine passing well and yet no
more than enough.

CYLINDRUS What guests have ye today, mistress?   130

EROTIUM Here will be Menaechmus and his parasite, and myself.

CYLINDRUS That's ten persons in all.

EROTIUM How many?

CYLINDRUS Ten, for I warrant you that parasite may stand for eight
at his victuals.   135

103–4 **Hercules . . . this** it was as difficult for
me to get this cloak as it was for Hercules
to get the girdle of Hippolyta (one of his
twelve labours)

107 **speed** success
109 **stood . . . in** cost me

EROTIUM Go, dispatch as I bid you, and look ye return with all speed.

CYLINDRUS I will have all ready with a trice.   *Exeunt*

2.1   *Enter Menaechmus ⸤the Traveller⸥, Messenio his slave, and*
        some sailors

MENAECHMUS THE TRAVELLER Surely, Messenio, I think seafarers never take so comfortable a joy in anything as, when they have been long tossed and turmoiled in the wide seas, they hap at last to ken land.

MESSENIO I'll be sworn, I should not be gladder to see a whole   5
country of mine own than I have been at such a sight. But, I pray, wherefore are we now come to Epidamnum? Must we needs go to see every town that we hear of?

MENAECHMUS THE TRAVELLER Till I find my brother, all towns are alike to me. I must try in all places.   10

MESSENIO Why, then, let's even as long as we live seek your brother. Six years now have we roamed about thus—Istria, Hispania, Massilia, Illyria, all the Upper Sea, all high Greece, all haven towns in Italy. I think if we had sought a needle all this time we must needs have found it, had it been above   15
ground. It cannot be that he is alive; and to seek a dead man thus among the living, what folly is it?

MENAECHMUS THE TRAVELLER Yea, could I but once find any man that could certainly inform me of his death, I were satisfied. Otherwise I can never desist seeking. Little knowest thou,   20
Messenio, how near my heart it goes.

MESSENIO This is washing of a blackamoor. Faith, let's go home, unless ye mean we should write a story of our travel.

MENAECHMUS THE TRAVELLER Sirrah, no more of these saucy speeches. I perceive I must teach ye how to serve me, not to rule   25
me.

MESSENIO Ay, so, now it appears what it is to be a servant. Well, yet I must speak my conscience. Do ye hear, sir? Faith, I must tell ye one thing: when I look into the lean estate of your purse and consider advisedly of your decaying stock, I hold it very   30
needful to be drawing homeward, lest in looking your brother we quite lose ourselves. For, this assure yourself: this town Epidamnum is a place of outrageous expenses, exceeding in all

---

138 **with a trice** in a twinkling   22 **washing . . . blackamoor** trying to make
2.1.4 **ken** catch sight of   a black man white, i.e. performing an
14 **haven** port   impossible task

194

riot and lasciviousness and, I hear, as full of ribalds, parasites,
drunkards, catchpoles, coneycatchers, and sycophants as it can   35
hold. Then, for courtesans, why, here's the currentest stamp of
them in the world. Ye must not think here to scape with as light
cost as in other places. The very name shows the nature: no
man comes here *sine damno*.

MENAECHMUS THE TRAVELLER Ye say very well indeed. Give me my   40
purse into mine own keeping, because I will so be the safer, *sine
damno*.

MESSENIO Why, sir?

MENAECHMUS THE TRAVELLER Because I fear you will be busy
among the courtesans and so be cozened of it. Then should I   45
take great pains in belabouring your shoulders. So, to avoid
both these harms, I'll keep it myself.

MESSENIO I pray do so, sir. All the better.

    Enter Cylindrus ⌈with a handbasket⌉

CYLINDRUS (*to himself*) I have tickling gear here, i'faith, for their
dinners. It grieves me to the heart to think how that cormorant   50
knave Peniculus must have his share in these dainty morsels.
But what? Is Menaechmus come already, before I could come
from the market?—Menaechmus, how do ye, sir? How haps it
ye come so soon?

MENAECHMUS THE TRAVELLER God-a-mercy, my good friend, dost   55
thou know me?

CYLINDRUS Know ye? No, not I. Where's Mouldychaps that must
dine with ye? A murrain on his manners!

MENAECHMUS THE TRAVELLER Whom meanest thou, good fellow?

CYLINDRUS Why, Peniculus, worship, that whoreson lick-   60
trencher, your parasitical attendant.

MENAECHMUS THE TRAVELLER What Peniculus? What attendant?
My attendant?— (*aside*) Surely this fellow is mad.

MESSENIO Did I not tell ye what coneycatching villains ye should
find here?   65

CYLINDRUS Menaechmus, hark ye, sir: ye come too soon back
again to dinner. I am but returned from the market.

MENAECHMUS THE TRAVELLER Fellow, here, thou shalt have money
of me. Go, get the priest to sacrifice for thee. I know thou art
mad, else thou wouldst never use a stranger thus.   70

---

34 **ribalds** vulgar persons
35 **catchpoles** (term of contempt for minor law officers)
  coneycatchers petty criminals, swindlers
39 *sine damno* L., 'without being damned' (a play on 'Epidamnum').
49 **tickling gear** excellent food
58 **murrain** plague
60-1 **whoreson lick-trencher** damned glutton (trencher = dish)

CYLINDRUS Alas, sir, Cylindrus was wont to be no stranger to you. Know ye not Cylindrus?

MENAECHMUS THE TRAVELLER Cylindrus or Coliendrus or what the devil thou art I know not; neither do I care to know.

CYLINDRUS I know you to be Menaechmus. 75

MENAECHMUS THE TRAVELLER Thou shouldst be in thy wits, in that thou namest me so right. But tell me, where hast thou known me?

CYLINDRUS Where? Even here, where ye first fell in love with my mistress, Erotium. 80

MENAECHMUS THE TRAVELLER I neither have lover, neither know I who thou art.

CYLINDRUS Know ye not who I am? Who fills your cup and dresses your meat at our house?

MESSENIO What a slave is this? That I had somewhat to break the 85
rascal's pate withal!

MENAECHMUS THE TRAVELLER At your house, whenas I never came in Epidamnum till this day?

CYLINDRUS O, that's true. (*Pointing to the house of Menaechmus the Citizen*) Do ye not dwell in yonder house? 90

MENAECHMUS THE TRAVELLER Foul shame light upon them that dwell there, for my part!

CYLINDRUS (*aside*) Questionless he is mad indeed, to curse himself thus.—Hark ye, Menaechmus.

MENAECHMUS THE TRAVELLER What sayst thou? 95

CYLINDRUS If I may advise ye, ye shall bestow this money which ye offered me upon a sacrifice for yourself, for out of doubt you are mad that curse yourself.

MESSENIO What a varlet art thou to trouble us thus?

CYLINDRUS (*aside*) Tush, he will many times jest with me thus. Yet, 100
when his wife is not by, 'tis a ridiculous jest.

MENAECHMUS THE TRAVELLER What's that?

CYLINDRUS This I say: think ye I have brought meat enough for three of you? If not, I'll fetch more for you and your wench, and Snatchcrust your parasite. 105

MENAECHMUS THE TRAVELLER What wenches? What parasites?

MESSENIO Villain, I'll make thee tell me what thou meanest by all this talk!

CYLINDRUS Away, jackanapes! I say nothing to thee, for I know thee not. I speak to him that I know. 110

---

73 **Coliendrus** Possibly a (weak) pun by
Menaechmus: *coleus* means 'testicle'.

99 **varlet** knave
109 **jackanapes** monkey, fool

MENAECHMUS THE TRAVELLER Out, drunken fool! Without doubt thou art out of thy wits.

CYLINDRUS That you shall see by the dressing of your meat. Go, go, ye were better to go in and find somewhat to do there whiles your dinner is making ready. I'll tell my mistress ye be here. 115

⌈*Exit to the courtesan's*⌉

MENAECHMUS THE TRAVELLER Is he gone? Messenio, I think upon thy words already.

MESSENIO Tush, mark, I pray. I'll lay forty pound here dwells some courtesan to whom this fellow belongs.

MENAECHMUS THE TRAVELLER But I wonder how he knows my name. 120

MESSENIO O, I'll tell ye. These courtesans, as soon as any strange ship arriveth at the haven, they send a boy or a wench to enquire what they be, what their names be, whence they come, wherefore they come, etc. If they can by any means strike 125 acquaintance with him, or allure him to their houses, he is their own. We are here in a tickle place, master; 'tis best to be circumspect.

MENAECHMUS THE TRAVELLER I mislike not thy counsels, Messenio.

MESSENIO Ay, but follow it, then. Soft, here comes somebody forth. 130 (*To the sailors, giving them money*) Here, sirs, mariners, keep this same amongst you.

Enter Erotium ⌈*from her house*⌉

EROTIUM (*calling within*) Let the door stand so. Away, it shall not be shut. Make haste within there, ho! Maids, look that all things be ready. Cover the board, put fire under the perfuming pans, let all 135 things be very handsome. Where is he that Cylindrus said stood without here?—O, what mean you, sweetheart, that ye come not in? I trust you think yourself more welcome to this house than to your own, and great reason why you should do so. Your dinner and all things are ready as you willed. Will ye go sit 140 down?

MENAECHMUS THE TRAVELLER Whom doth this woman speak to?

EROTIUM Even to you, sir. To whom else should I speak?

MENAECHMUS THE TRAVELLER Gentlewoman, ye are a stranger to me, and I marvel at your speeches. 145

EROTIUM Yea, sir, but such a stranger as I acknowledge ye for my best and dearest friend, and well you have deserved it.

MENAECHMUS THE TRAVELLER Surely, Messenio, this woman is also mad or drunk, that useth all this kindness to me upon so small acquaintance. 150

118 **lay** wager   135 **Cover . . . board** set the table

MESSENIO Tush, did not I tell ye right? These be but leaves which
fall upon you now in comparison of the trees that will tumble on
your neck shortly. I told ye here were silver-tongued hacksters.
But let me talk with her a little.—Gentlewoman, what acquaintance have you with this man? Where have you seen him?   155

EROTIUM Where he saw me, here in Epidamnum.

MESSENIO In Epidamnum? Who never till this day set his foot within the town?

EROTIUM Go, go, flouting jack.—Menaechmus, what need all this?
I pray, go in.   160

MENAECHMUS THE TRAVELLER She also calls me by my name.

MESSENIO She smells your purse.

MENAECHMUS THE TRAVELLER Messenio, come hither. Here, take
my purse. (*Giving him his purse*) I'll know whether she aim at me
or my purse ere I go.   165

EROTIUM Will ye go in to dinner, sir?

MENAECHMUS THE TRAVELLER A good motion. Yea, and thanks with
all my heart.

EROTIUM Never thank me for that which you commanded to be
provided for yourself.   170

MENAECHMUS THE TRAVELLER That I commanded?

EROTIUM Yea, for you and your parasite.

MENAECHMUS THE TRAVELLER My parasite?

EROTIUM Peniculus, who came with you this morning when you
brought me the cloak which you got from your wife.   175

MENAECHMUS THE TRAVELLER A cloak that I brought you which I
got from my wife?

EROTIUM Tush, what needeth all this jesting? Pray, leave off.

MENAECHMUS THE TRAVELLER Jest or earnest, this I tell ye for a
truth: I never had wife, neither have I nor never was in this   180
place till this instant. For only thus far am I come since I broke
my fast in the ship.

EROTIUM What ship do ye tell me of?

MESSENIO Marry, I'll tell ye: an old rotten weather-beaten ship
that we have sailed up and down in this six years. Is't not time to   185
be going homewards, think ye?

EROTIUM Come, come, Menaechmus, I pray, leave this sporting
and go in.

MENAECHMUS THE TRAVELLER Well, gentlewoman, the truth is you
mistake my person. It is some other that you look for.   190

EROTIUM Why, think ye I know ye not to be Menaechmus, the son
of Moschus, and have heard ye say ye were born at Syracuse,

---

153 **hacksters** prostitutes   159 **flouting jack** insolent fellow

where Agathocles did reign, then Pythia, then Liparo, and now
Hiero?

MENAECHMUS THE TRAVELLER All this is true.   195

MESSENIO Either she is a witch, or else she hath dwelt there and
knew ye there.

MENAECHMUS THE TRAVELLER I'll go in with her, Messenio; I'll see
further of this matter.

MESSENIO Ye are cast away, then.   200

MENAECHMUS THE TRAVELLER Why so? I warrant thee I can lose
nothing. Somewhat I shall gain—perhaps a good lodging during my abode here. I'll dissemble with her another while.—
Now, when you please, let us go in. I made strange with you
because of this fellow here, lest he should tell my wife of the   205
cloak which I gave you.

EROTIUM Will ye stay any longer for your Peniculus, your
parasite?

MENAECHMUS THE TRAVELLER Not I. I'll neither stay for him nor
have him let in if he do come.   210

EROTIUM All the better. But sir, will ye do one thing for me?

MENAECHMUS THE TRAVELLER What is that?

EROTIUM To bear that cloak which you gave me to the dyer's to
have it new trimmed and altered.

MENAECHMUS THE TRAVELLER Yea, that will be well, so my wife shall   215
not know it. Let me have it with me after dinner. I will but speak
a word or two with this fellow and then I'll follow ye in.
⌜*Exit Erotium*⌝
Ho, Messenio, come aside. Go and provide for thyself and these
shipboys in some inn, then look that after dinner you come
hither for me.   220

MESSENIO Ah, master, will ye be coneycatched thus wilfully?

MENAECHMUS THE TRAVELLER Peace, foolish knave. Seest thou not
what a sot she is? I shall cozen her, I warrant thee.

MESSENIO Ay, master.

MENAECHMUS THE TRAVELLER Wilt thou be gone?   225
⌜*Exit to the courtesan's*⌝

MESSENIO See, see, she hath him safe enough now. Thus he hath
escaped a hundred pirates' hands at sea, and now one land-
rover hath boarded him at first encounter.—Come away,
fellows.   ⌜*Exeunt*⌝

3.1   *Enter Peniculus*

PENICULUS Twenty years, I think, and more have I played the
knave, yet never played I the foolish knave as I have done this

morning. I follow Menaechmus, and he goes to the hall where
now the sessions are holden. There thrusting ourselves into the
press of people, when I was in the midst of all the throng he gave   5
me the slip, that I could nevermore set eye on him, and, I dare
swear, came directly to dinner. That I would he that first devised
these sessions were hanged, and all that ever came of him! 'Tis
such a hindrance to men that have belly business in hand. If a
man be not there at his call, they amerce him with a vengeance.   10
Men that have nothing else to do, that do neither bid any man
nor are themselves bidden to dinner, such should come to
sessions, not we that have these matters to look to. If it were so,
I had not thus lost my dinner this day, which I think in my
conscience he did even purposely cozen me of. Yet I mean to go   15
see. If I can but light upon the reversion, I may perhaps get my
pennyworth's. But how now? Is this Menaechmus coming
away from thence? Dinner done, and all dispatched? What
execrable luck have I!

> *Enter Menaechmus the Traveller ⌈from the courtesan's,*
> *carrying a cloak⌉*

MENAECHMUS THE TRAVELLER (*calling back into the courtesan's house*)
　Tush, I warrant ye, it shall be done as ye would wish. I'll have it   20
　so altered and trimmed new that it shall by no means be known
　again.
PENICULUS (*aside*) He carries the cloak to the dyer's, dinner done,
　the wine drunk up, the parasite shut out-of-doors. Well, let me
　live no longer but I'll revenge this injurious mockery. But first   25
　I'll hearken awhile what he saith.
MENAECHMUS THE TRAVELLER Good gods, whoever had such luck as
　I? Such cheer, such a dinner, such kind entertainment! And, for
　a farewell, this cloak, which I mean shall go with me.
PENICULUS (*aside*) He speaks so softly I cannot hear what he saith. I   30
　am sure he is now flouting at me for the loss of my dinner.
MENAECHMUS THE TRAVELLER She tells me how I gave it her and
　stole it from my wife. When I perceived she was in an error,
　though I know not how, I began to soothe her and to say every-
　thing as she said. Meanwhile I fared well, and that a' free cost.   35
PENICULUS (*aside*) Well, I'll go talk with him.
MENAECHMUS THE TRAVELLER Who is this same that comes to me?
PENICULUS O, well met, ficklebrain, false and treacherous dealer,
　crafty and unjust promise-breaker! How have I deserved you

3.1.4 **sessions** i.e. of the law courts　　　　34 **soothe** agree with
　10 **amerce** fine

should so give me the slip, come before and dispatch the dinner, 40
deal so badly with him that hath reverenced ye like a son?

MENAECHMUS THE TRAVELLER Good fellow, what meanest thou by
these speeches? Rail not on me, unless thou intend'st to receive
a railer's hire.

PENICULUS I have received the injury, sure I am, already. 45

MENAECHMUS THE TRAVELLER Prithee, tell me, what is thy name?

PENICULUS Well, well, mock on, sir, mock on. Do ye not know my
name?

MENAECHMUS THE TRAVELLER In troth, I never saw thee in all my
life, much less do I know thee. 50

PENICULUS Fie, awake, Menaechmus, awake! Ye oversleep yourself.

MENAECHMUS THE TRAVELLER I am awake. I know what I say.

PENICULUS Know you not Peniculus?

MENAECHMUS THE TRAVELLER Peniculus or Pediculus, I know thee 55
not.

PENICULUS Did ye filch a cloak from your wife this morning and
bring it hither to Erotium?

MENAECHMUS THE TRAVELLER Neither have I wife, neither gave I
any cloak to Erotium, neither filched I any from anybody. 60

PENICULUS Will ye deny that which you did in my company?

MENAECHMUS THE TRAVELLER Wilt thou say I have done this in thy
company?

PENICULUS Will I say it? Yea, I will stand to it.

MENAECHMUS THE TRAVELLER Away, filthy mad drivel, away! I will 65
talk no longer with thee.

PENICULUS (*aside*) Not a world of men shall stay me but I'll go tell
his wife of all the whole matter, sith he is at this point with me.
I will make this same as unblessed a dinner as ever he ate.
⌈*Exit*⌉

MENAECHMUS THE TRAVELLER It makes me wonder to see how 70
everyone that meets me cavils thus with me. Wherefore comes
forth the maid, now?

Enter Ancilla, Erotium's maid

ANCILLA (*offering a gold chain*) Menaechmus, my mistress
commends her heartily to you, and, seeing you go that way to
the dyer's, she also desireth you to take this chain with you and 75
put it to mending at the goldsmith's. She would have two or
three ounces of gold more in it and the fashion amended.

44 **hire** payment   71 **cavils** argues, disputes
55 **Pediculus** L., 'little foot', also 'flea'.

MENAECHMUS THE TRAVELLER (*taking the chain*) Either this or anything else within my power, tell her, I am ready to accomplish.

ANCILLA Do ye know this chain, sir? 80

MENAECHMUS THE TRAVELLER Yea, I know it to be gold.

ANCILLA This is the same you once took out of your wife's casket.

MENAECHMUS THE TRAVELLER Who? Did I?

ANCILLA Have you forgotten?

MENAECHMUS THE TRAVELLER I never did it. 85

ANCILLA Give it me again, then.

MENAECHMUS THE TRAVELLER Tarry. Yes, I remember it. 'Tis it I
gave your mistress.

ANCILLA O, are ye advised?

MENAECHMUS THE TRAVELLER Where are the bracelets that I gave 90
her likewise?

ANCILLA I never knew of any.

MENAECHMUS THE TRAVELLER Faith, when I gave this, I gave them
too.

ANCILLA Well, sir, I'll tell her this shall be done. 95

MENAECHMUS THE TRAVELLER Ay, ay, tell her so. She shall have the
cloak and this both together.

ANCILLA I pray, Menaechmus, put a little jewel for my ear to
making for me. Ye know I am always ready to pleasure you.

MENAECHMUS THE TRAVELLER I will. Give me the gold; I'll pay for 100
the workmanship.

ANCILLA Lay out for me. I'll pay it ye again.

MENAECHMUS THE TRAVELLER Alas, I have none now.

ANCILLA When you have, will ye?

MENAECHMUS THE TRAVELLER I will. Go, bid your mistress make no 105
doubt of these. I warrant her I'll make the best hand I can of
them.   *Exit Ancilla*
Is she gone? Do not all the gods conspire to load me with good
luck? Well, I see 'tis high time to get me out of these coasts, lest
all these matters should be lewd devices to draw me into some 110
snare. There shall my garland lie, because, if they seek me, they
may think I am gone that way. (*Laying down his garland*) I will
now go see if I can find my man Messenio, that I may tell him
how I have sped.   *Exit*

---

89 **are ye advised** do you agree
98–9 **put . . . making** order an earring to be
made
102 **Lay . . . me** advance me the money, pay

the bill for me
106 **hand** deal
110 **lewd** wicked

Appendix C

4.1   *Enter Mulier, the wife of Menaechmus the Citizen, and*
       Peniculus

MULIER Thinks he I will be made such a sot, and to be still his
   drudge, while he prowls and purloins all that I have to give his
   trulls?

PENICULUS Nay, hold your peace. We'll catch him in the nick. This
   way he came, in his garland, forsooth, bearing the cloak to the   5
   dyer's. And see, I pray, where the garland lies. This way he is
   gone. See, see, where he comes again now without the cloak.

MULIER What shall I now do?

PENICULUS What? That which ye ever do—bait him for life.

MULIER Surely I think it best so.   10

PENICULUS Stay. We will stand aside a little; ye shall catch him
   unawares.

       Enter Menaechmus the Citizen

MENAECHMUS THE CITIZEN It would make a man at his wit's end to
   see how brabbling causes are handled yonder at the court. If a
   poor man, never so honest, have a matter come to be scanned,   15
   there is he outfaced and overlaid with countenance. If a rich
   man, never so vile a wretch, come to speak, there they are all
   ready to favour his cause. What with facing out bad causes for
   the oppressors and patronizing some just actions for the
   wronged, the lawyers, they pocket up all the gains. For mine   20
   own part, I come not away empty, though I have been kept long
   against my will; for, taking in hand to dispatch a matter this
   morning for one of my acquaintance, I was no sooner entered
   into it but his adversaries laid so hard unto his charge and
   brought such matter against him that, do what I could, I could   25
   not wind myself out till now. I am sore afraid Erotium thinks
   much unkindness in me that I stayed so long; yet she will not be
   angry, considering the gift I gave her today.

PENICULUS (*to Mulier*) How think ye by that?

MULIER (*to Peniculus*) I think him a most vile wretch thus to abuse   30
   me.

MENAECHMUS THE CITIZEN I will hie me thither.

MULIER (*to Menaechmus*) Yea, go, pilferer, go with shame enough!
   Nobody sees your lewd dealings and vile thievery.

4.1.4 **nick** act
   9 **bait . . . life** taunt or torment him
      unmercifully
  14 **brabbling** litigious
  15 **scanned** judged

16 **outfaced** contradicted to his face
   overlaid . . . countenance crushed by
   mere show or pretence on the part of his
   adversaries
26 **wind . . . out** extricate myself

MENAECHMUS THE CITIZEN How now, wife, what ails thee? What is   35
the matter?

MULIER Ask ye me what's the matter? Fie upon thee!

PENICULUS (*to Mulier*) Are ye not in a fit of an ague, your pulses beat
so sore? To him, I say.

MENAECHMUS THE CITIZEN Pray, wife, why are ye so angry with   40
me?

MULIER O, you know not?

PENICULUS He knows, but he would dissemble it.

MENAECHMUS THE CITIZEN What is it?

MULIER My cloak.   45

MENAECHMUS THE CITIZEN Your cloak?

MULIER My cloak, man. Why do ye blush?

PENICULUS He cannot cloak his blushing.—Nay, I might not go to
dinner with you, do ye remember?—To him, I say.

MENAECHMUS THE CITIZEN Hold thy peace, Peniculus.   50

PENICULUS Ha! Hold my peace?—Look ye, he beckons on me to
hold my peace.

MENAECHMUS THE CITIZEN I neither beckon nor wink on him.

MULIER Out, out, what a wretched life is this that I live!

MENAECHMUS THE CITIZEN Why, what ails ye, woman?   55

MULIER Are ye not ashamed to deny so confidently that which is
apparent?

MENAECHMUS THE CITIZEN I protest unto you before all the gods—is
not this enough?—that I beckoned not on him.

PENICULUS O, sir, this is another matter.—Touch him in the   60
former cause.

MENAECHMUS THE CITIZEN What former cause?

PENICULUS The cloak, man, the cloak! Fetch the cloak again from
the dyer's.

MENAECHMUS THE CITIZEN What cloak?   65

MULIER Nay, I'll say no more, sith ye know nothing of your own
doings.

MENAECHMUS THE CITIZEN Tell me, wife, hath any of your servants
abused you? Let me know.

MULIER Tush, tush.   70

MENAECHMUS THE CITIZEN I would not have you to be thus
disquieted.

MULIER Tush, tush.

MENAECHMUS THE CITIZEN You are fallen out with some of your
friends.   75

MULIER Tush, tush.

51 **beckons on** gestures at

MENAECHMUS THE CITIZEN Sure I am I have not offended you.

MULIER No, you have dealt very honestly.

MENAECHMUS THE CITIZEN Indeed, wife, I have deserved none of
these words. Tell me, are ye not well?   80

PENICULUS (*to Mulier*) What, shall he flatter ye now?

MENAECHMUS THE CITIZEN I speak not to thee, knave.—Good wife,
come hither.

MULIER Away, away! Keep your hands off.

PENICULUS So, bid me to dinner with you again, then slip away   85
from me. When you have done, come forth bravely in your garland to flout me! Alas, you knew not me even now.

MENAECHMUS THE CITIZEN Why, ass, I neither have yet dined, nor
came I there, since we were there together.

PENICULUS Whoever heard one so impudent? Did ye not meet me   90
here even now and would make me believe I was mad, and said
ye were a stranger and ye knew me not?

MENAECHMUS THE CITIZEN Of a truth, since we went together to the
sessions hall I never returned till this very instant, as you two
met me.   95

PENICULUS Go to, go to, I know ye well enough. Did ye think I
would not cry quittance with you? Yes, faith, I have told your
wife all.

MENAECHMUS THE CITIZEN What hast thou told her?

PENICULUS I cannot tell. Ask her.   100

MENAECHMUS THE CITIZEN Tell me, wife, what hath he told ye of
me? Tell me, I say. What was it?

MULIER As though you knew not. My cloak is stolen from me.

MENAECHMUS THE CITIZEN Is your cloak stolen from ye?

MULIER Do ye ask me?   105

MENAECHMUS THE CITIZEN If I knew, I would not ask.

PENICULUS O, crafty companion! How he would shift the matter.—
Come, come, deny it not. I tell ye, I have bewrayed all.

MENAECHMUS THE CITIZEN What hast thou bewrayed?

MULIER Seeing ye will yield to nothing, be it never so manifest,   110
hear me, and ye shall know in few words both the cause of my
grief and what he hath told me. I say my cloak is stolen from me.

MENAECHMUS THE CITIZEN My cloak is stolen from me?

PENICULUS Look how he cavils.—She saith it is stolen from her.

MENAECHMUS THE CITIZEN I have nothing to say to thee.—I say,   115
wife, tell me.

MULIER I tell ye my cloak is stolen out of my house.

MENAECHMUS THE CITIZEN Who stole it?

97 **cry quittance** get even   108 **bewrayed** revealed

MULIER He knows best that carried it away.

MENAECHMUS THE CITIZEN Who was that?   120

MULIER Menaechmus.

MENAECHMUS THE CITIZEN 'Twas very ill done of him. What
  Menaechmus was that?

MULIER You.

MENAECHMUS THE CITIZEN I? Who will say so?   125

MULIER I will.

PENICULUS And I. And that you gave it to Erotium.

MENAECHMUS THE CITIZEN I gave it?

MULIER You.

PENICULUS You, you, you. Shall we fetch a kennel of beagles that   130
  may cry nothing but 'You, you, you, you'? For we are weary of
  it.

MENAECHMUS THE CITIZEN Hear me one word, wife. I protest unto
  you, by all the gods, I gave it her not. Indeed, I lent it her to use a
  while.   135

MULIER Faith, sir, I never give nor lend your apparel out-of-doors.
  Methinks ye might let me dispose of mine own garments as you
  do of yours. I pray, then, fetch it me home again.

MENAECHMUS THE CITIZEN You shall have it again without fail.

MULIER 'Tis best for you that I have. Otherwise think not to roost   140
  within these doors again.

PENICULUS (*to Mulier*) Hark ye, what say ye to me now, for bringing
  these matters to your knowledge?

MULIER I say, when thou hast anything stolen from thee, come to
  me and I will help thee to seek it. And so farewell.   145

⌈*Exit into her house*⌉

PENICULUS God-a-mercy for nothing! That can never be, for I
  have nothing in the world worth the stealing. So, now with
  husband and wife and all I am clean out of favour. A mischief
  on ye all!   *Exit*

MENAECHMUS THE CITIZEN My wife thinks she is notably revenged   150
  on me, now she shuts me out-of-doors, as though I had not a
  better place to be welcome to. If she shut me out, I know who
  will shut me in. Now will I entreat Erotium to let me have the
  cloak again to stop my wife's mouth withal, and then will I
  provide a better for her.—Ho, who is within there? Somebody   155
  tell Erotium I must speak with her.

Enter Erotium ⌈*from her house*⌉

EROTIUM Who calls?

MENAECHMUS THE CITIZEN Your friend more than his own.

EROTIUM O Menaechmus, why stand ye here? Pray, come in.

MENAECHMUS THE CITIZEN Tarry. I must speak with ye here.   160

EROTIUM Say your mind.

MENAECHMUS THE CITIZEN Wot ye what? My wife knows all the
matter now, and my coming is to request you that I may have
again the cloak which I brought you that so I may appease her.
And, I promise you, I'll give ye another worth two of it.   165

EROTIUM Why, I gave it you to carry to your dyer's, and my chain
likewise, to have it altered.

MENAECHMUS THE CITIZEN Gave me the cloak and your chain? In
truth, I never saw ye since I left it here with you and so went to
the sessions, from whence I am but now returned.   170

EROTIUM Ah, then, sir, I see you wrought a device to defraud me of
them both. Did I therefore put ye in trust? Well, well.

MENAECHMUS THE CITIZEN To defraud ye? No, but I say my wife
hath intelligence of the matter.

EROTIUM Why, sir, I asked them not; ye brought them me of your   175
own free motion. Now ye require them again, take them, make
sops of them! You and your wife together, think ye I esteem
them or you either? Go, come to me again when I send for you.

MENAECHMUS THE CITIZEN What so angry with me, sweet
Erotium? Stay, I pray, stay.   180

EROTIUM Stay? Faith, sir, no. Think ye I will stay at your request?
⌈*Exit into her house*⌉

MENAECHMUS THE CITIZEN What, gone in chafing, and clapped to
the doors? Now I am every way shut out for a very benchwhistler; neither shall I have entertainment here nor at home. I
were best to go try some other friends and ask counsel what to   185
do.   *Exit*

5.1 *Enter Menaechmus the Traveller* ⌈*carrying the cloak, and*⌉
Mulier ⌈*from her house*⌉

MENAECHMUS THE TRAVELLER Most foolishly was I overseen in giving my purse and money to Messenio, whom I can nowhere
find. I fear he is fallen into some lewd company.

MULIER I marvel that my husband comes not yet. But see where he
is now, and brings my cloak with him.   5

MENAECHMUS THE TRAVELLER I muse where the knave should be.

MULIER I will go ring a peal through both his ears for this his dis-
honest behaviour.—O sir, ye are welcome home, with your
thievery on your shoulders. Are ye not ashamed to let all the

---

164 **so** thus
179 **What** Why
182 **clapped to** slammed shut

183–4 **benchwhistler** idler, vagrant
5.1.1 **overseen** rash, imprudent

world see and speak of your lewdness? 10

MENAECHMUS THE TRAVELLER How now? What lacks this woman?

MULIER Impudent beast, stand ye to question about it? For shame, hold thy peace.

MENAECHMUS THE TRAVELLER What offence have I done, woman, that I should not speak to you? 15

MULIER Askest thou what offence? O shameless boldness!

MENAECHMUS THE TRAVELLER Good woman, did ye never hear why the Grecians termed Hecuba to be a bitch?

MULIER Never.

MENAECHMUS THE TRAVELLER Because she did as you do now: on 20 whomsoever she met withal she railed, and therefore well deserved that doggèd name.

MULIER These foul abuses and contumelies I can never endure, nay, rather will I live a widow's life to my dying day.

MENAECHMUS THE TRAVELLER What care I whether thou livest as a 25 widow or as a wife? This passeth, that I meet with none but thus they vex me with strange speeches.

MULIER What strange speeches? I say I will surely live a widow's life rather than suffer thy vile dealings.

MENAECHMUS THE TRAVELLER Prithee, for my part, live a widow till 30 the world's end if thou wilt.

MULIER Even now thou deniedst that thou stolest it from me, and now thou bringest it home openly in my sight. Art not ashamed?

MENAECHMUS THE TRAVELLER Woman, you are greatly to blame to 35 charge me with stealing of this cloak, which this day another gave me to carry to be trimmed.

MULIER Well, I will first complain to my father. (*Calling into her house*) Ho, boy! Who is within there?
⌈*Enter Boy*⌉
Vecio, go run quickly to my father. Desire him of all love to come 40 over quickly to my house. ⌈*Exit Boy*⌉
I'll tell him first of your pranks. I hope he will not see me thus handled.

MENAECHMUS THE TRAVELLER What i' God's name meaneth this madwoman thus to vex me? 45

MULIER I am mad because I tell ye of your vile actions and lewd pilfering away my apparel and my jewels to carry to your filthy drabs.

MENAECHMUS THE TRAVELLER For whom this woman taketh me I

11 **What lacks** what is the matter with   48 **drabs** sluts
23 **contumelies** insults

know not. I know her as much as I know Hercules' wife's father. 50
MULIER Do ye not know me? That's well. I hope ye know my
father. Here he comes. Look, do ye know him?
MENAECHMUS THE TRAVELLER As much as I knew Calchas of Troy.
Even him and thee I know both alike.
MULIER Dost know neither of us both, me nor my father? 55
MENAECHMUS THE TRAVELLER Faith, nor thy grandfather neither.
MULIER This is like the rest of your behaviour.
    Enter Senex
SENEX (*to himself*) Though bearing so great a burden as old age, I
can make no great haste; yet, as I can, I will go to my daughter,
who I know hath some earnest business with me that she sends 60
in such haste, not telling the cause why I should come. But I
durst lay a wager I can guess near the matter. I suppose it is
some brabble between her husband and her. These young
women that bring great dowries to their husbands are so mas-
terful and obstinate that they will have their own wills in every- 65
thing and make men servants to their weak affections. And
young men, too, I must needs say, be naught nowadays. Well,
I'll go see. But yonder methinks stands my daughter, and her
husband too. O, 'tis even as I guessed.
MULIER Father, ye are welcome. 70
    ⌜*They converse apart*⌝
SENEX How now, daughter? What, is all well? Why is your husband so sad? Have ye been chiding? Tell me, which of you is in
the fault?
MULIER First, father, know that I have not any way misbehaved
myself, but the truth is I can by no means endure this bad man, 75
to die for it, and therefore desire you to take me home to you
again.
SENEX What is the matter?
MULIER He makes me a stale and laughing stock to all the world.
SENEX Who doth? 80
MULIER This good husband here, to whom you married me.
SENEX See, see, how oft have I warned you of falling out with your
husband?
MULIER I cannot avoid it, if he doth so foully abuse me.
SENEX I always told ye you must bear with him, ye must let him 85
alone, ye must not watch him nor dog him nor meddle with his
courses in any sort.
MULIER He haunts naughty harlots under my nose.
SENEX He is the wiser, because he cannot be quiet at home.

76 **to die** if I have to die   79 **stale** butt of ridicule

MULIER There he feasts and banquets and spends and spoils.   90

SENEX Would ye have your husband serve ye as your drudge? Ye will not let him make merry nor entertain his friends at home.

MULIER Father, will ye take his part in these abuses and forsake me?

SENEX Not so, daughter. But if I see cause, I will as well tell him of   95
his duty.

MENAECHMUS THE TRAVELLER (*aside*) I would I were gone from this prating father and daughter.

SENEX Hitherto I see not but he keeps ye well. Ye want nothing— apparel, money, servants, meat, drink, all things necessary. I   100
fear there is fault in you.

MULIER But he filcheth away my apparel and my jewels to give to his trulls.

SENEX If he doth so, 'tis very ill done; if not, you do ill to say so.

MULIER You may believe me, father, for there you may see my   105
cloak, which now he hath fetched home again, and my chain, which he stole from me.

SENEX Now will I go talk with him to know the truth. (*Approaching*) Tell me, Menaechmus, how is it that I hear such disorder in your life? Why are ye so sad, man? Wherein hath your wife   110
offended you?

MENAECHMUS THE TRAVELLER Old man—what to call ye I know not—by high Jove and by all the gods I swear unto you, whatsoever this woman here accuseth me to have stolen from her, it is utterly false and untrue, and if I ever set foot within her doors I   115
wish the greatest misery in the world to light upon me.

SENEX Why, fond man, art thou mad to deny that thou ever sett'st foot within thine own house where thou dwellest?

MENAECHMUS THE TRAVELLER Do I dwell in that house?

SENEX Dost thou deny it?   120

MENAECHMUS THE TRAVELLER I do.

SENEX Hark ye, daughter, are ye removed out of your house?

MULIER Father, he useth you as he doth me. This life I have with him!

SENEX Menaechmus, I pray, leave this fondness. Ye jest too   125
perversely with your friends.

MENAECHMUS THE TRAVELLER Good old father, what, I pray, have you to do with me? Or why should this woman thus trouble me, with whom I have no dealings in the world?

MULIER Father, mark, I pray, how his eyes sparkle. They roll in his   130
head; his colour goes and comes; he looks wildly. See, see.

102 **filcheth** steals   103 **trulls** whores

MENAECHMUS THE TRAVELLER (*aside*) What? They say now I am mad. The best way for me is to feign myself mad indeed; so I shall be rid of them.

MULIER Look how he stares about, how he gapes! 135

SENEX Come away, daughter. Come from him.

MENAECHMUS THE TRAVELLER (*feigning madness*) Bacchus, Apollo, Phoebus, do ye call me to come hunt in the woods with you? I see, I hear, I come, I fly, but I cannot get out of these fields. Here is an old mastiff bitch stands barking at me, and by her stands 140 an old goat that bears false witness against many a poor man.

SENEX Out upon him, Bedlam fool!

MENAECHMUS THE TRAVELLER Hark! Apollo commands me that I should rend out her eyes with a burning lamp.

MULIER O father, he threatens to pull out mine eyes! 145

MENAECHMUS THE TRAVELLER (*aside*) Good gods, these folk say I am mad, and doubtless they are mad themselves.

SENEX Daughter!

MULIER Here, father. What shall we do?

SENEX What if I fetch my folks hither and have him carried in 150 before he do any harm?

MENAECHMUS THE TRAVELLER (*aside*) How now? They will carry me in if I look not to myself. I were best to scare them better yet.— Dost thou bid me, Phoebus, to tear this dog in pieces with my nails? If I lay hold on her I will do thy commandment. 155

SENEX Get thee into thy house, daughter. Away, quickly!

⌐*Mulier exits into her house*⌐

MENAECHMUS THE TRAVELLER She is gone.—Yea, Apollo, I will sacrifice this old beast unto thee; and, if thou commandest me, I will cut his throat with that dagger that hangs at his girdle.

⌐*He advances toward Senex*⌐

SENEX Come not near me, sirrah. 160

MENAECHMUS THE TRAVELLER Yea, I will quarter him and pull all the bones out of his flesh. Then will I barrel up his bowels.

SENEX Sure I am sore afraid he will do some hurt.

MENAECHMUS THE TRAVELLER Many things thou commandest me, Apollo. Wouldst thou have me harness up these wild horses and 165 then climb up into the chariot and so override this old stinking toothless lion? So, now I am in the chariot, and I have hold on the reins. Here is my whip. Hait! Come, ye wild jades, make a hideous noise with your stamping. Hait, I say! Will ye not go?

SENEX What, doth he threaten me with his horses? 170

---

168 **Hait!** (to the horses)

MENAECHMUS THE TRAVELLER Hark, now Apollo bids me ride over
  him that stands there and kill him. How now? Who pulls me
  down from my chariot by the hairs of my head? O, shall I not
  fulfil Apollo's commandment?

SENEX See, see, what a sharp disease this is, and how well he was   175
  even now! I will fetch a physician straight, before he grow too
  far into this rage.   *Exit*

MENAECHMUS THE TRAVELLER Are they both gone now? I'll then hie
  me away to my ship. 'Tis time to be gone from hence.   *Exit*
       Enter Senex and Medicus following

SENEX My loins ache with sitting and mine eyes with looking while   180
  I stay for yonder lazy physician. See now where the creeping
  drawlatch comes.

MEDICUS What disease hath he, said you? Is it a lethargy or a luna-
  cy, or melancholy, or dropsy?

SENEX Wherefore, I pray, do I bring you, but that you should tell   185
  me what it is and cure him of it?

MEDICUS Fie, make no question of that. I'll cure him, I warrant ye.
  O, here he comes. Stay, let us mark what he doth.
                                              ⌈*They stand aside*⌉
       Enter Menaechmus the Citizen

MENAECHMUS THE CITIZEN Never in my life had I more overthwart
  fortune in one day! And all by the villainy of this false knave the   190
  parasite, my Ulysses, that works such mischiefs against me, his
  king. But let me live no longer but I'll be revenged upon the life
  of him. His life? Nay, 'tis my life, for he lives by my meat and
  drink. I'll utterly withdraw the slave's life from him. And
  Erotium! She showeth plainly what she is, who, because I   195
  require the cloak again to carry to my wife, saith I gave it her,
  and flatly falls out with me. How unfortunate am I!

SENEX Do ye hear him?

MEDICUS He complains of his fortune.

SENEX Go to him.   200

MEDICUS (*approaching Menaechmus*) Menaechmus, how do ye, man?
  Why keep you not your cloak over your arm? It is very hurtful to
  your disease. Keep ye warm, I pray.

MENAECHMUS THE CITIZEN Why, hang thyself. What carest thou?

MEDICUS Sir, can you smell anything?   205

MENAECHMUS THE CITIZEN I smell a prating dolt of thee.

MEDICUS O, I will have your head thoroughly purged. Pray tell me,
  Menaechmus, what use you to drink? White wine or claret?

MENAECHMUS THE CITIZEN What the devil carest thou?

182 **drawlatch** laggard   189 **overthwart** contrary

SENEX Look. His fit now begins. 210

MENAECHMUS THE CITIZEN Why dost not as well ask me whether I eat bread, or cheese, or beef, or porridge, or birds that bear feathers, or fishes that have fins?

SENEX See what idle talk he falleth into.

MEDICUS Tarry, I will ask him further.—Menaechmus, tell me, be 215 not your eyes heavy and dull sometimes?

MENAECHMUS THE CITIZEN What dost think I am, an owl?

MEDICUS Do not your guts gripe ye and croak in your belly?

MENAECHMUS THE CITIZEN When I am hungry they do, else not.

MEDICUS He speaks not like a madman in that.—Sleep ye soundly 220 all night?

MENAECHMUS THE CITIZEN When I have paid my debts, I do. The mischief light on thee with all thy frivolous questions!

MEDICUS O, now he rageth upon those words. Take heed.

SENEX O, this is nothing to the rage he was in even now. He called 225 his wife bitch, and all to naught.

MENAECHMUS THE CITIZEN Did I?

SENEX Thou didst, mad fellow, and threatenedst to ride over me here with a chariot and horses, and to kill me and tear me in pieces. This thou didst. I know what I say. 230

MENAECHMUS THE CITIZEN I say thou stolest Jupiter's crown from his head, and thou wert whipped through the town for it, and that thou hast killed thy father and beaten thy mother. Do ye think I am so mad that I cannot devise as notable lies of you as you do of me? 235

SENEX Master Doctor, pray heartily, make speed to cure him. See ye not how mad he waxeth?

MEDICUS I'll tell ye, he shall be brought over to my house and there will I cure him.

SENEX Is that best? 240

MEDICUS What else? There I can order him as I list.

SENEX Well, it shall be so.

MEDICUS O, sir, I will make ye take neezing powder this twenty days.

MENAECHMUS THE CITIZEN I'll beat ye first with a bastinado this 245 thirty days.

MEDICUS Fetch men to carry him to my house.

SENEX How many will serve the turn?

218 **Do . . . croak** do you not have pains and rumbling
225–6 **called . . . all to naught** abused her vehemently
241 **list** wish
243 **neezing** sneezing
245 **bastinado** cudgel

MEDICUS Being no madder than he is now, four will serve.

SENEX I'll fetch them. Stay you with him, Master Doctor.   250

MEDICUS No, by my faith, I'll go home to make ready all things
    needful. Let your men bring him hither.

SENEX I go.   *Exeunt Medicus and Senex*

MENAECHMUS THE CITIZEN Are they both gone? Good gods, what
    meaneth this? These men say I am mad, who without doubt are   255
    mad themselves. I stir not, I fight not, I am not sick. I speak to
    them, I know them. Well, what were I now best to do? I would go
    home, but my wife shuts me forth o' doors. Erotium is as far out
    with me too. Even here I will rest me till the evening. I hope by
    that time they will take pity on me.   260

        Enter Messenio, the Traveller's servant

MESSENIO The proof of a good servant is to regard his master's
    business as well in his absence as in his presence, and I think
    him a very fool that is not careful as well for his ribs and shoul-
    ders as for his belly and throat. When I think upon the rewards
    of a sluggard, I am ever pricked with a careful regard of my back 265
    and shoulders, for in truth I have no fancy to these blows, as
    many a one hath. Methinks it is no pleasure to a man to be bast-
    ed with a rope's end two or three hours together. I have provid-
    ed yonder in the town for all our mariners, and safely bestowed
    all my master's trunks and fardels and am now coming to see if   270
    he be yet got forth of this dangerous gulf where, I fear me, he is
    overplunged. Pray God he be not overwhelmed and past help ere
    I come!

        Enter Senex, with four lorarii (porters)

SENEX (*to the porters*) Before gods and men, I charge and command
    you, sirs, to execute with great care that which I appoint you. If 275
    ye love the safety of your own ribs and shoulders, then go take
    me up my son-in-law. Lay all hands upon him. Why stand ye
    still? What do ye doubt? I say, care not for his threatenings nor
    for any of his words. Take him up and bring him to the physi-
    cian's house. I will go thither before.   *Exit*   280

        ⌈*The porters seize Menaechmus*⌉

MENAECHMUS THE CITIZEN What news? How now, masters? What
    will ye do with me? Why do ye thus beset me? Whither carry ye
    me? Help, help! Neighbours, friends, citizens!

MESSENIO O Jupiter, what do I see? My master abused by a
    company of varlets.   285

MENAECHMUS THE CITIZEN Is there no good man will help me?

---

285 **varlets** rogues

MESSENIO Help ye, master? Yes, the villains shall have my life before they shall thus wrong ye. 'Tis more fit I should be killed than you thus handled. Pull out that rascal's eye that holds ye about the neck there. I'll clout these peasants. Out, ye rogue! Let   290 go, ye varlet!

MENAECHMUS THE CITIZEN I have hold of this villain's eye.

MESSENIO Pull it out, and let the place appear in his head. Away, ye cut-throat thieves! Ye murderers!

ALL THE PORTERS (*crying pitifully*) O, O, ai, ai!   295

MESSENIO Away! Get ye hence, ye mongrels, ye dogs. Will ye be gone? Thou rascal behind there, I'll give thee somewhat more. Take that.   ⌜*Exeunt porters*⌝
It was time to come, master; you had been in good case if I had not been here now. I told you what would come of it.   300

MENAECHMUS THE CITIZEN Now, as the gods love me, my good friend, I thank thee. Thou hast done that for me which I shall never be able to requite.

MESSENIO I'll tell ye how, sir: give me my freedom.

MENAECHMUS THE CITIZEN Should I give it thee?   305

MESSENIO Seeing you cannot requite my good turn.

MENAECHMUS THE CITIZEN Thou art deceived, man.

MESSENIO Wherein?

MENAECHMUS THE CITIZEN On mine honesty, I am none of thy master. I had never yet any servant would do so much for me.   310

MESSENIO Why, then, bid me be free. Will you?

MENAECHMUS THE CITIZEN Yea, surely. Be free, for my part.

MESSENIO O, sweetly spoken! Thanks, my good master. (*To himself*) Messenio, we are all glad of your good fortune.—O master—I'll call ye master still—I pray, use me in any service as ye did   315 before; I'll dwell with you still, and when ye go home I'll wait upon you.

MENAECHMUS THE CITIZEN Nay, nay, it shall not need.

MESSENIO I'll go straight to the inn and deliver up my accounts and all your stuff. Your purse is locked up safely sealed in the casket,   320 as you gave it me. I will go fetch it to you.

MENAECHMUS THE CITIZEN Do, fetch it.

MESSENIO I will.   *Exit*

MENAECHMUS THE CITIZEN I was never thus perplexed. Some deny me to be him that I am and shut me out of their doors. This fel-   325 low saith he is my bondman, and of me he begs his freedom. He

293 **place** empty socket
319–20 **deliver . . . stuff** pay my bill and collect your baggage

will fetch my purse and money. Well, if he bring it, I will receive
it and set him free. I would he would, so he go his way. My old
father-in-law and the Doctor say I am mad. Whoever saw such
strange demeanours? Well, though Erotium be never so angry,   330
yet once again I'll go see if by entreaty I can get the cloak of her
to carry to my wife.   *Exit* ⌈*to the courtesan's*⌉
          Enter Menaechmus the Traveller, and Messenio

MENAECHMUS THE TRAVELLER Impudent knave, wilt thou say that I
    ever saw thee since I sent thee away today and bade thee come
    for me after dinner?   335

MESSENIO Ye make me stark mad! I took ye away and rescued ye
    from four great big-boned villains that were carrying ye away
    even here in this place. Here they had ye up. You cried, 'Help,
    help!' I came running to you. You and I together beat them
    away by main force. Then, for my good turn and faithful service, 340
    ye gave me my freedom. I told ye I would go fetch your casket.
    Now in the meantime you ran some other way to get before me,
    and so you deny it all again.

MENAECHMUS THE TRAVELLER I gave thee thy freedom?

MESSENIO You did.   345

MENAECHMUS THE TRAVELLER When I give thee thy freedom, I'll be
    a bondman myself. Go thy ways.

MESSENIO Whew! Marry, I thank ye for nothing.
          Enter Menaechmus the Citizen

MENAECHMUS THE CITIZEN (*calling into the courtesan's house*) For-
    sworn queans, swear till your hearts ache and your eyes fall   350
    out! Ye shall never make me believe that I carried hence either
    cloak or chain.

MESSENIO (*to Menaechmus the Traveller*) O heavens, master, what do
    I see?

MENAECHMUS THE TRAVELLER What?   355

MESSENIO Your ghost.

MENAECHMUS THE TRAVELLER What ghost?

MESSENIO Your image, as like you as can be possible.

MENAECHMUS THE TRAVELLER Surely not much unlike me, as I
    think.   360

MENAECHMUS THE CITIZEN (*to Messenio*) O my good friend and
    helper, well met! Thanks for thy late good help.

MESSENIO Sir, may I crave to know your name?

MENAECHMUS THE CITIZEN I were to blame if I should not tell thee
    anything. My name is Menaechmus.   365

---

330 **demeanours** behaviour
349–50 **Forsworn queans** lying whores

364 **I . . . blame** it would be very wrong of
    me

MENAECHMUS THE TRAVELLER Nay, my friend, that is my name.

MENAECHMUS THE CITIZEN I am of Syracuse in Sicily.

MENAECHMUS THE TRAVELLER So am I.

MESSENIO (*to Menaechmus the Citizen*) Are you a Syracusan?

MENAECHMUS THE CITIZEN I am.   370

MESSENIO Oho, I know ye! (*Pointing to the Citizen*) This is my master; I thought he there had been my master, and was proffering my service to him. Pray pardon me, sir, if I said anything I should not.

MENAECHMUS THE TRAVELLER Why, doting patch, didst thou not   375
come with me this morning from the ship?

MESSENIO My faith, he says true. (*Pointing to the Traveller*) This is my master; you may go look ye a man.—God save ye, master!— You, sir, farewell. This is Menaechmus.

MENAECHMUS THE CITIZEN I say that I am Menaechmus.   380

MESSENIO What a jest is this! Are you Menaechmus?

MENAECHMUS THE CITIZEN Even Menaechmus, the son of Moschus.

MENAECHMUS THE TRAVELLER My father's son?

MENAECHMUS THE CITIZEN Friend, I go about neither to take your father nor your country from you.   385

MESSENIO O immortal gods, let it fall out as I hope! And, for my life, these are the two twins, all things agree so jump together. I will speak to my master.—Menaechmus?

BOTH What wilt thou?

MESSENIO I call ye not both. But which of you came with me from   390
the ship?

MENAECHMUS THE CITIZEN Not I.

MENAECHMUS THE TRAVELLER I did.

MESSENIO Then I call you. Come hither.
    ⌈*He takes Menaechmus the Traveller aside*⌉

MENAECHMUS THE TRAVELLER What's the matter?   395

MESSENIO This same is either some notable cozening juggler or else it is your brother whom we seek. I never saw one man so like another. Water to water nor milk to milk is not liker than he is to you.

MENAECHMUS THE TRAVELLER Indeed, I think thou sayst true. Find   400
it that he is my brother, and I here promise thee thy freedom.

MESSENIO Well, let me about it.
    ⌈*He takes Menaechmus the Citizen aside*⌉
    Hear ye, sir, you say your name is Menaechmus?

MENAECHMUS THE CITIZEN I do.

375 **patch** fool   387 **jump** precisely
378 **look ye** look for

MESSENIO So is this man's. You are of Syracuse?   405

MENAECHMUS THE CITIZEN True.

MESSENIO So is he. Moschus was your father?

MENAECHMUS THE CITIZEN He was.

MESSENIO So was he his. What will you say if I find that ye are
brethren and twins?   410

MENAECHMUS THE CITIZEN I would think it happy news.

MESSENIO Nay, stay, masters both. I mean to have the honour of
this exploit. Answer me: your name is Menaechmus?

MENAECHMUS THE CITIZEN Yea.

MESSENIO And yours?   415

MENAECHMUS THE TRAVELLER And mine.

MESSENIO You are of Syracuse?

MENAECHMUS THE CITIZEN I am.

MENAECHMUS THE TRAVELLER And I.

MESSENIO Well, this goeth right thus far. What is the farthest thing   420
that you remember there?

MENAECHMUS THE CITIZEN How I went with my father to Tarentum,
to a great mart, and there in the press I was stolen from him.

MENAECHMUS THE TRAVELLER O Jupiter!

MESSENIO Peace, what exclaiming is this?—How old were ye   425
then?

MENAECHMUS THE CITIZEN About seven year old, for even then
I shed teeth; and since that time I never heard of any of my
kindred.

MESSENIO Had ye never a brother?   430

MENAECHMUS THE CITIZEN Yes, as I remember I heard them say we
were two twins.

MENAECHMUS THE TRAVELLER O Fortune!

MESSENIO Tush, can ye not be quiet?—Were ye both of one name?

MENAECHMUS THE CITIZEN Nay, as I think, they called my brother   435
Sosicles.

MENAECHMUS THE TRAVELLER It is he. What need farther proof? O
brother, brother, let me embrace thee!

MENAECHMUS THE CITIZEN Sir, if this be true I am wonderfully glad.
But how is it that ye are called Menaechmus?   440

MENAECHMUS THE TRAVELLER When it was told us that you and our
father were both dead, our grandsire, in memory of my father's
name, changed mine to Menaechmus.

---

423 **mart** market
  press crowd
428 **shed teeth** lost baby teeth
441–3 Warner was misled by a lacuna in the

text of Plautus. The father was Moschus;
Menaechmus was named for his lost
brother (see 'The Argument').

MENAECHMUS THE CITIZEN 'Tis very like he would do so, indeed. But
let me ask ye one question more: what was our mother's name?   445
MENAECHMUS THE TRAVELLER Theusimarche.
MENAECHMUS THE CITIZEN Brother, the most welcome man to me
that the world holdeth!
MENAECHMUS THE TRAVELLER Ay, joy, and ten thousand joys the
more, having taken so long travail and huge pains to seek you.   450
MESSENIO See now how all this matter comes about. (*To
Menaechmus the Traveller*) Thus it was that the gentlewoman had
ye in to dinner, thinking it had been he.
MENAECHMUS THE CITIZEN True it is, I willed a dinner to be pro-
vided for me here this morning, and I also brought hither   455
closely a cloak of my wife's and gave it to this woman.
MENAECHMUS THE TRAVELLER (*showing the cloak*) Is not this the
same, brother?
MENAECHMUS THE CITIZEN How came you by this?
MENAECHMUS THE TRAVELLER This woman met me, had me in to   460
dinner, entertained me most kindly, and gave me this cloak and
this chain.
⌈*He shows the chain*⌉
MENAECHMUS THE CITIZEN Indeed, she took ye for me, and I believe
I have been as strangely handled by occasion of your coming.
MESSENIO You shall have time enough to laugh at all these matters   465
hereafter. Do ye remember, master, what ye promised me?
MENAECHMUS THE CITIZEN Brother, I will entreat you to perform
your promise to Messenio. He is worthy of it.
MENAECHMUS THE TRAVELLER I am content.
MESSENIO Io, triumph!   470
MENAECHMUS THE TRAVELLER Brother, will ye now go with me to
Syracuse?
MENAECHMUS THE CITIZEN So soon as I can sell away such goods as
I possess here in Epidamnum, I will go with you.
MENAECHMUS THE TRAVELLER Thanks, my good brother.   475
MENAECHMUS THE CITIZEN Messenio, play thou the crier for me and
make a proclamation.
MESSENIO A fit office. Come on. Oyez! What day shall your sale
be?
MENAECHMUS THE CITIZEN This day sennight.   480
MESSENIO (*making proclamation*) All men, women, and children in
Epidamnum or elsewhere that will repair to Menaechmus'
house this day sennight shall there find all manner of things to

464 **handled** treated
470 **Io** (exclamation of joy).

480 **This day sennight** (seven-night) one
week from today

sell: servants, household stuff, house, ground, and all, so they
bring ready money.—Will ye sell your wife too, sir?   485

MENAECHMUS THE CITIZEN Yea, but I think nobody will bid money
    for her.

MESSENIO (*as Epilogue*) Thus, gentlemen, we take our leaves, and if
    we have pleased, we require a *Plaudite*.   *Exeunt*

489 **require a *Plaudite*** ask applause

EXTRACTS FROM THE GENEVA BIBLE (1560)

SPELLING and punctuation are modernized. Verse numberings are those
of the Geneva Bible. The marginalia are omitted.

Acts 19

1 And it came to pass, while Apollos was at Corinthus, that Paul, when he
passed through the upper coasts, came to Ephesus, and found certain
disciples . . .

11 And God wrought no small miracles by the hands of Paul,
12 So that from his body were brought unto the sick, kerchiefs or hand-
kerchiefs, and the diseases departed from them, and the evil spirits went
out of them.
13 Then certain of the vagabond Jews, exorcists, took in hand to name
over them which had evil spirits the name of the Lord Jesus, saying, 'We
adjure you by Jesus whom Paul preacheth.'
14 (And there were certain sons of Sceva a Jew, the priest, about seven,
which did this.)
15 And the evil spirit answered and said, 'Jesus I acknowledge and Paul I
know, but who are ye?'
16 And the man in whom the evil spirit was ran on them and overcame
them, and prevailed against them, so that they fled out of that house,
naked and wounded.
17 And this was known to all the Jews and Grecians also which dwelt at
Ephesus, and fear came on them all, and the name of the Lord Jesus was
magnified.
18 And many that believed, came and confessed and showed their works.
19 Many also of them which used curious arts brought their books and
burned them before all men, and they counted the price of them and found
it fifty thousand pieces of silver.
20 So the word of God grew mightily and prevailed.

23 And the same time there arose no small trouble about that way.[1]
24 For a certain man named Demetrius, a silversmith, which made silver
temples of Diana,[2] brought great gains unto the craftsmen,

---

[1] That is, about the new, Christian, way that Paul and the disciples were
preaching.
[2] Presumably replicas of the famous temple at Ephesus, bought by pilgrims as
souvenirs.

25 Whom he called together, with the workmen of like things, and said, 'Sirs, ye know that by this craft we have our goods.

26 Moreover, ye see and hear that not alone at Ephesus but almost throughout all Asia, this Paul hath persuaded and turned away much people, saying that they be not gods which are made with hands,

27 So that not only this thing is dangerous unto us, that the state[3] should be reproved, but also that the temple of the great goddess Diana should be nothing esteemed, and that it would come to pass that her magnificence, which all Asia and the world worshippeth, should be destroyed.'

28 Now when they heard it, they were full of wrath and cried out, saying, 'Great is Diana of the Ephesians!'

29 And the whole city was full of confusion, and they rushed into the common place with one assent, and caught Gaius and Aristarchus, men of Macedonia, and Paul's companions of his journey.

30 And when Paul would have entered in unto the people, the disciples suffered him not.

31 Certain also of the chief of Asia which were his friends sent unto him, desiring him that he would not present himself in the common place.

32 Some therefore cried one thing and some another, for the assembly was out of order, and the more part knew not wherefore they were come together.

35 Then the town clerk, when he had stayed the people, said, 'Ye men of Ephesus, what man is it that knoweth not how that the city of the Ephesians is a worshipper of the great goddess Diana, and of the image which came down from Jupiter?

36 Seeing then that no man can speak against these things, ye ought to be appeased and to do nothing rashly.

37 For ye have brought hither these men, which have neither commit[ted] sacrilege, neither do blaspheme your goddess.

38 Wherefore if Demetrius and the craftsmen which are with him have a matter against any man, the law is open and there are deputies: let them accuse one another.

39 But if ye enquire anything concerning other matters, it may be determined in a lawful assembly.

40 For we are even in jeopardy to be accused of this day's sedition, forasmuch as there is no cause whereby we may give a reason of this concourse of people.'

41 And when he had thus spoken, he let the assembly depart.

---

[3] The marginal gloss explains that Demetrius refers to 'their art and occupation'.

Ephesians 5

22 Wives, submit yourselves unto your husbands, as unto the Lord.

23 For the husband is the wife's head, even as Christ is the head of the Church, and the same is the saviour of his body.

24 Therefore as the Church is in subjection to Christ, even so let the wives be to their husbands in everything.

25 Husbands, love your wives, even as Christ loved the Church and gave himself for it,

26 That he might sanctify it and cleanse it by the washing of water through the word,

27 That he might make it unto himself a glorious Church, not having spot or wrinkle or any such thing, but that it should be holy and without blame.

28 So ought men to love their wives as their own bodies; he that loveth his wife, loveth himself.

29 For no man ever yet hated his own flesh, but nourisheth and cherisheth it, even as the Lord doth the Church.

30 For we are members of his body, and of his flesh, and of his bones.

31 For this cause shall a man leave father and mother, and shall cleave to his wife, and they twain shall be one flesh.

32 This is a great secret, but I speak concerning Christ and concerning the Church.

33 Therefore every one of you, do ye so: let every one love his wife even as himself, and let the wife see that she fear her husband.

Ephesians 6

1 Children, obey your parents in the Lord, for this is right.

2 Honour thy father and mother (which is the first commandment with promise)

3 That it may be well with thee, and that thou mayst live long on earth.

4 And ye fathers, provoke not your children to wrath, but bring them up in instruction and information of the Lord.

5 Servants, be obedient unto them that are your masters, according to the flesh, with fear and trembling in singleness of your hearts as unto Christ . . .

9 And ye masters, do the same things unto them, putting away threatening; and know that even your master also is in heaven, neither is there respect of person with him.

10 Finally, my brethren, be strong in the Lord and in the power of his might.

11 Put on the whole armour of God, that ye may be able to stand against the assaults of the devil.

12 For we wrestle not against flesh and blood, but against principalities, against powers, and against the worldly governors, the princes of the darkness of this world, against spiritual wickednesses which are in the high places.

13 For this cause, take unto you the whole armour of God, that ye may be able to resist in the evil day, and having finished all things, stand fast.

14 Stand, therefore, and your loins gird about with verity, and having on the breastplate of righteousness,

15 And your feet shod with the preparation of the Gospel of peace.

16 Above all, take the shield of faith wherewith ye may quench all the fiery darts of the wicked,

17 And take the helmet of salvation, and the sword of the spirit which is the word of God.

Further echoes of the Geneva Bible's headnotes may be detectable in the play; at least the coincidences are worth noting. In Galatians, one finds 'An Angel from heaven'; 'Testimony of the Spirit'; 'Works of the flesh'; 'Redemption in Christ'; as well as 'Free & bond'. And in Ephesians: 'One body, one spirit'; 'Put on the new man'; 'Awake from sleep'; 'Christian armour'.

As Christine Buckley points out to me, passages from the two letters were read as the Epistles at Holy Communion on the thirteenth to the twenty-first Sundays after Trinity. Easter Day fell on 31 March in 1594, thus these passages were read between 25 August and 20 October. In particular, passages from Ephesians 4–6 were set for the nineteenth, twentieth and twenty-first Sundays; for example, Ephesians 6: 10–20, containing the passage about the whole armour of God, was appointed for the twenty-first Sunday after Trinity (20 October). The six chapters of Ephesians were also set for Evening Prayer in late October. If, as has been argued earlier, Shakespeare was working on or planning *Errors* in the months leading up to Christmas 1594, Ephesus and Paul's letter to its early church may well have been more than usually present to his consciousness.

INDEX

THIS is a *selective* index to the Introduction and Commentary. It includes names of persons—including literary authors and theatre practitioners (but not modern critics, nor previous editors of the play cited only in collations or commentary)—and works, other than *The Comedy of Errors*, mentioned or cited in the Introduction and Commentary. Characters' names are listed only if they are discussed in the Commentary; the Appendices are not indexed. A large majority of the glossed words and phrases are included; key words and phrases in proverb citations are indicated by '(P)'. Entries that supplement *OED* are marked by an asterisk (*).

Index

Dench, Judi p. 76
Dennis, John p. 65
Derby, Earl of (Lord Strange) p. 4
devil/devil's pp. 42, 56
Diana (goddess) pp. 32, 36, 38
dilate in full 1.1.121
disannul 1.1.142–3
discharged 4.1.32
disparagement 1.1.147
distemperatures 5.1.82
diviner 3.2.145
door . . . hatch (P) 3.1.33
doth it shame 2.1.113
doubtful warrant 1.1.67
*doubtfully 2.1.50, 53
Dowsabel 4.1.110
draw cuts for the senior 5.1.425
draws dryfoot 4.2.39
Drayton, Michael p. 7
Dromio (name) 2.2.197
drop of water (P) 1.2.35–40
drudge 3.2.145
Drury Lane p. 60
Dryden, John pp. 25, 27 n. 1, 43, 60
ducats p. 49; 4.1.30
Dunlop, Frank p. 77

ears 4.4.31
earthy gross conceit 3.2.34
Echard, Lawrence p. 25
ecstasy 4.4.52
Edwards, Thomas p. 7
either at flesh or fish 3.1.22
ell 3.2.112
elm and vine (P) 2.2.177
elves 2.2.193
end 1.1.84
ensconce 2.2.35–9
entrelacement p. 45
Ephesians (New Testament book) pp.
37, 39, 41; 2.1.110–14, 133;
3.2.150
Ephesus pp. 17–18, 31–5, 37–9, 42,
49–50, 52–5, 68; 4.1.1
Epidamnus pp. 17–19, 32–4, 36–8,
50; 1.1.41; 1.2.97–102; 5.1.356–60
Epidaurus pp. 32, 34; 1.1.92;
5.1.356–60
Equivoci, Gli (Storace) p. 62
ergo 4.3.56
Essex, Earl of p. 2
Etherege, George p. 27 n. 2
everlasting 4.2.33

evil angel 4.3.19
excrement 2.2.79
exempt 2.2.174

face me down 3.1.6
failing 1.2.37
fair 2.1.99
fairy 4.2.35
*falsing 2.2.95
Far from her nest the lapwing (P)
4.2.27
farce pp. 42–4, 57, 59, 67, 79
felicity 5.1.408
Feydeau, Georges p. 43
fine and recovery 2.2.74–5
First Folio (1623) pp. 10–11, 13,
15–16, 37
*First Part of the Contention (2 Henry
VI), The* pp. 6, 8, 23
Fletcher, Giles p. 7
Fletcher, John p. 6
flout 1.2.91; 2.2.22
Flower, C. E. p. 67
folded 3.2.36
fondly 4.2.56
fool 2.2.27
fool-begged 2.1.41
for 1.1.56, 126
for fashion 1.1.72
formal 5.1.105
formes, setting by p. 14
foul papers pp. 12–13
Fourth Folio (1685) p. 16
France 3.2.126–7
freightage 4.1.87

Galatians (New Testament book) p. 41
Gammer Gurton's Needle p. 5 n. 1, 12;
4.4.40.1
Gardner, Edmund p. 70
Geneva Bible pp. 38–41
genius 5.1.333
Gesta Grayorum pp. 1, 2 n. 1, 4–5, 10,
23
Gesta Romanorum pp. 28, 30
Gildon, Charles pp. 65–6
Giraudoux, Jean p. 25
glass 5.1.419
globe 3.2.116
Globe theatre pp. 10–11
goblins 2.2.193
Godfrey of Viterbo p. 28
gold/golden p. 49; (P) 2.1.112–13